SHATT

Rebecca Asher has worked in television news
and current affairs and as the Deputy Editor of
Woman's Hour and an Executive Producer at BBC
Radio 4. She lives in London with her husband
and two children. *Shattered* is her first book.

REBECCA ASHER

Shattered

Modern Motherhood and the
Illusion of Equality

VINTAGE BOOKS
London

Published by Vintage 2012

2 4 6 8 10 9 7 5 3 1

First published in Great Britain in 2011 by
Harvill Secker

Vintage
Random House, 20 Vauxhall Bridge Road,
London SW1V 2SA

www.vintage-books.co.uk

Addresses for companies within The Random House Group Limited
can be found at: www.randomhouse.co.uk/offices.htm

The Random House Group Limited Reg. No. 954009

A CIP catalogue record for this book
is available from the British Library

ISBN 9780099548843

The Random House Group Limited supports The Forest Stewardship
Council (FSC®), the leading international forest certification
organisation. Our books carrying the FSC label are printed on FSC®
certified paper. FSC is the only forest certification scheme endorsed
by the leading environmental organisations, including Greenpeace.
Our paper procurement policy can be found at
www.randomhouse.co.uk/environment

Typeset in Dante MT by Palimpsest Book Production Limited,
Falkirk, Stirlingshire

Printed in Great Britain by Clays Ltd, St Ives plc

Contents

Introduction: Confinement 1

1   'All I Did was Have a Baby' 11
2   The Baby and the Bath Water 35
3   A Word of Advice, Dear 59
4   A Job For Life 84
5   Man Power 113
6   The Enemy Within 137
7   Foreign Policy 152
8   The Birth of Equality 184

Afterword: On the Threshold 211
Acknowledgements 215
Further Reading 217
Notes 220

Introduction

Confinement

There is a photograph of me holding my son when he is two months old. He is in rude health. His complexion is peachy, his eyes shine with liveliness and curiosity, and his impressive thatch of hair sits naturally in a boy-band twist. In contrast, I appear to be in the grip of a life-sapping disease. My skin is sallow and drawn, the grey offset only by aubergine accents below the eyes. My cheeks are hollow. My shoulders are hunched. But I am smiling a stunned, enraptured smile, driven by an overwhelming love to nurture my adored child, who drains me of my strength in order to build up his own. A few months later I appraise myself in the landing mirror on the return leg from a night feed. There has been no improvement: I still look deathly. My dressing gown is covered in an appliqué of baby snot and nappy cream. My T-shirt, an old Fawcett Society number, is stiff with stale breast milk. I look down. Among the stains it is possible to pick out a slogan. It reads: *This is What a Feminist Looks Like*.

What has happened to me?

I worried about being a parent long before I became one. I had a decent line of work that, though it didn't make me rich or powerful, allowed me to think of myself as an independent, capable woman and gave me just enough cash and free time to live a varied and spontaneous existence. I fretted about the inevitable compromises to my life and relationship with my husband that having a child would bring. We wrestled with the issue off and on for a few years. Then, as I hurtled towards the wrong end of my thirties, we took the plunge and I hoped for the best.

The result has been both much better and worse than I'd imagined. I have discovered the intense joys of parenthood. I have been floored by the fierce love and protection I feel towards my child, my heart-stopping happiness at his pleasure and my dismay at his upset. I experience a rush of rapture at his wonder for the world and recognise the elation of others when his spotlight falls on them. I am entranced by his beauty, the wriggling softness of his body and his fearless physicality. I delight at the love affair that has developed between my son and his grandparents. And, through him, I have revisited my own childhood, recalling the joy of discovery in books and television characters, paint pots and toys, infant friendships and games.

Yet I have also learnt that the inequality mothers in the UK experience in raising their children is not simply the cause of occasional bouts of angst, but the very foundation on which their daily existence is built and future prospects determined. I was well aware of the penalties that women pay on becoming mothers: the burden of care that falls to them and the consequences that flow from it. But I have had to live that experience to appreciate the defining magnitude of it.

In the lead-up to the birth of our son I thought we were getting ready for his arrival. The house filled up with a cot, bedding and bodysuits. Bottles and bibs were stacked in cupboards. The sitting room acquired a pram. The parenting books my husband and I had bought were studied with a new intensity, pages marked. But having acquired these tools of the trade I was no more equipped for my part in raising our child than I had been before we started. I knew to expect the hard work of looking after a baby and I was delighted and relieved to feel devoted to my child in return. But I was entirely unprepared for the fundamental undoing of the life and identity I'd carefully constructed for myself over the previous fifteen years and, in particular, the demolition of the equality that I'd thought to be at the heart of my relationship with my husband. This illusion of equality was completely shattered.

The day after our son was born we walked home from hospital a new family of three. We were entranced and so were our families. I was ecstatic to be the mother of my son. My husband took his two weeks' statutory paternity leave. We spent that fortnight in a jet-lagged haze, barely getting any sleep but surviving on exhilaration, adoration for our child and, initially, in my case, the remnant whack-out from the drugs the doctors had supplied. We met up with friends, took long walks by the river and called into pubs. Our portable little baby was a compliant passenger in our lives.

But then my husband went back to work, our baby ceased sleeping all day and the music stopped. My devotion to my son was unshakeable but I was now faced with day after day in which for twelve or more hours I was solely responsible for an infant who was entirely dependent on me, utterly resistant to being put down and never minded to take a nap. Abruptly the severe challenges of new motherhood were brought home to me: the loss of autonomy and the self-abnegation were instant and absolute. The independence, affirmation and daily purpose that I'd been used to gave way to gruelling, unacknowledged servitude. My life became unrecognisable to me. The uncertainty I'd felt about having a child had vanished. I loved my son. But a new emotional complexity took its place: despite this love I came to resent motherhood itself. The coexistence of these two apparently contradictory feelings defined my days.

Having had a busy and purposeful life I now occupied a universe where, apart from the grindingly repetitive tasks centred on feeding and cleaning my child, activity existed in the main simply to fill the time. I went to a parent and baby group and found myself singing nursery rhymes with other grown women as our tiny children lay impassive on the floor. I took my baby swimming, swishing him about in the pool as if washing a precious piece of cloth, while he blinked the water from his eyes and stared straight ahead. I walked every inch of my neighbourhood, discovering cut-throughs, corner shops and architectural quirks that until then had been hidden. Having been used to environments where I mixed with women and men of all ages, circumstances and life stages, I now lived in a world where I only ever seemed to be in the company of other new mothers and their young charges. Collectively shell-shocked, our topics of conversation appeared limited to the merits of various pram models and how to tackle colic. I vacillated between a desperate hunger for tips on encouraging my child to sleep and a head-pounding boredom with this narrow, entirely baby-centric world. It felt as if I'd entered a bizarre female sect in which we novices nervously twittered about our infant deities. Every day I was brought up sharp by the dismantling of my former life. En route to one of my time-filling activities, hooded anorak at the ready in case of rain, my box-fresh pram feeling as conspicuous and unwieldy as a supermarket trolley, I would pass young women determinedly heading off to work dressed immaculately and with the luxury of a solitary bus ride ahead of them. I was filled with envy.

I'd known that life with a newborn would be tough but what made it hard to bear was the disparity that was emerging between my existence and that of my husband. Having a child meant sacrifice in return for a richer existence, but why was the sacrifice all mine? Up until now we'd followed the same path: pursuing careers, forging independent identities for ourselves at work, socially and through our other interests, and then coming back to each other at the end of the day. Now my husband alone pushed ahead with his exterior life as I was left at home, holding the baby. Rather than taking on the challenges and pleasures of life as equals, I found myself waving him off to work from the doorstep, our child in my arms.

Up and out of the house by eight in the morning, scrubbed and suited, I suspected that he was only too glad to flee the domestic disorder he left behind. In my thoughts I jealously shadowed my husband's day: a silent, uninterrupted walk to the office, mulling over the day's work ahead; a coffee at his desk while looking over his emails and the day's newspapers; perhaps some meeting at which men in pale blue shirts sat across the table from each other making serious points with emphatic hand gestures and nodding sagely at what each other had to say; lunch followed by some finite, urgent task involving frenzied activity and high-spirited camaraderie once it had been completed. In short, a day in which he had time to himself, exercised his brain and kept his career on track. No wonder then, that when he came through the front door in the evening as I was clearing up the baby's wreckage, my clothes covered in that day's combination of shit, snot and unguent, he was sometimes met with tears or sulking. Bound up in my enforced domesticity, I gave no thought to my husband's own entrapment in the world of work.

When a couple chooses to have children, all the gains women have supposedly made over the past few decades suddenly vanish, as the time machine of motherhood transports us back to the 1950s. In so many ways modern society is intent on overcoming biological constraints, from assisted conception to athletic prowess. Yet giving birth and breastfeeding permanently define a woman's life, and differentiate it from a man's, in a way that is drearily unimaginative and restrictive. Society chooses to base the entire parenting structure on this one biological fact. We magnify the differences between men and women instead of recognising that their commonalities are greater and acknowledging that both parents can play a part in the day-to-day care of their children as well as in the wider world.

In my distress, when my husband was around, I wanted him to experience how hard it could be to look after a young baby. Perversely I willed our son to puke and scream when he was with him. At those times when this wish was granted I would look on coldly, offering no assistance, glad that he was finding it difficult. On other occasions, when he was changing the baby's nappy, putting him in the pram, or dressing him, I would bossily interject, scolding my husband for his ineptitude and taking over the task. I wanted him to understand how gruelling it was to live my new life. Yet in the way I went about it I risked discouraging him from getting involved.

By the time my child was twelve months old we were all more than ready for me to return to work. I saw that my son was keen to branch out into new environments and widen his circle of friends. I was certain that my husband wanted a change from my foul temper and demands that he do more and yet do things exactly as I would. And I was definitely ready to earn my own money, rebuild a social life and have a place in 'the world' again. Having at last got to the top of the nursery waiting list we grabbed the opportunity for a shake-up of family life.

Now that I've returned to paid work, my shock and anger have peaked and we've settled down in to a more or less amicable family set-up. My husband and I work flexibly and this, together with our son's nursery place and invaluable help from our own parents, means that we are both able to pursue our work while sharing the care of our son. The polarisation of our lives that took place immediately after his birth is over. But, as the dust settles, it is clear that this process has changed our respective roles and status irrevocably.

Despite our now quite determined efforts to share the parenting equally, a combination of habit, social structures, cultural norms and cold hard earning power means that I have become, and remain, the foundation parent. We have resisted the worst of these forces yet they are so powerful that they still leave their mark. Subtly yet certainly the tectonic plates that underpin our relationship have permanently shifted and the disparity in our early experience of parenthood has left its legacy. Despite both spending a great deal of time with our son, I do the majority of planning and errands for him, such as buying his clothes, making his medical appointments and finding out about playgroups: all tasks that I became accustomed to while on maternity leave. When the nursery staff need to get hold of us, I'm the parent they call; unsurprising given that I signed him up to their care in the first place. I manage his burgeoning social diary, organising weekend meet-ups and activities with his friends.

I have found so much to celebrate in becoming a mother. I have given birth to, and nurtured, a child with whom I have an ever deepening and evolving bond. At one moment clinging to me like a chimp, at another dismissively telling me to 'go away', every day he both tests and rewards my love. In my eyes, he's full of delight and inquisitiveness and even in his more non-cooperative moods I can't help but admire his strength of personality. I'm frustrated and awed by his focus on his own satis-faction and comfort and can only imagine that, even as he matures and begins to accept explanation and compromise, the balance of love and sacrifice will remain in his favour for many years. Understanding and accepting this as the necessary state of parent-hood is one of the great ongoing challenges for me but adapting to it – and digging deep for resources of patience, resilience and energy that I would never before have thought I possessed – brings its own satisfaction. So too does the knowledge that in attempting to teach our son to be responsible and kind, my husband and I are hoping to contribute a little to the long-term common good.

All of this instils a sense of fellow feeling with other parents. I now recognise the panic of running to collect a child at the end of the day after having been detained at work, the walk of shame when dragging a mid-tantrum infant up the street, the terror when a child tumbles from a climbing frame. Most of all I share the often-voiced frustration that all this care work mainly falls to women. In the midst of my own early shock and disorienta-tion, I realised that the abrupt divide that my husband and I were experiencing was being replicated all around me. My exchanges with other parents in playgrounds and baby clinics signalled that ours was part of a wider story. It gave me the first, almost unconscious, inkling to investigate contemporary parenthood, the expectations and hopes that mothers and fathers have of life while raising children and the reality that then emerges.

So I was prompted to move beyond casual discussion and set out on a deliberate and structured inquiry, beginning with in-depth conversations with mothers and fathers around the UK. For reasons this book will explore, many of them feel that they are currently unable to express and realise their full selves when they become parents, and that there must be a better way to organise their family lives. I have also spoken to mothers and fathers bringing up children in other countries, from America to Iceland, and discovered much that the UK could learn from approaches elsewhere in the world. Some of these countries have made a real difference to family life within the space of a few decades, demonstrating that, if we determine to bring about change in this country, the possibilities for what we might achieve are enormous.

These conversations with parents form the backbone of this book: their lucid and vivid accounts act as a floodlight, illuminating aspects of the world of parenting, its thrills and its strains. Alongside these interviews, the book draws together academic and social research in a quest to understand why, for contemporary women, becoming a mother entails such a profound break from our past lives and expectations, why the disparity between men's and women's experiences of parenthood is so great and why progress towards sexual equality on the home front so far has moved with such glacial slowness. I examine the government policies, public services, cultural and commercial forces, employment structures and personal beliefs and attitudes that shape the UK's parenting culture. I argue that this entire structure is built on the unquestioning assumption that mothers will take on primary care for their children. At the same time, fathers are treated as extras in the drama centred on their own children. And these children are denied the full contribution to family life that fathers might bring. Society promotes and perpetuates this set-up, to the degree that parents become swallowed up by it (although, tellingly, this trend is bucked by lesbian and gay parents, as I discuss in Chapter 8). Some couples genuinely wouldn't have had it any other way, but most will not have had the opportunity to consider other options, never mind embrace them. It's women whose illusions are shattered, but it's mothers, fathers and, most importantly, their children who lose out under our broken system.

Ultimately, this book is an attempt to discover if there is another way of organising our homes, communities and workplaces which would enable both women and men to give wholeheartedly to their children and to experience the joy of a deep connection with them, while retaining other fulfilling elements of their lives. If the vote was the primary target of first-wave feminists, and the workplace that of the second wave, we now need to set our sights on family life. I come to this as a mother and as a feminist, and the challenges that women confront are my initial and primary concern. But in writing this book it has become clear to me that many other social problems flow from the inequality suffered by mothers and that in addressing this core inequality we will begin to address those too, including child poverty, relationship breakdown, unequal life chances, and social atomisation. We all stand to gain from reinventing family life for modern times.

The UK Coalition Government has promised to 'encourage shared parenting'.[1] 'Shared parenting', along with phrases such as 'involved fathers', is a slippery, vague term. If, as it should, the government means encouraging the option of *equally* shared parenting so that both mothers and fathers can be *actively* involved in their children's daily lives, then genuine commitment and concerted effort will be required. If mothers and fathers are going to change how they structure their family lives, they have to be enabled to do so by the state, and by employers. And as parents, we also need to ask some searching questions about what we want for ourselves, and for our children, in the decades to come. It is in the power of parents to bring about great change within their own families, as well as looking to others to facilitate this endeavour. It is only by proactive reform – within the family and outside it – that our current system of parental apartheid can be overhauled. In achieving this, I believe that not only will mothers and fathers have more balanced, varied and fulfilling lives, but that their children will reap the benefits of love and active involvement from both parents. And the positive knock-on effect of that for society will be enormous. Mothers and fathers want the best for their children. While acting in our children's interests, we will also be delivering the best for ourselves and our communities, as well as benefiting employers and the state. This would be the least bloody of revolutions.

1

'All I Did was Have a Baby'

'My mum is a traditional housewife . . . I look at her and I think I can understand how it would have been for her generation . . . But I hoped that by the time it got to me it would be different and I always assumed before I had my daughter that it *would* be different, that it *had* to be different, but it isn't . . . I work but I'm still expected to look after the babies.'

Sam, a full-time researcher and mother of one, sits in her neat-as-a-pin Somerset home, her work files tidily stacked next to children's toys, and voices her deeply felt frustrations. 'I am kind of working class done good. I was able to go to university and my parents had aspirations for me to get an education, to get a good professional job . . . I guess the assumption was that it would be different for me because I saw equality at university, I saw equality at work, I just saw equality . . . I just assumed that would continue if I chose to have a baby. So yes, it's been a harsh reality check . . . And I think my daughter will be sitting here in thirty years' time having the same conversation with your little one. Nothing has changed.'

Despite all the developments in women's lives since the 1970s, when Sam's mother was starting her family, one fact remains the same: women are expected to take primary responsibility for their children. This expectation appears to withstand all social change and is handed down intact from generation to generation. Today more young women than men stay on at school and college beyond the age of sixteen.[1] They are more likely to study for and be awarded vocational qualifications.[2] And in recent years, for the first time, just over half of women between the ages of seventeen and thirty have entered higher education in the UK.[3] Despite the hike in university fees and the abolition of the education maintenance allowance, higher and further education are set to remain common cultural experiences, with all the confidence and hope that they bring. In 2010 and 2011 young women's earnings began to inch ahead of those of young men as a consequence.[4] Professionals in their twenties believe that equality between women and men is a done deal.[5] But as things stand, they too are in for a shock. Women are being set up for a fall, their ambitions compromised by the unfair burden of domesticity.

In 1976, as Sam and I were both beginning primary school, the artist Mary Kelly was scandalising the media with an exhibition of her work-in-progress, *Post-Partum Document*, at the Institute of Contemporary Arts in London. The piece featured her son's stained nappy liners, together with other relics of motherhood through which she explored her psychological, social and physical relationship with her child. *Post-Partum Document* brought the raw physicality of motherhood and the detritus of infant-rearing into public view: it shocked the men of the press, unused to the private (female) world of domestic child-rearing making itself visible in all its literal shittiness. Today Kelly's work lies in storage, part of the Tate collection and a stone's throw from London's Tate Modern, the public work of art returned to invisibility, unseen by all the mothers who while away the hours in there with their own children. Yet the intensity and singularity of motherhood is still as much a feature of their lives as it was for Mary Kelly all those years ago.

Now, as then, inequality is woven into the seam of women's daily experience when they become mothers. Once autonomous and assertive, women are wrenched from their life's moorings and dragged into a restricted existence they had not expected, nor would have chosen. For a generation of women used to freedom and confident of holding its own against men, the implications are profound. As the scales fell from my own eyes, I saw my shock mirrored in others I met. Every Tuesday morning I made the pilgrimage to a local parent and baby group. The parents – all mothers – retreated afterwards to a nearby park café, ignoring the snarls of local dog walkers, as their space was invaded by a caravan of twenty-odd women and their complicated buggies. We'd sit awkwardly, baby in one hand and coffee in the other, savouring ten minutes of semi-stillness before the coffee spilt, an infant screamed and we experienced one of the numerous ways in which the hastily sewn-together quiet moments of our lives became unstitched.

The conversation on these occasions was taken up with obsessive note-swapping about the minutiae of our babies' lives. Can she sit up? Is he crawling? I love her jumper, where did you get it? How's it going with tummy time? What is tummy time? Are you weaning yet? What did you start her on pear or carrot? But in smaller groups and pairs, as we straggled out of the park towards home, we turned to the bewilderment we felt about our new circumstances. Anecdotes were told of domestic strains and of rows with partners about their failure to come home early enough to share bath-time or their lack of interest in planning weekend family activities. Common frustrations became apparent: it would be great if, just once, he would come through the door and say that he'd put the baby to bed while I put my feet up; he'll do things for the baby when I ask him, but he won't take the initiative; he never calls me from work to ask how we are doing. And then there were the bigger-picture grievances, signalling fundamental changes in our lives: my boss doesn't think it's possible for me to return to my old job part time; my boyfriend's fine about giving me money but I hate asking; every day he comes home with news about big meetings or major bust-ups at work, and all I've got to contribute to the conversation is how many nappies I have changed and what our neighbour thinks about the new street parking system. Collectively it was dawning on us that motherhood brought with it an inequality we couldn't dodge. Being a parent would determine the course of our lives to a far greater degree than was the case for our partners. We weren't stupid women. We'd heard about what happened to your status, career and autonomy when you had children. But we'd felt equal to the men we were close to in our child-free years. We thought we could resist the inequality of motherhood, or that it wouldn't be enough to hold us back. We thought we could beat the statistics.

In the early months of motherhood, as we cope with the incessant needs of our helpless infants, dizzy with infatuation, exhaustion and lack of confidence, the physical and emotional shock of our new existence is intense. Jane lives in Leeds and is currently on maternity leave from her teaching job, having had her second child six months ago. Her partner works full time in urban planning. She recalls her experience of first becoming a mother: 'However hard I'd worked before there had always been an end point and suddenly there is no end point – especially if you are breastfeeding . . . It just goes on and on and on until six months have gone by. It's a funny sensation because with a young baby you are busy all the time, aren't you? And yet there is this sense of all this time stretching ahead . . . so it's possible to be with a baby all day and be on your own . . . That was definitely a problem – you are sitting there and feeding and your brain is whirring at a hundred miles an hour . . . And when you are at home you are busy, busy, busy, but you've got nothing to show for it – you are doing well, in fact, if there's nothing to show at the end of the day. It's just clean up the poo, put the nappy on, make the food, wash up, make some more for the next day. Of course, there is something to show for it because you hopefully have two well-adjusted adults in twenty years' time but on a daily basis you feel that . . . all you are doing is holding back this tide. I was quite shocked by how much of looking after small children, particularly, is actually just drudgery. It's what women for centuries were stuck doing.'

New mothers cope not just with the relentless physical grind of early parenting, but, worse than that, with the realisation that they must do much of it alone, despite shifting cultural expectations of fathers over recent decades. Helen is a full-time mother in Oxford. She remembers clearly the moment she realised her partner, who works five days a week for the NHS, would take a back seat. 'When my daughter was very young she suffered from colic. She was screaming in the middle of the night one time and I was holding her. I asked my husband, "What else should I do?" And he just said, "I can't handle this any longer," and left the room to go and sleep downstairs. It's then I realised, "OK, this is how it is going to be from now on. I'll do the child-rearing and he will do other things."'

Having lived in partnerships of equals, we enter motherhood expecting to share the parenting. But we are soon brought up short. Olive is a mother of two from London. Her husband and she are both academics, and she now works part time in order to spend some of the week looking after her youngest child. 'I think, "How did it get to this?" . . . My husband just ambles into the house, as though it's nothing to do with him. He will be reading a newspaper and I will be feeding one child and the other will be sitting on my head, and eventually he will look up and say, "Do you need some help?" It's like he's kind of wandered into this life involving a wife and two children . . . And I am the loser. I don't think I put up my hand at the beginning and said, "I volunteer to be the one who is fucked up by this."'

Mandy, a mother of five from Newcastle, is equally exasperated. Neither she nor her husband is in paid work, yet she finds that the vast majority of the childcare and domestic work falls to her. 'My husband is quite happy to sit back and let me sort it out . . . I mean, when he changes a nappy my jaw hits the floor . . . He doesn't realise that it's really hard to do housework and look after five children . . . In an ideal world I thought that the parenting would be shared.'

In instances where women look afer their children alone, following a relationship split, this sense of inequality can be particularly acute. Elaine has a young son with her partner of twelve years and works as a childminder in London. She also has two older children, the first of whom she had when she was a teenager herself. She recalls the time when she separated from their father and took on the sole care of their children. 'I expected ideally to work together to bring them up. It was a bit of a shock to my system when I ended up being a single parent . . . I used to take my daughter over to my mum at five in the morning so that I could be at my café job at six and I felt really resentful towards him over the years . . . I felt that I had just been lumbered.'

The shock of being 'lumbered' also hit Linda, a mother of two and health worker from Swindon. Unusually, she was brought up by her father after her mother left home, although she still saw her regularly. 'From my upbringing I've been taught that it's a group of people that bring up a child, not an individual,' Linda says. But as an adult, she split up with the father of her oldest child who then moved to a different part of the country and gradually lost contact. 'I was quite surprised to get out in the world and discover that men didn't necessarily take responsibility for children . . . For me, it was very hard for someone to come along and not do that at all. I was, like, "Oh, right, I thought men wanted to look after children and they just couldn't because people wouldn't let them. But you don't want to."'

Linda went on to have a second child with another partner and, even though they too separated, they share the care between them. She now feels that she has a family life that suits her. 'Looking back on it, I feel it's enriched my life. I would never not want to have my children, there's no question. Over the last couple of years I've been very happy and fulfilled in my role as a mother and very proud of my children and the life that we lead . . . It totally focuses you down on what happiness is . . . This

love is just so overwhelming . . . I feel much happier now.'
She adds, 'But I don't think that anybody should have to have
sole responsibility for a child . . . I think it's far too much pressure on both the adult and the child for just one person to be
responsible.'

If fathers will not share the care when children come along,
mothers are forced to make all the necessary compromises themselves. The difference becomes particularly stark and significant,
of course, over the question of employment. Becky is an administrator from Durham. She works part time and spends the rest
of the week looking after her son. She'd been looking to change
career but, when she found out she was pregnant, she decided
to stay put, as her job is secure and she's able to work flexibly.
There was some talk of her partner going part time too so they
could share the weekday childcare between them but it didn't
happen as he'd just changed jobs and said it would be difficult
to ask his new employer. She observes, 'Your options do narrow,
there's no getting around that, in a way that they don't for men.
And I do feel a little bit – not resentment – but, "Ah, OK, I didn't
realise that this is how it works but obviously it is." My partner
is working full time, he's always worked full time. Although
he's a little bit more tired, there's not a huge amount that has
changed for him . . . But it's not the same as being unable to get
a full-time job or to get another job, which is how I feel at the
moment.'

Emma is also agitated by this new disparity between her life
and that of her husband. Struggling to combine a full-time job
as a housing manager in Cardiff with raising their two-year-old
daughter, she feels that her husband is not making the same effort
with family life as she does. He is a teacher and often coaches
at sports fixtures at weekends, in addition to his five days at
school. The strain is beginning to affect their marriage seriously:
'We have just become like strangers, you know? . . . It feels like
my life is completely turned upside down and really his life
hasn't changed a great deal . . . So things are pretty grim, to be

perfectly honest . . . I wanted to have a happy, solid family . . . I think, "All I did was have a baby and look what happened!" Plenty.'

This sense of choices shutting down extends to the most apparently progressive of relationships and causes significant tension within them. Maggie is a photographer and mother of three based in London. She and her partner, an IT manager, both work flexibly in order to share the care of their children: she undertakes freelance projects and he works a four-day week in his permanent job. 'We have a set routine around sharing the dropping off and picking up from school but if there's ever anything extra, we will talk about it. There's never an assumption that I will pick up the pieces. He knows what I think and he is sensitive. But . . . he feels OK about the fact that I do the majority of the childcare. He's not beating himself up about it. So, in spite of the fact that we negotiate most things and we are pretty high on the modern couple scale, nevertheless, when you start to interrogate the detail, there are quite a lot of fundamental differences between not just what we do, but how we do it, how we go about it . . . We did recently have a real blow-out and I knew I was being really very angry and it came from nowhere – he'd done loads of work and loads of evenings and I came into the room and he was there again one night on his fucking laptop and I just lashed out and he was nearly in tears saying, "I'm so stressed, I really don't need this." And I said, "Well fuck it, because you are going to get it." I said to him, "Actually your working like this, you think this is just an issue for you to manage and it makes me feel like the one who is being really needy. But actually, implicitly, you are making loads of demands on me by not being around."'

Men and women's lives head in separate directions when they have children, as distinct pressures on each pull them apart. Mothers take on responsibility for raising children, in most cases combining this with a paid job, while fathers continue to concentrate on bringing in the money.[6] As the UK's Family and Parenting

Institute revealingly puts it, 'The full-time *breadwinner* [my italics] and female part-time worker have become the most common arrangements in the UK.'⁷ Unsurprisingly, then, over three quarters of mothers say that they have primary responsibility for the day-to-day care of their children in the home.⁸ And, although the amount of childcare that men do has risen from between three and eight minutes a day (depending on their educational achievement) in 1975 to between thirty-two and thirty-six minutes a day in 2000, the time women spend with their children has also increased in that period, from between eight and twenty-one minutes to between fifty-one and eighty-six minutes a day.⁹ Reinforcing this gendered split between paid and unpaid work, mothers take on primary responsibility for the home as well as the childcare. Indeed the time required for domestic chores, in part generated by having children, is more than double the time spent on childcare itself.¹⁰ The changes over the last three decades have given rise to what is termed the 'modified breadwinner' model, in which mothers spend more time on paid work and fathers on domestic work than in the past but the expectation remains that women will do most of the childcare and work around the house.¹¹

The adoption of the housekeeper role creeps up on women. Usually more often at home than their partners, they build up a greater awareness of the domestic chores that need doing and fit odd jobs into the nooks and crannies of time between paid work and childcare. So, typically, en route from leaving work and collecting the children, mothers pick up something for dinner. When they get home they prepare the adults' evening meal while their children are eating. And, once the children have had their bath, they scoop up their dirty clothes, sort out the laundry, put on a wash and take the dinner out of the oven just in time for their partner to step through the front door after a long day at the office. Incrementally women become fully entrenched in what the American feminist writer Adrienne Rich brilliantly calls 'the work of love'.¹² Men, too, become entrenched, in their jobs.

In terms of hours, neither person in the couple is doing significantly more work than the other but they are doing markedly different work.[13]

Jane describes her own experience of this process: 'You do slip into that sort of behaviour, I think. I would have said before we had children that we had an egalitarian relationship. We were two individuals who both had jobs and we lived together and had a relationship together and everything was pretty equal. But once you are at home you think, "Well it's easier for me to put the washing on, I'm here all day." Or, "I can run the hoover over when I have five minutes." Or, "I'll phone the plumber because I've got to be here when he comes." And before you know where you are you end up running a household and being a housewife. And I thought, "Well I didn't sign up to that." I agreed to have kids – well, it was my idea – but I never really wanted to become a wife, you know? I'm not a wife and I don't want to become one.'

As Jane has found, once mothers return to paid work after maternity leave, the responsibility for the domestic chores accrued in that time remains with them. In fact, women carry on performing almost the same amount of domestic tasks when they switch from looking after their children full time to working outside the home part time.[14] And even if they work outside the home full time they are still more likely to take responsibility for household chores than their partners and to take time off work to look after an ill child.[15] Early in 2010, as I began writing this book, most of the country was covered in snow and the news bulletins were full of dispatches from areas around the UK where schools had been forced to close. There was concern about the economic cost of parents taking time off work to look after their school-deprived children. Some of these parents were vox popped: they were all women.

Isla is the mother of two primary-school-aged children living in Manchester. When her children were very young she looked after them full time while her husband worked. But when he lost his job they both began applying for work in order to increase the chances of a salary coming into the house. She was the first to be offered employment, as a full-time researcher, and, in order to enable her to take the job, her husband began doing far more of the childcare. Since then her husband has developed his own business, which started as a part-time enterprise but is now taking up an increasing amount of his week. She has continued to work full time but still finds herself responsible for the majority of work around the house. 'There have been certain points when I've felt overworked in every way due to me pushing myself in my career and family life at the same time . . . I've felt overwhelmed by how much I have to do and I do feel overwhelmed by housework. I have quite low standards for housework but my husband has even lower standards; I don't know where they bottom out but it's really, really low, such that if people dropped by you would be thoroughly ashamed. So that side of things I do sometimes find a bit unbearable . . . You get home and there's a mountain of stuff to do.'

In addition to carrying out most of the childcare and household chores, mothers find themselves overseeing all of it. Although the amount of time fathers spend on childcare has increased in recent decades, this tends to revolve around particular tasks and falls short of taking primary responsibility for their children.[16] The assumption that this responsibility rests with mothers is an even greater source of resentment among women than the amount of hands-on domestic and childcare work they actually do. Even women who have always done the lion's share of household planning find this becomes more oppressive once they have a family. It's no longer possible to take it or leave it. Chores that in the past might have been put to one side now have to be undertaken because they affect their children's welfare.

Mary has two children and lives in London. She has recently returned to a job in the media after the birth of her second son. Her oldest son is at primary school. She works a three-day week.

Her husband, who is freelance, works full time and intensively when employed, interspersed with periods of drumming up new business. Mary speaks for many when she says, 'Sometimes I get quite resentful because not only am I the main carer but also I am the one that has to sort out a lot of things – tedious and time-consuming hassle . . . like the after-school clubs and swimming lessons . . . In terms of the hours spent with the children, yes, it's true that I do more because I work part time and when my husband is working he works full time, but I think it's not that that I feel resentful about, because I think he probably does spend quite a lot of time with them. It's more that I have to take the responsibility for them, if you see what I mean . . . I don't think my husband has ever taken them off to buy them a pair of shoes. He has never bought them clothes – never. He quite often says, "Where are their socks?" My oldest son's socks have been in the same place for seven years, you know? That sort of thing . . . makes me feel resentful towards him . . . Because it's all quite time consuming that stuff, and boring.' But the more women become used to managing and carrying out the childcare and domestic tasks, the easier it seems to just do it themselves. In this way, arrangements are perpetuated. Through an unholy alliance of assumptions about the mother's role, expediency and habit, women become the foundation parents.

Parenting demands compromise, it demands the 'work of love'. It is the price we pay for a richer life and a fulfilling relationship with our children. But this price is paid disproportionately by women. Their responsibility for family life restricts the other aspects of their existence. Women do not have the opportunity to develop their careers, public roles or personal interests to the same degree as men because they take on the work of the private sphere in a way fathers do not. They suffer a consequential reduction in their economic worth, independence and social status and experience their power in the relationship diminish. Dependent on their partners for money and status, women are sitting ducks. If the relationship breaks down, they face the prospect of trying to remain in an unhappy partnership or taking on the significant, added challenges of single parenthood often without the financial back-up of a progressing career.

The care imbalance and its knock-on effects are themselves common causes of conflict in relationships.[17] Rather than enhancing our lives as a couple, the strain that having children places on a relationship – stirred up in a bitter brew of dog-tiredness, lack of free time and state-sponsored sexism – means that the years immediately following a child's birth can be hard ones, in particular for those whose daily experience diverges the most.[18] Only 15 per cent of babies are born to parents who are not co-resident, and even of those a quarter of the mothers and fathers are living together at least some of the time when their baby is one year old.[19] Yet one in four dependent children ends up living in a lone-parent home.[20] Men and women want to make a go of it as a family but something goes wrong along the way. Among married women, marital satisfaction is significantly affected by whether or not they are content with the division of household tasks.[21] And research published in 2010, drawing on a longitudinal study involving married couples in the UK who had their first child in 1970, shows that a man's failure to share in childcare and housework increased the risk of divorce over the following sixteen years, regardless of whether or not the mother was in paid work.[22]

The expectation that the mother is primarily responsible for the children and family home disfigures our relationships. Mother and child are claustrophobically bound together as the father hovers on the sidelines. This is a perfect breeding ground for feelings of entrapment and exclusion, for misunderstandings and resentment, producing unhappy families that harm themselves and others. In a risk-averse society in which we fret about the dangers of school trips and social networking sites and pay for insurance against everything from injured pets to our own death, we unthinkingly take a huge gamble with our happiness, and that of our children, by segregating family roles.

This powerlessness and rancour was very far from what I had expected of adult life when I was growing up. Despite the hard economic times of the Thatcher years, my home city of Newcastle still managed a swagger in its walk. Along with the new metro system and the football team, one of its attractions was Mandala Wholefoods. Situated deep in the brown-rice belt of the city, a distinctive aroma of lentils, ground coffee and inattentive personal hygiene greeted you as you pushed open its door and fought your way through the beaded curtain. Among its many period details – shelves stacked with tofu, banana chips and carob bars – was a selection of postcards. This included a set with the confident slogan *It's Really Good Being a Girl* under a picture of three smiling young women, arms around each other's shoulders.

For my generation, it really did feel good to be a girl. We were raised by mothers born as Simone de Beauvoir lit the long touch paper to second-wave feminism in *The Second Sex* and who came of age in the 1960s. At the beginning of that decade Betty Friedan exposed and denounced 'the feminine mystique' and looked forward to a time when women 'are finally free to become themselves'.[23] Four years later, in 1967, the Abortion Act was passed in the UK. This, together with the earlier availability of the pill on prescription, significantly advanced reproductive control for women. With the second wave in full swing, the seventies brought legislation enshrining women's rights at work in Britain. The Equal Pay Act in 1970 was followed by the Sex Discrimination Act and the Employment Protection Act five years later. For those who qualified, this latter Act entitled them to statutory maternity leave, some maternity pay and the right to return to the same job after having a baby. Feminists writing at the time inspired and reflected the excited determination that gripped women in Western liberal democracies. At the beginning of the decade three landmark books – *Sexual Politics* by Kate Millett, Germaine Greer's *The Female Eunuch* and Shulamith Firestone's *The Dialectic of Sex* – were published in quick succession. They laid bare and challenged male oppression and successfully focused attention on women's humanity and their rights. Mothers demanded more than the fulfilment gained from nurturing children. In the late seventies, Adrienne Rich (herself the mother of three sons) declared in *Of Woman Born*:

> We need to imagine a world in which every woman is the presiding genius of her own body. In such a world women will truly create new life, bringing forth not only children (if and as we choose) but the visions, and the thinking, necessary to sustain, console, and alter human existence – a new relationship to the universe. Sexuality, politics, intelligence, power, motherhood, work, community, intimacy will develop new meanings: thinking itself will be transformed.
> This is where we have to begin.[24]

Women were forcing their concerns onto the agenda within a male-dominated civil society and achieving significant political, social and cultural change. All this meant that girls in the 1970s and '80s grew up in an environment where women's entitlements had been forcefully asserted. Taking our lead from the mothers who raised us and paved the way with the advances they secured, we considered ourselves unstoppable. In our childhood and early teens we had our pick of seemingly invincible women to inspire us. A trio of blondes dominated: Margaret Thatcher, Madonna and Princess Diana. Too young to understand the historical enormity of it when she came to power, for girls growing up in the UK in the 1980s, it seemed unremarkable that a woman led the country. Whatever our views on her politics, there was no denying her force as she faced down trades unions, Europe and dissenters in her own political party. From across the Atlantic, Madonna also featured large in our lives, conquering the world's charts, taking up with film stars, and dictating fashion trends. When she sashayed down the stairs in the 'Material Girl' video, sizing up and dismissing suppliant men and their gifts, her unimpressed demeanour was the cue for our own view of the opposite sex. The UK even had its own glamorous blonde in Princess Diana. Her personal turmoil yet to unfold, she held the world in thrall. In retrospect, it is risible that any of these three – a Prime Minister who cared nothing for equality, a tawdry pop star and a young woman calculatedly picked as a suitable consort by the country's most powerful family – were seen as representing female emancipation; but they were effective decoys, leading us to believe that society had travelled further than it really had.

More everyday influences also shaped our sense of self and of the possibilities ahead of us. Many of our mothers entered the labour market, as more and more women became permanent additions to the workforce rather than temporary substitutes for men at war as in the past.[25] They offered us in-house examples of women combining family life with an existence outside the home. Yuppies, Thatcher's darlings, became the defining tribe of the time. We heard sensational stories of professional young women keeping only champagne and Perrier in their integrated fridges and flying over to New York for the weekend. From the cover of *Just Seventeen* more glamorous females beamed out at us, their easy confidence as aspirant as the age in the magazine's clever title. The sappy femininity of old-school publications was replaced between its covers with something more assertive. Among the fashion, pop and gossip appeared 'It's a Living', a recurrent feature on working women (a pilot, a RADA graduate, a helicopter engineer). The problem pages urged correspondents to stand up to exploitative boyfriends, bosses or relatives. Even the magazine's more troubling content – pieces on rape, other sexual abuse and domestic violence – felt empowering. The blame was firmly laid at the door of the perpetrator and readers were left armed with knowledge and sources of advice and help. When we were flicking on the telly rather than through magazines, our programmes of choice – *Brookside*, *Neighbours* and *Grange Hill* – featured independently minded women and girls confident in their relationships and their place in the world. Surrounded by these examples, we grew into our own roles as young women, stomping around in an androgynous uniform of Levi 501s, T-shirts and Dr Marten shoes.

It seemed there was everything to play for. Boys were viewed as peers rather than superiors and, by the late 1980s, our educational attainment more than bore this out. The introduction of coursework and GCSEs marked the start of girls outperforming boys at school,[26] and many of us went on to higher education where, in the mid 1990s, women began to exceed men.[27] We then entered the labour market in the same numbers.[28] If we thought of motherhood at all, it raised few fears as we imagined agilely negotiating a temporary break from our careers thanks to ever more generous maternity and flexible working rights, steered through Westminster from 1997 by the women in the Blair government.

But the actual experience of motherhood, for all its pleasures, was to challenge our assuredness about the progress that had been made. We were too quick to take these apparent advances at face value, too complacent about what had been achieved and too optimistic about what lay in store. Our old Riot Grrrl CDs were no help to us now. We were to learn a hard lesson: feeling 'empowered' wasn't the same as being powerful. Those of us who had curled our lips at the consumerist faux liberation that blossomed in the 1990s hadn't been as clever as we thought. So we saw *Sex and the City* for what it was: but what use was that in the face of a screaming child, an absent partner and a kitchen floor strewn with puke-stained bed linen?

Discrimination takes more complicated forms than in the past and is better hidden, but it is still powerfully present. Women haven't gained equality with men. We've settled for the illusion of a loosening of the leash. Our apparent emancipation extends to holding down badly paid, part-time jobs which free us up to spend half the week in sole charge of our children or doing the cleaning, the better-off occasionally scraping the money together for a 'me-time' spa package. And yet, the patriarchal double knot ensures that those who dare complain about any of this risk the accusation of being spoilt, naive, un-maternal, or, worst of all in our novelty-obsessed age, boring. Mothers have never had it so good; what did you expect when you had children; you mustn't love them if you don't always want to be with them; you are not the first woman to have a baby: each of these put-downs keeps us in our place.

Looking back to the feminist writing of the 1970s, it is not only optimism for the future that is striking. What is also apparent is the similarity to the present day: this despite the heralding of radical change. In the mid 1970s the renowned feminist socio-logist Professor Ann Oakley interviewed sixty-six women in London who were having their first child. She wrote up her work in two books, *Becoming a Mother* (1979 – later reprinted as *From Here to Maternity*) and *Women Confined: Towards a Sociology of Childbirth* (1980). The comments made by the new mothers she interviewed are startlingly resonant now. Even though these women were becoming mothers in, to some extent, very different times (they would be far less likely than now to return to the workplace, for example), their concerns are instantly recognis-able. Professor Oakley writes, 'More than a third of women said they found becoming a mother a difficult experience. Eight out of ten said it had been different from what they had expected. The same proportion thought the pictures of pregnancy, birth and motherhood conveyed in antenatal literature, women's maga-zines and the media in general were too romantic, painting an over-optimistic portrait of happy mothers and fathers, quiet contented babies, and neat and shining homes that bore little resemblance to the chaos, disruption and confusion of first-time motherhood.'[29]

Professor Oakley quotes one woman, Sarah Moore, as saying, 'My views have changed, become more radical. I do think that women are – oppressed is a very emotive word, isn't it? But they are to a certain extent . . . I do think you're thought of as a second-class citizen . . . It's taken Jonathan for me, and for me to be at home, for me to realise this. It's strange, isn't it, because before when I was working, I wouldn't say I was a liberated woman by any means, but I was certainly holding my own at work and running a home. And so I should have then been in favour of women's lib. Let's be honest, once you've got an education behind you, you're not discriminated against as much as other women, are you? And you don't experience it: it's all very chatty, you go down to the pub at lunchtime with the fellows from work and what's this women's lib all about. My God.'[30] This account of feminist coming-to-consciousness on becoming a mother could just have well been articulated today.

Much has changed since the 1970s but too much remains the same. Adrienne Rich, writing in the middle of that decade, provides further proof of this as she describes the disconcertingly familiar lives of the mothers in her block of flats. 'Women are still raising children alone, living day in and day out within their individual family units, doing the laundry, herding the tricycles to the park, waiting for the husbands to come home. There is a baby sitting pool and a children's play room, young fathers push prams on weekends, but childcare is still the individual responsibility of the individual woman. I envy the sensuality of having an infant of two weeks curled against one's breast; I do not envy the turmoil of the elevator full of small children, babies howling in the laundromat, the apartment in winter where pent up seven- and eight-year-olds have one adult to look to for their frustrations, reassurances, the grounding of their lives.'[31]

So the great change foretold in _Of Woman Born_ is coupled with a description of segregated family life that still holds true. Hannah Gavron, in her 1966 sociological study of London mothers, _The Captive Wife_,[32] cites this nugget from a 1953 _Daily Herald_ article announcing the arrival of the more hands-on father. She quotes, '"Young men are now family men in a way that former generations were not. They push prams, do the washing up and bath the baby."' But this excited mid-twentieth-century twittering of transformation in family roles has still to be followed through with anything more significant and widespread among fathers. As Adrienne Rich points out, a father pushing a pram does not in itself constitute a reinvention of the family. Yet, it continues to be proffered as a signifier of change, even today. In 2009 a columnist in the *Guardian* remarked, 'Every time I see a dad pushing a buggy, children hanging on to the handle-bars, biscuit crumbs down his coat, pockets stuffed with toys, there is silent applause in my head.'[33] But male pram-pushing, while no doubt more common among today's fathers than in previous generations, stops far short of developing into anything really meaningful. Over half a century on from the change trumpeted in the *Daily Herald*, fathers are still on the fringes of childcare rather than making fundamental changes to their public lives in order to share equally in the raising of their children. And so still, in my darker hours, I feel the 'quiet desperation' that Betty Friedan described almost fifty years ago in *The Feminine Mystique*.

More recent writing, from the turn of the millennium, tells a tale with even greater resonance. I recognise the 'acute social demotion' on becoming a mother that Naomi Wolf describes in *Misconceptions*, the 'brittle' dynamic in couples who are new parents, and the men in those relationships 'pulling rank'.[34] I identify with Rachel Cusk in *A Life's Work* when she writes of her 'desire to shed my motherly persona, a persona I cannot seem to support without injury to what I have come to know as myself'.[35] In the UK, we recently lived through thirteen years of a relatively socially progressive Labour government, with senior female politicians promoting women's rights as part of a broader equality agenda, and yet the experience of mothers writing at the beginning of that period still rings very true.

Second-wave feminists may raise their eyebrows at my generation's shock at our predicament. After all, have we not reaped the rewards of their hard work, not to mention that of the first wave of activists? And even if the inequality suffered by mothers is still alarming, these women writers and campaigners had set it all out in stark terms, so how can it be such a nasty surprise?

Part of the answer is that, no matter what has been written, nothing can prepare a woman for the experience of motherhood and the fundamental upending of her life that it entails. But the main reason is that my generation grew up keeping pace with the opposite sex, markedly more so than in the past. Although the economic, social and physical toll of motherhood may have lessened since the 1960s and '70s, women's expectations today are far higher. So the gap between our lives up until the point we become mothers and the reality of motherhood that confronts us and sets us apart from fathers is still great, even if we begin from a better starting point. Our expectation, along with our experience, has shifted: both goalposts have moved so the impact is still significant. The disillusion this causes is intensified if women start a family in their thirties or later, as many now do.[36] This enables them to establish themselves in their careers before taking time off to have a child. It also means that women can have a decade or more of completely independent living, in contrast to the past, when they frequently moved from their parents' house straight into running their own marital home. But women now risk having further to fall if they lose their footing on becoming mothers. They see a chasm open up not just between themselves and their partners but also between their former and present lives.

Frieda, a mother of one, works four days a week running a charity in London. She was born in the 1970s as second-wave feminism was at full throttle. She describes her experiences and expectations as she grew up. 'I came from a background that was very much you can do what you want to do, sort of thing. Although my mother didn't go to university and stayed at home with the children, she ran her own business and she's always been feisty . . . I never internalised any sense that I couldn't do exactly what I wanted . . . [At school] I began reading *The Female Eunuch* and other feminist literature and became interested in women's rights and competitive with the boys at sixth form. I was then Women's Officer at university and was involved in women's rights stuff there . . . I had quite high expectations of my relationship and of equality and my partner has always been proud to call himself a feminist as well and that's always been quite important to me . . . It's fantastic that he never questions our equality, that we think the same things on those issues. But, before I had a long-term relationship, I had imagined a utopia where everyone shared the domestic chores equally and I some-times feel bitter about that, because that's not how it's worked out . . . I sometimes think that I've made it worse for myself because I had a vision that we would have a perfectly equal rela-tionship. I had very high expectations but actually I have had to make compromises . . . I think I have been disappointed and depressed by living through what is obviously such a mother-centric type of culture: you go to playgroups and there's the odd man but it's mainly women. Lots of people view it as a female domain . . . And it does make you reflect on how far have we come?'

Karen, too, has suffered from the mismatch between her expect-ations for her life and her experience as a mother. An academic and mother of one son, she and her husband are now expecting another child. 'I am the first in my entire extended family to go to university, and I watched these very traditional, quite unhealthy, often quite violent, oppressed marital relationships within the family. I just felt that – you know, it's that old adage that for me education was escape – through social mobility I could find a different life . . . I had watched my mother and aunts being pretty much tied to the house and to their children and that was not what I wanted for myself . . . I think slowly my husband and I came round to thinking we would have a child. All that time I was thinking that in an ideal world we will . . . share it equally. But we had these discussions and it became acutely apparent that that was not going to be the case. He works in law, it's one of the most traditional employment sectors and a lawyer is always going to earn more than an academic . . . And so you think, "OK,

I can stick by my principles but what is going to make the most practical, financial sense?" And so, you know, it became fairly obvious if we were going to have children then I would . . . bear the brunt of dealing with family life.'

Women have made great strides since the 1970s. Most notably, many more mothers have entered the labour market.[37] They have new rights at work that enable them to continue to forge identities outside the home and retain a degree of economic autonomy. But this 'green shoot' of progress must be very heavily qualified, as I explore in later chapters.

It would be a mistake to assume that we are moving inexorably towards equality between women and men, or that the progress that has been made cannot be reversed. The spending cuts announced by the UK government in 2010 and 2011 were proof of that. They are being felt most sharply by families with children, particularly those on low incomes.[38] Because women still have to take on primary responsibility for raising children, they must fit together jobs and family life, often relying on tax credits and childcare services to make it work. They are employed disproportionately in the public sector because it offers greater flexibility than the private sector.[39] Deep cuts to benefits and public sector employment and services are pulling the rug from under women's feet. Many have lost their jobs, and others have lost the childcare services and subsidies that enabled them to work. Female unemployment has risen as a consequence.[40]

Progress towards equality is fragile and can falter all too easily. It is vital that we don't grow complacent. Now, more than ever, women must insist on their rights to the same opportunities as men. The efforts of feminists in past decades notwithstanding, society has failed to bridge the divide between the sexes because family roles have barely changed. For women to have a realistic chance of equality outside the home they must have equality within it. We must be clear-sighted about the implications of this. In seeking to empower women, we have to recognise the imperative to release men from their own confines also, enabling mothers and fathers to share in the effort and rewards of life both inside and outside the home. This will not only liberate parents, but benefit the rest of society too, as we all undertake the whole of the work of life. Unless we begin to tackle proscribed gender roles seriously, the gap between young women's expectations for their lives and the hard reality will get wider and wider. It was really good being a girl in the 1980s. But being a mother could be so much better than it is now.

2

The Baby and the Bath Water

'I found it started when you were pregnant they began to separate you from your partner then. My husband was only able to come to one of the antenatal classes anyway and even then they talk about men as if they are another species.'

The antenatal experience described by Kate, a mother of two from Hampshire, is illustrative of what happens to couples as soon as they learn that they are having a baby. Different and unequal expectations are placed on mothers and fathers even before their children are born. In the months leading up to the birth, gendered norms are established, setting patterns of parental involvement that endure throughout a child's life and beyond. The mother is destined to take on the caring role while the father remains focused on life outside the home. For a woman, feeling your baby kicking inside you and then holding it close to you as you first feed it is a bewildering yet precious experience. But this sweet biological bond soon tightens to the point of constriction. Society allows no attempt to loosen its ties, to let the mother breathe more freely or to allow the father equal status in relation to his child.

At the heart of this process is the 'woman-centred' maternity care provided in the UK by the NHS. Although they may not know it, prospective parents enter a politically charged world as they prepare for the birth of their child. Up until the eighteenth century maternity care was a woman's domain. Midwives took charge of pregnant and labouring women and female assistants attended the birth. In the 1700s male medics began to encroach, bringing with them a new invention – obstetric forceps. This fancy new gadget was attractive to aristocratic women who, knowing only too well the high risk of death in labour, hired medical men to ensure safer births. From this point onwards, childbirth came to be viewed as a medical event rather than a female rite of passage. By the second half of the twentieth century hospital births were the norm.[1] Far fewer mothers died in childbirth.[2]

But the medics' bedside manner left a lot to be desired. Women giving birth were routinely induced so that their labour would fit around doctors' timetables. Their pubic hair was shaved and enemas administered to make life easier for hospital staff. Those who questioned all this were scolded for risking the lives of their children. Understandably, women began to challenge these medical interventions by (mainly male) obstetricians. In 1956 the Natural Childbirth Association (later to become the National Childbirth Trust) was set up, rapidly followed in 1960 by the Association for Improvements in Maternity Services. Both organisations were founded by women determined to promote 'natural' or 'normal' childbirth. Maternity care became a feminist cause. Campaigners argued that male medics were wresting control from women of their own bodies. Over time, the care of pregnant women and how they gave birth became a key battleground in the fight against patriarchy and the defence of women's identities.

Midwives also joined in the fight. They wanted to support the women in their care – and defend their turf on the labour ward. In 1976 the Association of Radical Midwives was formed and joined the resistance movement. The fight pushed childbirth up the health policy agenda, so that by the early 1990s the preference for 'woman-centred' care – defined by the Royal College of Midwives as 'maternity care that gives priority to the wishes and needs of the user'[3] – had been accepted as government policy and clincial credo.

But what has this struggle really achieved? Women (at least in theory) are given a choice of where to give birth, including in their own homes or in midwife-led, low-tech birth centres, as well as in consultant-led labour wards. No antenatal tour of a hospital's maternity services is complete these days without a peek at the birthing pool and potted-plant-filled relaxation room. Yet at the same time childbirth is more medicalised than ever before. Caesarean section rates have risen from 3 per cent in the UK in the 1950s[4] to 12 per cent in 1990[5] to 24 per cent in 2008.[6] Meanwhile the home birth rate has gone from being the norm to the experience of a tiny minority, and it continues to fall.[7] Whatever the arguments for or against this increasing medicalisation, women giving birth for the first time would be forgiven for thinking that the event will be characterised by whale music and candles, when the reality may be very different.

Besides this risk of a great gap between expectations and experience, there is a less discussed consequence of the current state of 'woman-centred' care. In the rush to grab back control from male obstetricians, fathers have been marginalised. Women carry a child to term but both parents can be responsible for its welfare. By focusing so intensively on the mother, the father is undermined. This sets a poor precedent for his role as a parent, indicating that he will play only a secondary part in the life of his child. For the mother, the exclusion of the father means that her role will be all the more demanding: parenting will be largely down to her. The women's empowerment agenda has backfired. In privileging the mother at this point, the NHS sets her up as the main carer in the years to come, a role that in its solitude becomes a burden and disenfranchises women in every other aspect of their lives.

The Royal College of Midwives' Position Statement on *Woman*

Centred Care exemplifies the problems with this misguided approach. It notes that 'woman-centred' care should take 'a holistic perspective, encompassing emotional, psychological and social as well as physical needs'. It should encompass 'a focus on pregnancy and childbirth as the start of family life, not just as isolated clinical episodes, taking full account of the meanings and values each woman brings to her experience of motherhood'.[8] Despite this insistence that the care of women should be seen in the round, within the context of family life and not just as a physical event, there is no explicit mention in the whole document of fathers and the role they should play in the maternity period and in preparation for family life. And yet it is RCM members – midwives – that the NHS, individual hospitals and the government would have leading most births.

Opinions vary on whether fathers have been deliberately excluded by health professionals in the bid to focus on the needs of the mother. The National Childbirth Trust, while acknowledging that men 'have been paid relatively little attention by policy-makers and service providers',[9] intimates that this is an oversight rather than anything more deliberate. The male obstetrician that I saw for an appointment before I gave birth to my son told a different story. He alluded to a sex war in his hospital in which the staff was made up of 'hawks and doves', the former comprising female midwives and obstetricians who aggressively called the shots in an attempt to sideline both male medics and fathers.

Roger Olley was one of the first male health visitors in the north-east of England before he joined the charity Children North East where he ran their Fathers Plus Service for ten years. He is now a consultant working with health, family and other services to make them more accessible for men. He is frank: 'I think what is happening is that we are getting an overt statement of intention to include men. But covertly it's viewed as an intrusion into [the midwives'] role, their focus, woman to woman. And I think midwives have got a huge cultural shift to go through.'

From the get-go the NHS signals to fathers that they will play second fiddle. The government colludes in this. Women are expected to attend antenatal care appointments and classes and are entitled to paid time off work to do so. Men are not. Antenatal appointments (including check-ups with a GP or midwife, and hospital scans) are viewed by the NHS as narrowly female-focused medical occasions. But although men are not required to present themselves for monitoring and prodding, there are medically sound reasons to include fathers in antenatal appointments. Fathers who smoke risk the health of their partner and their child.[10] Heavy drinking among fathers-to-be is linked to drinking by expectant mothers,[11] and drug use by either parent can compromise their ability to raise children effectively.[12] But it is only the mother's lifestyle that comes under scrutiny from maternity services. She is lectured on the dangers of smoking and drinking, and instructed on a moderate diet and appropriate exercise. With the child yet to be born, responsibility for its well-being as a foetus is firmly laid at her door. Rather than both parents being given information, her behaviour is interrogated while the father's remains his own business. The chance to educate him about his lifestyle choices, and to understand and share in those of his partner, is lost. The message is clear: mothers are to take the greater responsibility for the health of their children, setting them apart from their partners.

Linda, the mother of two children from Swindon, tells of the behaviour of her former partner and father of her youngest child: 'One of the things we used to do together was take drugs and obviously when I was pregnant that was not going to happen. And he still – well, he was free to do things that I wasn't and did them. And I found that not supportive at all and with the hormones and everything, it was all very rocky.' As the experience of Linda shows, while pregnant women make adjustments to their lifestyle and mindset in preparation for life as a parent, fathers may remain detached. Maternity services get off to a bad start in their failure to show men that they too have an immediate role to play in the health of their children. More broadly, the opportunity is lost to engage both women and men as equals in preparing for their role of parents.

In its advice for fathers, the NHS awkwardly manoeuvres around this inequality. Its information urges men to attend antenatal appointments yet at the same time makes plain that nothing will be done to facilitate this: 'Pregnant women might have lots of tests and scans, including ultrasound scans to check the baby's development. These can cause anxiety, so go with her *if you can* [my italics].'[13] This implies that the man is there to assist his partner through *her* anxiety. Seemingly, it is only the woman who will feel worried about tests and scans, as if the foetus is primarily her concern. The fact that fathers have no rights to paid time off work to attend antenatal check-ups codifies this inequality.

Fiona, herself an inner-city GP as well as a mother of two, echoes this emphasis on the practical rather than social aspects of antenatal appointments: 'I do antenatal care and I virtually never see a partner there unless they are translating for their wife. I think it would be great if men were more involved from the very start – that would be better for increasing their roles after the baby is born. But all these appointments are usually during the day and so it is often not that practical. The NHS is constantly under pressure to open extended hours in the evenings and weekends. And maybe antenatal care is an ideal thing to be moved to these times because generally these women are healthy and that would be an ideal way to involve the partners. But often it just boils down to, "Well, what practically needs to be done here, actually?" My experience of antenatal care is usually, "OK, well it's your blood test this week, and you are going for a scan next time. So how much is there to be gained by sharing that experience?"'

GPs and midwives, with limited time for each patient, will inevitably focus on immediate medical issues and the (female) body that needs to be examined in this process. But as Fiona says, antenatal appointments present an ideal opportunity to engage men in preparing for their lives as fathers. And health professionals, through organisations such as the Royal College of Midwives, purport to be alive to these wider social concerns. The assumption that there is nothing to be gained from a father going along to a blood test and 'sharing that experience' is short-sighted and reductionist. It isn't just an appointment for a routine medical test, it's also an opportunity for both parents to track the pregnancy, discuss their own, relevant health issues, and begin to focus as a couple on their life with the child once it is born.

Antenatal appointments are, in theory, supplemented by ante-natal classes where, it might be imagined, there is greater scope for talking through planning for parenthood, including how roles and responsibilities will be shared. This would be particularly useful for new parents. Yet just over one third of first-time mothers do not attend antenatal classes.[14] Despite legal provision to allow them to take paid time off work, and attempts by some NHS trusts to hold classes at weekends or in the evening, which might be more convenient for some, women are prevented from attending because of cost and timing, as well as the location and availability of classes in the area.[15] These are all factors that will apply to their partners too.

Nevertheless, almost 80 per cent of all women who attend ante-natal classes are accompanied by their partners.[16] Men make real efforts to be involved. But the invitation extended to them can be ambivalent. One Sure Start leaflet I came across listed: 'Antenatal classes: Workshops for pregnant women on labour, breastfeeding and early weeks with parent and baby run by a Sure Start midwife.'[17] No need for men to bother themselves with that, it implies.

Follow-up research with parents after the birth shows that they would have liked more information and discussion about infant care and the effect of babies on couple relationships.[18] But, with the emphasis often on getting the baby out, the role of fathers, beyond their support to partners in labour, is overlooked. Unsurprisingly they feel sidelined. Karl is a father of one daughter. He lives in County Durham with his partner and is currently unem-ployed and looking for work. In early adulthood he joined the army, but on leaving the forces he drifted into drug abuse and in and out of prison before meeting his girlfriend. Expecting a baby and determined to make his family life work, he attended antenatal classes at his local hospital. 'I went to three classes. I wanted to go along and see what it felt like . . . But not again – just sit down, boring, holding their stomach. What they were saying and that, it was like, "Nah, that's not for me." . . . They were always talking about the mams and stuff like that and not to the dads . . . I was proud of myself because I was the father but it was not for me. My girlfriend was asking questions but they weren't asking me questions, "How do you feel? Is this your first one?" I was, like, "What about me?" I just thought, "It's not for me this." And I stopped going.'

NHS online information for fathers expecting a child (a potentially important source of guidance for those unable to attend classes or appointments) is also belittling. It assumes that dads are idiotic, pathologically nervous and sex obsessed. Tips include, 'Decide how you'll get to the hospital . . . If you're using your own car, make sure it works and has petrol.'[19] A list of top-ten issues for dads includes, '3. I'm not ready to be a dad! . . . 4. Having sex won't hurt the baby.' The latter helpfully points out: 'If you are not having sex, you can still be affectionate in other ways, such as hugs.'[20]

This information reinforces the view that fathers are to take on a supporting function, stereotyping the roles of men and women in one fell swoop: 'Your partner may be used to doing most of the housework as well as going out to work. If she continues to do all this work she'll tire herself out. Now is the time to start sharing the housework, if you don't already do so. There are two areas where you can be helpful. Cooking: in the early months the smell may put her off. If you cook, she's more likely to eat what she needs. Carrying heavy shopping can put a lot of strain on her back, so do the shopping yourself or together.'[21] According to the NHS, the father should assist (or 'be helpful') in traditionally female tasks until the woman is back on her feet. At a time when men like Karl are excited and proud about the arrival of their child and potentially open to changing their lifestyles and attitudes to parenting, they are made to feel marginalised and patronised instead. Rather than seriously thinking through the approach to childcare that will really work for them, couples are shepherded into conventional set-ups.

There is another reason why maternity services keep fathers at arm's length: they are seen as a threat. This is not entirely irrational. Over 30 per cent of domestic violence starts in pregnancy and more than 14 per cent of maternal deaths occur in women who have reported to a health professional that they are in a violent relationship.[22] An Australian review of international research has concluded that between four and nine pregnant women in every hundred are abused in pregnancy or shortly after childbirth.[23] The Royal College of Midwives explains in its Position Statement on *Domestic Abuse* that, 'Where abuse is suspected, the RCM urges midwives to further ask the woman explicitly but carefully and sensitively.'[24] This is a sensible intervention, taking advantage of the fact that women are likely to come into contact with health services and so potentially have the opportunity to access support at this time. However, consciousness of this issue is at such a peak it risks becoming the dominant image of men. The National Childbirth Trust acknowledges this: 'There is a perception of men as a threat to children, particularly non-resident fathers.'[25] The RCM Position Paper on *Domestic Abuse in Pregnancy* notes among 'Behavioural signs of abuse': 'The partner accompanies the woman, insists on staying close and answers all questions directed to her – may also undermine, mock or belittle her.'[26] Later it says: 'Where abuse is suspected, the midwife should discuss this with the woman in a quiet, private environment where confidentiality can be assured. If the woman is with her partner (or any other person) at every appointment then the midwife will need to ask to see her on her own at least once – tactfully and carefully, without rousing suspicion.'[27] Distinguishing between an interested father-to-be and an abusive one may be very difficult to judge in some instances, and creating opportunities for private questioning when women are attending sessions accompanied by partners may be difficult. Given these problems, and the risk of not detecting domestic violence, some midwives may think it easier to discourage men's attendance at antenatal sessions altogether.

At my first appointment with a midwife the only mention of my partner, beyond a question about his occupation, came when she asked if he was violent towards me. The one image of a man in the antenatal section of the hospital I attended was on a poster warning of domestic violence. At a children's centre I visited to speak to new parents, the entrance hall featured a large noticeboard starkly entitled the 'Domestic Abuse Board' covered in posters warning of domestic violence and situated beside the soft seating and children's books. The centrepiece was a poster that warned, *The Dominator is his name/Controlling women is his game*. Below this the 'Dominator' personality type was split into subsets: 'The Sexual Controller', 'The King of the Castle', 'The Bad Father', 'The Liar', 'The Headworker', 'The Bully', 'The Jailer', 'The Persuader'. Each was then described in more detail. In a rack of leaflets further down the corridor, if fathers were resilient enough to make it that far, one lone handout reflected a positive image of men. It listed 'Activities for Dads and Male Carers', and aimed to entice fathers in with promises of 'Fun, information and refreshments'.

The warnings of the dangers of domestic violence are necessary. Health professionals must be alert to signs of domestic violence and encourage women to seek help. But the balance between supporting fathers and viewing them as a threat is out of kilter. How many men will feel welcome if they are forced to run the gauntlet of noticeboards such as that at the children's centre I visited? If fathers are treated first and foremost as a potential danger, they are disenfranchised as parents.

If the woman's primary parenting role has not been firmly impressed on the parents before the birth it will be very clear by the time they leave hospital with their baby. Almost all births happen in a hospital or birth centre,[28] and almost all fathers now attend the birth.[29] Yet the majority of those fathers will be turfed out once their child is born. Classed as 'visitors', they are ejected from the bedside when visiting time is over, unable to stay the night in hospital with their partner and new baby. I was struck by the pathos of this account of a birth written for an NCT magazine by a new mother: 'I was so elated to see [our baby] – he was nine days late, and me and my husband were desperate to meet him. Seeing him for the first time was wonderful. Definitely the best day of my life even considering the pushing, yelping and the stitches. We got down to the ward at five a.m., said goodbye to Daddy, and went to bed – Josh in his tiny cot by my bedside.'[30] Freshly born, the baby is already saying 'goodbye to Daddy'. On UK maternity wards, fathers become callers on their own family, popping in on the mother and child.

Dean is an electronic engineer and the father of one daughter, from Glasgow. He was separated from his wife and newborn child for five nights while they remained in hospital after the birth. 'I was a bit disappointed in this day and age that a couple couldn't spend the night together after the birth of their child . . . I just find it very strange that it isn't considered . . . They said it was a hospital rule that all dads must leave . . . [My wife] was finding it very hard.'

Even in the hours that men are allowed access to the most precious people in their lives there are no facilities for them; no meals provided, nowhere to make a cup of tea or grab a nap. Ben, a former factory worker from the north-east of England, is currently unemployed and attending a college training programme. He and his wife have three children. 'You feel awkward because they don't have any food for you. My wife used to give me bits of her food. If there was a dads' facility there – a room with showers or just to sit down – that would help.' With demands for beds and on staff so high, enabling fathers to stay over in hospital may at first appear an unrealistic aspiration. As Isla, a mother of two, observes, 'I think it's a good option but . . . I would just have liked not to be in labour on a general ward in front of people's families eating grapes.' But enabling fathers and mothers to be together in these formative first hours and days isn't a frill, it's an acid test of the goverment's commitment to 'shared parenting'. As it is, couples set out from the birth of their child with very different roles and expectations thrust upon them.

When nine o'clock in the evening comes and visitors are asked to leave, women are on their own. Bev, from Northumberland, is the mother of three children. She and her husband had their first two children in the 1990s and then a third child in 2005. She found that, between these two decades, hospitals had done nothing more to cultivate joint parental responsibility. She recalls her husband leaving the hospital after the birth of her first child. 'I was just bereft. I couldn't believe that he was expected to go home. And he went home and watched darts and came to get me in the morning. Our first child came very quickly with a two-hour labour and I was whisked to hospital and the baby came out and then within a couple of hours he'd gone and I was thinking, "What the hell? What kind of society is this that he's gone home?" So he came back at six in the morning and I then just went home at eight. We walked home. I just had to get out . . . [With our third child] again he had to go home and I felt so, so sad and I couldn't sleep and the baby didn't have a name and it was absolutely hideous . . . I was on my own and I hated it . . . It would have been nice to have him there and the other children to come if they had wanted to and spend the night together . . . rather than just arriving home with this baby.'

As Bev describes, this practice has a huge immediate emotional impact on mothers and fathers. Bill from London, a picture editor and father of a young daughter, recalls the nights that he left his wife and baby to come home from hospital. 'I was there from nine in the morning until nine at night, really. Then I would come home and I would drink whisky and cry.'

The ruthless speed with which fathers are ejected is unnecessarily harsh. Ben tells the alarming tale of his treatment after the birth of his first child. 'My wife had a Caesarean at night-time, three o'clock in the morning, and afterwards . . . she was taken through to the ward and I went with her and we started falling asleep on the bed. Then the nurse comes along and says to me, "What are you doing here?" And I said, "I'm with my wife: we've just had a baby." And she said, "There's no men allowed on this ward, get out now." This was, like, three thirty in the morning. So I go downstairs in the hospital and I ring up my dad and say, "Dad, can you come and pick us up please? I'm struggling here." Nobody had said anything [about the overnight rule] in the theatre room or the recovery room that she was put into afterwards. I walked all the way through to the ward with the nurses. We got into the ward, they put the curtains round, gave her a few tests, walked away, and I never saw them again . . . I was panicking for my wife, really. She was left alone at night for a week. She couldn't move or pick up the baby.'

Shortly after the birth, parents are cruelly separated and the burden of care is placed on the mother, whatever her own physical state. As her partner and any of their other children leave, the ward lights dim, the nurses melt into the background, and the mother is left to cope alone. Having been there with her through birth, the father is removed from the scene at the point that he could contribute care tasks as well as psychological strength. Three years on I remember the experience of my one night in hospital with my newborn son all too well. While my care through birth was excellent, memories of that night are like nightmarish flashbacks. As the other babies on the ward settled into drifts of sleep, my son remained awake and screaming. Despite the fresh wounds of childbirth, an accessorising catheter and feeling seasick with exhaustion, some remnant of social embarrassment kicked in and I felt obliged to remove the disturbance from the room. I hobbled down empty, fluorescent-lit corridors until I came to a storage room filled with clapped-out wheelchairs. Having found my sanctuary I collapsed into one of the seats and tried to comfort my startled son, forcing myself to return to the ward only when he emitted the extraordinary, tar-like shit of the newborn. I am as thankful for the drugs numbing my emotions on that night as numbing my pain during the birth. We were both bewildered and terrified. By the time my husband returned the next morning, my son and I had travelled across a universe of experience together.

Many new low-tech, midwife-led birth centres now provide facilities for fathers and older children to stay overnight, proving to the doubters that security and logistical concerns can be over-come. But only 5 per cent of mothers give birth at these centres.[31] Too few parents spend their crucial first nights together. And it is doubly perverse that those who don't have access to birth centres because they have had more complicated births, neces-sitating a longer recovery time and possibly more nights in hospital, are denied the overnight presence of their partners, while those who have had more straightforward births and stand a greater chance of not needing to stay overnight at all can have their partners with them.

Fiona, herself a doctor and mother of two, agrees: 'I was absolutely completely miserable on both occasions when my husband left. It is just ridiculous, actually. I mean, fine if you can go home that day, but if you are not going home you are probably in an emotional state either because you've just had a baby or because something has gone wrong and you are having to stay there . . . It feels like such a heartless thing to be doing to chuck the fathers out.'

By the time the family is reunited the mother has been through the steepest of learning curves. Overnight she accumulates a level of practice and expertise that puts her ahead of her partner. Aside from possibly breastfeeding, she has learnt to comfort her child, calm it, clean it, change it and wrap it up warm, all of which could be carried out by the father just as well. But already she is less fazed by the baby's moods and needs and more adept at ensuring its well-being. She has also come to realise that no matter how weak she is following the birth, the care of the baby is regarded as her concern, not the father's. She and the baby are now wrapped up in a cocoon of care that it is difficult for him to penetrate.

While the father is neglected by the hospital, the mother is unlikely to escape through its doors, pamphlets and product samples in hand, without a stern lecture on the merits of breast-feeding. This is often accompanied by the requirement that she demonstrate her mastery in order to win her freedom. The UK signs up to the World Health Organization's target for women to breastfeed exclusively for the first six months of a baby's life. Despite recent scientific research that suggests that some benefits of breastfeeding (such as lowering the risk of asthma, allergies and obesity, or contributing to a high IQ) may have been overstated,[32] breast is still judged irrefutably best with no compromise tolerated. The NHS is fixated by this target, bombarding women with leaflets, lectures and workshops on breastfeeding as soon as they become pregnant. Yet, this mass effort notwithstanding, the campaign fails miserably. Less than 1 per cent of women in the UK are exclusively breastfeeding their babies at six months.[33] And it's not hard to see why. For those able to breastfeed for any length of time, its appeal as a healthy, convenient and cheap bonding experience can soon wear off. It becomes instead a hugely restrictive obligation, an act that women feel compelled to continue for fear of otherwise disadvantaging their infants. The mother is unable to leave her baby for more than two or three hours at a time in case it needs a feed. In her brief gasps of freedom she is constantly preoccupied by thoughts of her child, worried that it might be ravenous in her absence, its temporary carer unable to do anything but look on helplessly. The mother alone must get up during the night – multiple times in the early weeks – to feed her child. The slightest whimper is judged by others to be a sign of hunger and the mother once more has to stop what she is doing and take the child to her breast. 'She's hungry!' the father adamantly states, as once again he hands over a crying child because 'she needs her mother.' The child could, in fact, be crying out of boredom or because it needs winding or a wet nappy changed but, with a nipple in its mouth, the crying stops and apparently its need has been answered.

The demands made by the NHS of the breastfeeding mother are extreme. She is instructed by midwives to breastfeed on demand, day and night. She can forget about trying to space out the feeds, set a routine or give herself a break. She must watch what she drinks, avoid spicy food and pulses and major on carbohydrates and water. She must give herself up completely to the feeding of her infant. Any attempt to introduce methods that would enable the father to contribute to this is frowned upon. Expressing milk to feed from a bottle causes 'nipple confusion', she is told. The occasional use of formula invokes shudders: breastfeeding is promoted to the extent that formula feeding is consequently demonised. When I mentioned over the phone to my health visitor that I was thinking of introducing a daily formula feed I was summoned to her clinic. Women are pushed to the point of exhaustion while fathers are left unable to share night feeds or to take the baby off for half a day to give their partners a break. Both parents are trapped in a miserable cycle, while trying to 'do the best' for their child. This post by a father on the homedad.org.uk website describes the misery the breastfeeding dogma causes: 'We are first-time parents and my wife is breastfeeding . . . [She] is absolutely shattered . . . I do what I can but when baby wants feeding there is nothing I can do and have to wake the wife . . . We saw the midwives today and they seemed reluctant for my wife to express so I could feed the baby and give the wife a rest. They said it could upset the way [the baby] feeds coming off the breast then onto a bottle then back onto the breast . . . We tried for so long and now [our daughter] is here my wife feels it her duty to try and be the complete mum without any consideration to herself, it really cuts me up knowing she is trying so hard.'[34]

Over time, breastfeeding leads to the mother taking responsibility for all of the baby's care, as Becky, a mother of one son,
found: 'When you are breastfeeding the baby only wants to go
to you anyway and only you can calm him. And when the baby
was crying a lot my partner used to find that very difficult. More
stressful than I found it . . . We had quite a few rows about that.
My partner would say, "I can't settle him – you go through." And
a couple of times – especially when I was ill, I had a cold or
something – we used to have a row about it. I just wanted one
night unbroken. I just wanted him to take responsibility without
having to default it to me.'

Breastfeeding casts the mother as the child expert in the home,
her (literal) attachment to the baby mistaken for some innate
skill. Karen, also the mother of one son, observes, 'My husband's
assumption, I think, was always that I was the mother, I was
the one doing the breastfeeding, albeit really awfully, in an
ineffective way, so I must therefore be the expert. Many of our
earliest rows were about that. "I am not the expert, he is your
son too! I don't know what I am doing."'

It is no wonder that nearly half of all women who start out
exclusively breastfeeding soon give up. Women may go back to
work well before six months are up. They may want their bodies,
their autonomy and their sleep back. They may also want their
partner to play a role in the core parental function of feeding the
child. Yet rather than understanding the reasons why women can't,
or choose not to, continue breastfeeding, perhaps even suggesting
compromises such as 'topping up' with formula milk or providing
efficient, hospital-grade expressing pumps at drop-ins and baby
clinics, the NHS insists on promoting breastfeeding alone and
by implication stigmatises most mothers for apparently putting
themselves before their babies.

But the mental health of the mother should trump the breastfeeding of the child. What is the point of attempting to pump
a child with 'superfood for babies' as the NHS patronisingly dubs
breast milk[35] if the mother is tearful, too exhausted to interact

with her child meaningfully, or in pain? What good does that do the child? Or the mother? Sensitivity and responsiveness are essential to infants' healthy emotional and cognitive development.[36] In some cases, breastfeeding may hinder rather than help this. Some women sail through six or more months of breastfeeding, but for the rest the effort, heartache and guilt, together with the exclusion of fathers, are suffered in pursuit of an overly restrictive goal.

Breastfeeding, of course, is one of the reasons cited in defence of the UK's grossly iniquitous parental leave system. For the crucial first months of a baby's life, the mother must look after the child alone. For employed mothers, maternity leave lasts up to twelve months, thirty-nine weeks of which are paid (the majority at a flat rate lower than the full-time minimum wage, though individual employers may supplement this).[37] Eligible fathers are allotted only two weeks' paternity leave when their baby is first born; again this is paid at the same low flat rate that may be topped up by employers.[38] Both parents are also entitled to take up to one month of unpaid parental leave in the first year of their child's life, if back at work within this period.[39]

Since April 2011 mothers who return to work before their child is twelve months old have been able, in effect, to transfer any outstanding leave (up to twenty-six weeks) to the father.[40] This Additional Paternity Leave is a welcome step that enshrines in law the possibility of sharing care for very young children more equitably. But there are significant barriers to pursuing this option. Parents may worry about fathers taking the earnings hit involved (Additional Paternity Leave is paid at the same level as the last twenty-six weeks of maternity leave: that is, at the usual flat rate for the first three months, after which nothing is paid at all). Fathers may fear alienating bosses by going on extended paternity leave. Families in which mothers can afford not to return to work earlier than twelve months may be minded to stick with the status quo: habits within the household have already been formed by this stage in the leave period; and women may be reluctant to give up what has been established as 'their' leave. Even the Labour government, which introduced this legislation before it lost the 2010 General Election, estimated that only 4 to 8 per cent of eligible fathers would take up the right to a greater share of the leave.[41] At the time of writing, the Coalition Government has additionally proposed that from 2015 parents be given greater flexibility in sharing leave and fathers allotted a further four weeks. Although this is another positive move, the leave would still be paid at a low flat rate and the proportion ring-fenced for fathers, whilst increased, would remain low. Once again, even the Government itself expects that any impact would be minor.[42]

The widespread severance of men from domestic life takes a great emotional toll on parents. Ben describes his feelings on returning to work: 'I was working in the factory and the offer I got was – you can take your two weeks, the first week on full pay, the second week you get sick pay. So I only took the first week. I felt robbed. Especially as my wife had had a Caesarean and she couldn't walk around or anything. It was hard. She was doing too much – what she shouldn't have been doing – because I wasn't there to help. I was feeling dreadful. I was at work looking at my phone about a million times. In that first week back, I thought the child was safer than my wife was.'

The inadequacy of the UK's paternity leave provision means that women who have undergone surgery and are advised to refrain from basic activities such as lifting and driving are left to cope at home unaided because their partners are forced back to work rather than taking time out to do a greater share of the parenting. And all women – whatever the circumstances of the birth – are left alone caring for newborn children for hours on end, day after day. Even in families where fathers can afford to take paternity leave, the pitifully short length of time passes very quickly. As Jane, on maternity leave herself, observes, 'Two weeks' paternity leave is nothing when you have a small baby. It goes in the blink of an eye.'

While the father is once again pulled back into working life, the mother is propelled into her role as primary carer. The resulting isolation is recalled by Michelle, a full-time mother of three from Gloucestershire whose husband works away from home during the week. 'I just thought I could sit on the kitchen floor and cry some days and nobody would even know I was there.' Mothers feel that the repetitive grind of looking after a small child goes unrecognised by partners who have little knowledge of that world. The circumstances are ripe for rancour. 'Although it is a privilege to have all that time with your baby I think that what is so shocking about maternity leave is that you literally separate into these different worlds,' remembers Maggie. 'The number of girlfriends I have got who have the same issues I did – which is that when my partner came home from work I just wanted to tell him all about my day because I'd hardly spoken to anyone and he wanted to come in and not do anything for an hour and there was me gabbling away. It's very divisive potentially and you have to work very hard at overcoming that.'

At a time when a relationship inevitably comes under stress anyway, because of the demands of a very young baby, UK maternity and paternity leave entitlements serve to ratchet up the pressure. And in this period, dynamics and patterns of behaviour are set from which it is very hard to move on. The mother spends all day, every day with her baby. As a result she becomes very familiar with her child and how best to care for it. This is an opportunity denied to fathers but it comes at a price. The mother becomes accustomed to taking the lead in provision and organisation for the child; and the father assumes a supporting role. This is perpetuated as the child, naturally, begins to turn to the mother in preference to the father, and so the mother becomes more and more expert at caring for it. This new order within the household is then embedded.

Celeste, a full-time mother of three children from Bristol whose husband works six days a week as a market trader, recalls that when her first child was very young her husband, 'Just left me to it and I remember feeling quite bewildered and scared really because I didn't know a thing about how to deal with a child. His explanation was that he felt he wanted to leave me to bond with my child and that's why he went out a lot . . . But maybe also he didn't know how to deal with a newborn.'

Unlike mothers, fathers are not obliged to face their fear of the responsibility involved in looking after a very young child. They are able to escape this situation and so the fear is never conquered. As a result, they may never feel entirely at ease with their children, in the way that the mother does after her months of compulsory practice.

Outside of the household, as women go about their new business as child carers, they build up networks and resources of knowledge that consolidate their expertise and reinforce their role as the main parent. They get to know the appointments system at the local GP surgery and which doctors to ask for and those to avoid. They are the first to realise that the child needs new shoes, or a thick winter coat, and to work out where best to buy them. Women hunt out local playgroups, swimming sessions and parks, and build up a mental database of where to go, when, and how to get there. The woman establishes an intricate web of information and contacts in her role as mother. As maternity leave progresses, her lead in the realm of childcare becomes the norm. Having done it from the start it seems natural – and easier – to carry on.

Diane works in finance and is a mother of one from London. Even though she took only a short period of maternity leave, returning to work after three months, she believes that this has set the pattern of care between her husband and herself ever since: 'The childcare is entirely down to me . . . There is so much that one keeps in one's head that it's not an easy thing for two people to share the responsibility for and that is where the problem comes from . . . It starts from when they are born and you are having to think about, "When did they last have a feed? When did they last do a poo? When are they going to next need a sleep?" All those kind of things. And it just goes from that to, "What time is the nanny coming round? When's the shopping—

being delivered? When do I need to get back to be there to meet them?" You just switch one for the other.'

Along with her repertoire of care skills, the mother's visits to parks and playgroups mean that her social circle has expanded to include countless other women and their children. It's easy, and often enjoyable, for her to take off with the children and meet up with friends in the park, leaving her partner to read the Sunday papers or set about a bit of home improvement. According to an Equal Opportunities Commission report in 2005, mothers not only do over three quarters of the childcare during the week but also two thirds of it at the weekend.[43] This habit, once formed, continues right through childhood. The less the father takes the children out by himself the less comfortable an option it seems. Yet the mother's playground social circle keeps on expanding and some deep and lasting bonds are forged. As Becky, now back at work part time after her maternity leave, observes, 'I have my baby friends and going to see them is really good because two adults looking after two children seems to be easier than one adult and one child. But obviously I met them through being on maternity leave and going to groups and being with my son all the time and having people chat to you when you are with your child and all that sort of thing and my partner doesn't really have that.'

Mothers also talk about giving their partners time to themselves after the rigours of their working week, distinguishing between paid work and the unpaid work of childcare. 'At weekends I definitely do more than my partner. Partly that is because I don't feel that I need as much of a break as he does because he's been working all week,' Becky adds. Mothers themselves internalise the prevailing view that childcare is less important, and less demanding, than paid work.

Despite the long-term benefits associated with fathers' close involvement in the early care of their children as attachment and responsiveness develop,[44] any man who attempts to break into post-natal groups soon finds that they are not intended for him. Kate tells of her husband's visit to a baby clinic: 'He took one of our children for her second set of jabs . . . Every other person in the room with a baby was a woman. They called everybody else out to see the nurse before him, including women who had arrived later than him with their babies. Eventually there was nobody else left in the room with a baby except him and they came over, frowned, looked round the room and went back in to the office again, came back out again and called our child's name and looked round the room again. So my husband said to them, "Well, clearly it's me. I have the only baby left in the room. I think this is the baby you are looking for, what do you think?" And they said, "Oh sorry, do come in." And he was furious by that stage as he'd sat there for forty-five minutes. And he went into the nurse's room and he was asked if he'd taken the baby in for jabs before. He said he hadn't and he asked what he should do. And they said, "Hold her as if you were breastfeeding her"! And he felt stupid and humiliated and all the things that you wouldn't want him to feel.'

In 'woman-centred' services men are made to feel as if their care for a child is an anomaly, something to be ridiculed rather than encouraged. Having experienced a situation such as this, most fathers would be unlikely to put themselves forward for future visits to the baby clinic.

The woman's public role as a mother gives her access to a communal maternal world but also traps her in it. Despite official pledges to 'encourage shared parenting from the earliest stages of pregnancy',[45] both the UK's 'woman-centred' maternity services and its inequitable antenatal and parental leave provision focus on mothers and fail to engage fathers. The cumulative effect is that the state promotes and facilitates the sexist notion that women should be the main carers for their children – simply because they give birth to them. This discourages the most willing of fathers and gives an official green light to the less willing to take a back seat. Meanwhile the mother has no choice but to take on the primary care of her children. This blinkered and unimaginative approach means that, even before the child is born, parents are assigned gender roles that will shape the rest of their lives.

The birth and early care of a child is one of the most exhilarating, nerve-racking and joyful periods in a couple's life. It is a watershed moment, in which we examine our priorities, values and relationships with a rare intensity. Terrifyingly yet thrillingly, all our cards appear to be thrown up in the air.

Society should not dictate how they fall. We can seize that moment to enable men and women to immerse themselves in the rewarding work of nurturing a young child and then, with the benefit of this experience, to configure their family lives as they see fit. As I discuss later, in countries that genuinely embrace shared parenting from the start, fathers are choosing to take a greater role in the lives of their young children and the positive benefits are being felt across society. The UK must change too: the birth of a child should mark the opening up of our lives, rather than the closing down of options.

3

A Word of Advice, Dear

'I just feel like we have had children at a point in time where it is difficult to win the game. There is so much pressure to be a successful person and to not let your standards slip . . . to be the biggest, fucking earth mother, but an earth mother that doesn't walk around looking like an earth mother, who looks great. So you look great while you are puréeing the food and you don't leave your child to cry, you sit with him all night, you know what I mean?'

Olive, an academic and mother of two from London, reflects on the judgemental and unsolicited advice that she feels she was forced to swallow on becoming a mother, and the severe loss of confidence she experienced as a result. 'I felt I was just a quivering wreck. How could I be such a failure at this? How could it be so hard?' While the government and public services like the NHS frame the woman as the primary parent, their efforts are bolstered by the parenting industry, whose propaganda confronts her at every turn. This fosters an atmosphere of claustrophic self-doubt for mothers, as Olive discovered.

Raising children is a woman's role, we are told by the media, campaigners, research groups and retailers. A trip to any shopping centre drives this point home. Supermarkets convene 'mum's choice' panels to review products, and offer a 'mum and baby bundle' in exchange for signing up to their parents' club. Food manufacturers produce 'mum's own' ranges and splash images of nurturing mothers and delighted children on their labels. Chemists promote their 'mother and baby' sections. Toiletry brands push 'pampering' products aimed at 'busy mums'. Nappy manufacturers feature mothers with their babies on their packaging. Catalogues show women delightedly bathing infants, conscientiously employing safety equipment to protect their children against household hazards and lending their offspring a hand to play an age-appropriate DVD. Department stores are packed with goods that crow 'Mums' favourite' on their wrapping. Products from ready meals to clothes ranges come accompanied by a blurb relaying folksy tales of the doughty CEO mum who spotted a gap in the market. Children's books dutifully convey messages of diversity, acceptance and ethical living and yet stories invariably feature a mother as the main carer, comforter, social organiser and cook.

The media, too, fixes its gaze on mothers. When women appear on the news, they are twice as likely as men to be identified by their family status.[1] Broadcasters and the press, gorging on the grub fed to them by researchers and charities, churn out an endless round of stories about how it is mothers who secure – or else risk – their children's happiness, health and intellectual prowess. The apex of this is the issue that the media and academics refuse to let die: the effect of so-called 'working mothers' on children's well-being. In 2009, while I was researching this book, two headline-grabbing reports came out that illustrated this phenomenon. The Institute for Child Health published research on the apparently negative effect of 'working mums' on child health, linking women alone to their children's welfare. 'Children of working mums "have unhealthier lifestyles"', announced its accompanying press release, a story jumped on by media outlets including the BBC, the *Guardian*, the *Daily Telegraph* and the *Daily Mail*.[2] In the same year, the Children's Society's Good Childhood Inquiry, although a very detailed and wide-ranging piece of work with many sensible policy suggestions, clumsily connected women's entry into the workplace with the increase in family break-up. Again, much of the media focused on this one angle.[3] For good measure such stories are routinely accompanied by photographs and footage of mothers engaged in either exemplary or transgressive parenting behaviour, as the tenor of the report and research dictates.

Beyond the news pages, in the lifestyle sections, female columnists are employed to offer 'been there' advice and humorous observation on 'coping with kids'. Children's television trailers reach out to mothers, depicting women at home with their children mining a channel's educational resources. Gossip pages are filled with speculation about famous mothers, from icy, pulled-together A-listers, snapped with oversized bags in the crook of their tiny arms, to frowsy reality fodder papped falling out of clubs. One minute admired for combining motherhood and glamour, the next found wanting in their commitment to their children, these celebrities are both a rebuke and a warning to civilian mothers. Ghouls are paraded before us as reporters pick over the lives of those depicted as sad mothers (Denise Fergus, the mother of James Bulger), as bad mothers (Karen Matthews) and as somewhere in between (Kate McCann): their public grief or shame a means of keeping us all in check.

Raising children, the parenting industry tells us, is a woman's function.[4] Yet despite supposedly being born to this role, women are not trusted in it. The parenting industry consistently questions our ability as mothers. Its very existence relies on the implicit assumption that we are not up to the job and that we require guidance and censure from a higher authority. On becoming a mother, a woman who has been used to a degree of respect and responsibility in her life finds herself being treated like an inept novice in an undervalued, unpaid role. Being a mother, we are to understand, is a risky business. Our children's and society's well-being and future happiness are at stake. We must not take this lightly, or even in our stride. Rather, the focus of each day should be to ensure the optimum outcome for our offspring. Television consumption, diet, discipline, internet use, social activities and friendship groups must all be carefully managed by mothers. We must not busk it. If we do, we risk our offspring developing more slowly than other children, becoming social misfits or being recruited into street gangs. The way to insure against this is to hand ourselves over to the self-appointed experts who will instruct us in carrying out the onerous task of parenting to the highest of standards. Exploiting our insecurity, which it has deliberately stirred up, the parenting industry then offers us the benefit of its wisdom: at a price.

And goodness knows there are enough of these experts around to check up on us. The contemporary professionalisation of motherhood is unprecedented. Even though mothers are now more likely to work than in the past, they still spend more time looking after their children than used to be the case because they've cut back on everything else in their lives – social events, leisure time and sleep – in order to dedicate themselves to their charges.[5] When women are with their children it is a far more focused affair than for previous generations, whose offspring were out in the street or the park all day while they got on with domestic chores, or played around their feet as they cooked and polished. Motherhood is no longer a state of being: it's a project. The writer of a 1977 research paper on 'Sexism in Parenting Manuals' exclaimed at the time that, 'there are more than fifty books on the market today for parents'.[6] Today Amazon lists more than 40,000 of them.[7] Meanwhile, newsagents' shelves groan under the weight of *Practical Parenting & Pregancy*, *Mother & Baby*, *Prima Baby & Pregnancy*, *Junior* and their like. Websites minutely detail the preparations required of the expectant mother; advise on breastfeeding, weaning and providing a balanced diet for children; and steer women through parenting toddlers, primary-school-age children, tweenies, and adolescents. Television parenting programmes, a phenomenon of the new millennium, blast out narratives of parental despair and salvation from gurus helicoptered in for the cameras.

Sam is the mother of one daughter from Somerset. She and her husband both work full time. She is very aware of an idealised image of motherhood perpetuated by the parenting industry, in relation to which she judges herself a failure: 'Good mothering [is depicted as] a wife, slim, heterosexual, middle class, privileged, stay at home. And I fit some of those categories but not very many . . . This idea of being a bad mum: I do think it comes from all angles . . . There was an example yesterday. One of those supermarket magazines came through the post and there was a debate in it about working mothers. Every single example that they gave of a working mother was a part-time working mother . . . Anything that talks about working mothers, I always think this might actually make me feel better about myself and every example they give is a part-time mum, at most three days a week. Or working from home with their children round them. Those enterprising mums that realise their daughters love their jam so much they are going to make it into a career, that sort of thing. "I made a headband for my daughter and everyone wanted one, now I'm a multi-millionaire." . . . those sort of people. Every time I read these articles I just really feel worse . . . I kind of get the feeling from these magazines that for the mums their babies are like handbags. I am not joking . . . those mums are just immaculate and they look beautiful and you see them and they are all matching, particularly little girls and mums . . . They talk about being a fashionable mum and that is good motherhood . . . Did you get your figure back quickly? Did you manage to not let yourself go? . . . It's in the normal magazines, mum magazines – how quickly can you get into your designer jeans? . . . They just didn't seem to reflect me . . . It's about buy this, buy that, it will make you a better mum . . . But actually I don't think that is necessarily helping, it makes people feel bad. It makes me feel bad about myself, makes me feel bad about being a mum, it makes me feel bad that I am not doing what perhaps I feel I should be doing . . . I see what I do as deviant and against the norm and kind of irresponsible.' By holding up domestic paragons before the rest of us, what constitutes a 'good' mother is made clear: devoted, self-sacrificing, with a natural affinity for the educational and nurturing tasks of parenthood; a woman who has reached the zenith of fulfilment in her role as a mother and homemaker.

Modern mothers take a double hit. Not only are they less prepared than previous generations for the inequality engendered by parenthood, but they are also expected to meet far more exacting and proscribed standards of mothering than in the past. No detail of a mother's approach to parenting is too small to require strict direction and criticism.

Take, for example, the choice of a pram. One might imagine that such a decision would come down to basic practicalities: which models are affordable, will take up least room at home, will be easy to get on public transport or to fold up into a car, and are comfortable to sit in and to push? Yet this list of considerations is far too limited for the experts. There's the weighty issue of child development to take into account. Which pram best advances your child's communication skills? Liz Attenborough, manager of a campaigning outfit called Talk to Your Baby (TTYB), has firm views on this issue: forward-facing, bad; inward-facing, good. The acceptable, inward-facing pram encourages interaction with a child while on the move; forward-facing prams prevent it. This is no minor matter. The campaign website warns: 'Early years professionals tell us that the unsociable design of children's buggies is a factor contributing to the poor language and communication skills of many children starting nursery or school. Young children need face-to-face communication to fully develop as sociable talkers and learners. If every parent owned a pusher-facing, sociable buggy, more toddlers would receive the one-to-one communication they need.'[8]

In an interview in the *Guardian* newspaper (accompanied, naturally, by images of women pushing children in prams and featuring references only to mothers) Liz Attenborough's thesis is explained further. According to this piece, 'She thinks cooing and chattering and singing should be statutory because the amount you talk to your children influences all sorts of things, not just how they learn to talk, but also their ability to make friends, and progress academically.'[9] Speech difficulties when children start school, 'she warns darkly, can lead to behavioural problems, exam failure, delinquency perhaps even prison'.[10] Forward-facing pram owners be warned. 'We know we've got a problem with communication skills and buggies aren't helping,' states the nation's buggy monitor.[11] 'Where I live in Richmond there is nothing but [forward-facing, three-wheelered prams] and you see lots of little people hanging over the edge looking unspeakably bored . . . One reason that people come up with [for not talking to their babies] is they don't know what to say, so they don't say anything, which makes you want to weep, quite frankly.'[12]

Well, quite frankly, pushing 'little people' around in forward-facing buggies often provides a welcome break from the sometimes joyful, frequently mind-numbing, interaction that goes on the rest of the time. The chance to gather your thoughts while getting some fresh air and exercise on the way to the supermarket can be sorely needed. In my case, my pram may have prevented me from wringing every last interactive opportunity out of the day but it did wonders for my mental health. Besides which, there's the issue of cost: one big factor in the all-important pram purchasing decision is that 'sociable' prams are more expensive. This is something to which Dr Suzanne Zeedyk, an academic who carried out research published by TTYB, is earnestly alive: 'Suddenly we have the possibility of a socio-economic divide. Middle-class parents can afford buggies that are good for babies, but parents from a different class can't.'[13] Unfortunately this terrible future world populated by the gormless offspring of the buggy underclass appears unavoidable. The average spend in the UK on a child in its first year is now just over nine thousand pounds.[14] Enough parents are prepared to dig deep for expensive baby paraphernalia, so there's no incentive for manufacturers to lower their prices. On trend designs, 'celebrity mum' endorsement and the chance to get ahead in the interaction stakes mean that posh prams are big business for those that can afford them. It doesn't stop there. Shops are filled with everything from toys that develop social skills through to biscuits that promote hand–eye coordination. Parents are easy prey, readily emptying their pockets in their desire to do the best for their child and give them a leg-up in life.

In a climate of such overstated benefits and risks, every choice we make concerning our children becomes loaded with import. One wrong move and their life chances could be severely hampered. No decision can be taken lightly, so we must do our research. One mother explains to *The Times* newspaper why she gave up her job after she had her child: 'I did some research and decided it would be bad for [my son's] psychological health if I went back to work . . . They don't want to be in a nursery, but they get used to it. They suppress their feelings and suppress who they really are. This might not be good for them later in life.'[15] Those who don't thoroughly investigate each step of the way in raising their children are frowned upon. 'My sis doesn't read anything, she's just right in there with her sleeves rolled up at the elbows, purifying [sic] food for weaning and doing [controlled crying] with no hint of research!' cries one woman on the website Mumsnet.[16]

Research is an essential part of the modern mother's job and the main tools at her disposal are parenting manuals and the internet. As the statistics show, the number of books about raising children has hugely increased in recent decades. 'Regretfully, many parents today are victims of information overload,' observes Tracy Hogg,[17] author of eight parenting manuals.[18] This productivity is all the more remarkable given that the majority have been published since she died in 2004, her profitable line in wise words living on beyond the grave. The use of the word 'parent' in these manuals is nothing more than a nod to politically correct niceties, for they really have women in their sights. The expansive 'parenting' sections of bookshops are awash with pastel book jackets, featuring doting mothers as well as their well-scrubbed, attractive offspring. Underneath the packed rows of books for parents (aka mothers), there's a small straggle of parenting books for men. These have a distinctive tone. They are jokey (*The New Dad's Survival Guide*), blokey (*The Bloke's Guide to Babies*), confessional (*The Reluctant Fathers' Club*) and self-deprecating (*The Dysfunctional Father's Guide to Pregnancy, Birth and Babies*), perpetuating all the usual stereotypes about fathers. But this awkward little collection is merely a blip before the row mutates into guides for grandparents. In fact, fathers are such an irrelevance in the world of the parenting manual that some bookshops don't even bother pretending, having instead sections that tell it as it is: 'Mother and Baby'.

These shelves upon shelves of manuals are aimed squarely at women, overwhelmed as they are by the inflated expectations placed on them, and crying out for company. First-time mothers, in particular, are desperate for someone to lean on. Although mothers with much younger siblings, or women who live with extended families, may have some recent experience of helping out with the care of children, most do not. Twenty-nine is now the average age for a woman to have her first baby.[19] Having usually moved out of her own childhood home to work or study elsewhere years ago, she lives apart from relatives other than her partner. Yet on becoming a mother she finds herself plunged into the role of primary parent to an entirely dependent child. Almost certainly feeling emotional and insecure, she turns to the slew of parenting self-help books.

Trish and her husband both work full time in London while their daughter attends nursery. From her maternity leave onwards Trish has been the main carer for their daughter. She felt in need of advice: 'I have got nieces and nephews but they live abroad so I have never been involved in babysitting for them or looking after them at all. Quite a lot of my friends like me had children later, you know, early to mid thirties. So I was never submerged in babies before that. So I needed something to point me in the right direction. I needed somebody to tell me, or tell us, what we should be doing.' Rational, educated women, who are used to furthering their knowledge through research and reading, turn to books for guidance. As Helen, a full-time mother from Oxford, observes, 'There's that bit, isn't there, where suddenly it all goes wrong and they stop sleeping all the time and they start requiring you to go for four-hour walks when you think, "I need a book!"? And I think that's part of having children later and you are not surrounded by babies as you might be in other cultures. So you feel the need to get some support and information from somewhere else . . . We live in an information culture and, especially maybe if you've come from work, you want answers to things.'

From colic and tantrums through to school transition and adolescent angst, the stages in the parenting journey are unknown to the first-time mother. And here, by the roadside, hovers the 'expert', waving her down and peddling advice. These people appear as friendly yet authoritative guides, setting out a stall of charts, quizzes and key principles alongside reassuringly familiar case studies of similarly clueless parents who were saved by following their system. Uncertain of the way, and of ourselves, we gladly stump up the cash for their wisdom.

The 'experts' have mothers over a barrel because they are the only ones coming up with solid suggestions about how to manage life with children. For many women, their partners are at work much of the time and so unable to figure things out alongside them; their parents may only be sporadically involved because of geographical distance, their own work commitments, or both; and advice from health visitors can be difficult to access.[20] On the occasions when a midwife or health visitor turned up at our door after our son was born they'd look at the books lying around, pityingly shake their heads and say something maddening along the lines of, 'Babies don't read, dear. Follow your instincts.' But I had no instinct. I loved my baby and I felt strongly protective of him but I didn't know how to care for him. It was only in time that I learnt to parent the way we all learn, through trial and error.

Isla, a Manchester mother of two, felt similarly lacking in this elusive instinct. 'I was just completely bewildered and had no idea what to do and people would say things like, "Don't you recognise the different cries?" and I was thinking, "No, I can just hear a yelling sound – I'm obviously not tuned into my baby." I had no experience with children – it's all very well to say turn to your inner mothering instinct but mine appeared to be absent. I'd held a baby once in my adult life – I didn't live in a world of babies – how could you know what to do with a baby? I didn't know how to handle babies, I didn't know what babies needed, what sleep or food they needed, how to breast-feed – anything. There's a reason that people turn to those books and it's because they don't have any parenting experience and therefore they have to rely on things like manuals because who the heck would tell them what to do? People don't have large families, they don't care for their younger siblings, they don't before the age of thirty have lots of babies in their lives – a lot of people don't anyway. This intuition isn't intuition, it's learnt behaviour – and if you take that away from people and you leave them on their own without any supportive community or family on their own in a house with a baby, yes they are going to need a manual.'

For Isla and many others these manuals offer genuine help, a landmark in the blizzard of early motherhood. But they also exert a covert pressure on women, subtly shaping the expectation that they will be the primary parent and codifying how they should perform this role. While they refer to 'parents' in general terms, these books contain instructions issued specifically to mothers. In Tracy Hogg's *Secrets of the Baby Whisperer* readers are encouraged to freeze a range of home-cooked meals in good time before 'you're due'.[21] In *The New Contented Little Baby Book*, Gina Ford admits free time is limited when following her routines but adds,

'Believe me, mothers who are not following a routine have even less spare time.'[22] The Continuum Concept philosophy involves the baby 'being constantly carried in arms or otherwise in contact with someone, usually his mother'.[23]

Having button-holed the mother, these manuals set out exacting care regimes. In addition to extensive home cooking, *Secrets of the Baby Whisperer* lists a string of other requirements. Mothers must give their new babies a tour of the house while someone else prepares 'chamomile tea or another calming beverage'. They must learn their babies' language, spot the meaning behind their different cries and interpret their movements. They must draw a 'circle of respect' around their child and ask its permission to embark on an all important baby massage session. They are instructed to follow Tracy Hogg's EASY (Eat, Activity, Sleep and You-time) routine and to diagnose their children as Angel, Textbook, Touchy, Spirited or Grumpy and treat them accordingly.[24]

The New Contented Little Baby Book, too, sets out an ambitious programme for the mother. Bed linen, changing table, wardrobe, chair, curtains, carpeting and lighting must be set up in the child's room to the book's precise specifications. Precise numbers of 'day outfits' should be bought and woollen clothes should be hand-washed. It advises that minutely detailed, labour-intensive daily routines be followed to the letter – 'half an hour can have a knock-on effect which disrupts the rest of your day and, possibly, your night' – as must the weaning programme. This begins with baby rice and works up to a menu including 'Fish cakes with cabbage and lyonnaise potatoes'.[25] Less routine-centred schemes are just as demanding: the Continuum Concept baby must experience 'constant physical contact', 'sleeping in his parents' bed', 'breast-feeding "on cue"' and 'having caregivers immediately respond to his signals'.[26]

From rigorous schedules, to being child-led or permanently attached to your child, each strategy demands that the mother give herself up entirely to its approach. The reward for this slavish devotion is a 'contented' baby,[27] a 'healthier, happier baby',[28] or a child that has achieved 'optimal physical, mental and emotional development'.[29] Following the instructions will deliver us the advertised dream child. But the weight of responsibility is a heavy one. 'Raising a child is a lifelong commitment,' Tracy Hogg intones in *Secrets of the Baby Whisperer*, 'something you must take more seriously than any mission you've ever accomplished. You are responsible for helping to guide and shape *another human being*, and there is no greater, higher assignment.' 'Try not to lose perspective,' she cheerily adds.[30] But, paradoxically, it is likely to increase the sales of these books if some do lose perspective: because the less perspective we have, the less sure we will be of ourselves, and the more dependent on such books we become. With the well-being of children at stake, women run themselves ragged trying to live up to the programme of 'good' mothering set out in these manuals. Some follow a regime of 'controlled crying', enduring weeks of their children screaming while confined to their cot in an effort to introduce regular bedtimes. Others, disciples of the let it all hang out gang, tolerate bun fights and flung toys while valiantly trying to distract their malevolent child with hand puppets or suggestions of potato printing. Throughout this time the mother berates herself for failing to match the successful model set out in the books, and so her confidence in herself as a parent – and as a person – ebbs away. Driven by despair to give most of the manuals a go in my time, I remember agonising over the fact that my baby insisted on sleeping after being fed rather than engaging in rigorous mini-gym exercise, as favoured by Tracy, and hanging my head in shame when I didn't get it together to express milk by seven o'clock in the morning, as advised by Gina.

This sense of failure was also Helen's experience: 'I got to the point where I felt actually these books are making it worse because all they do is make me feel inadequate and guilty all the time for not doing this or not having a baby who conforms to whatever pattern they set out . . . It's probably going to drive you to despair trying to get your wee little thing to feed every four hours and not wake you up, at all, ever.'

Deborah, a full-time mother of two children from Gloucestershire, also found the bombardment of instruction after the birth of her first child difficult to cope with. Having co-slept with her daughter, practised extended breastfeeding and eventually set up a flexi-home-schooling arrangement that enables her to educate her daughter at home for part of the week, she feels that she has always swum against the tide of mainstream advice. 'I can be quite obsessive if the situation isn't right . . . And when my daughter came along she was my main focus and she didn't sleep how I thought she was supposed to. I thought when she got to six weeks she would sleep through and she didn't and then I started to read books and the books weren't the right books for me . . . The book was saying, "She should be doing this, she should be doing that," and my daughter wasn't. I had always worked in an environment where if something wasn't working you put a plan together, you followed it and you resolved it. And it doesn't work with children . . . And so when someone you perceive as an expert, because you don't know any better, says, "They should be doing this and they should be doing that," then you take it very personally . . . My natural instincts didn't really match society's and so I was just being challenged continually and I got very obsessive about her sleep and I ended up with post-natal depression.'

When, despite the intensive efforts of mothers such as Deborah, a child's behaviour doesn't go to plan, the experts are apt to claim it is because the mother has failed to follow the advice correctly. It seems it is never the fault of the advice itself or simply the child's nature – or even the lack of effective input the mother is receiving from her partner or health professionals. There appear no suggestions for dealing with behaviour beyond the range permitted in the case studies, charts and systems, as Helen discovered: 'I remember thinking, "So you go on and you pat your baby on the back and what happens if that doesn't work?" There's lots of advice up to a point, but when it's not working it's no good.' But in our belief that the answer to our child's apparently errant behaviour must be out there somewhere, and that we alone are responsible for finding it, we frantically keep on searching. Mothers trade their valuable information, swapping tips and instructions: 'Gina says . . .', 'Annabel suggests . . .' 'Tracy advises . . .' We are on first-name terms with these sages. We become women with a one-track mind: motherhood. It matters too much, we think about it too much. Against Tracy Hogg's instructions, we lose perspective.

When women define themselves by motherhood their parenting decisions become integral to their self-perception. Like our taste in music or clothes, we see our School of Parenting choice as a statement about ourselves. And so we are affronted by others' different decisions: it's a rejection of something we have bought into heavily, and therefore a rejection of us, and even of our children. Mothers are driven into a downward spiral of comparison, competition and feelings of inadequacy. Michelle, a full-time mother of three from Gloucestershire, remarks, 'Women aren't very supportive of other women, there is that competition It's a very isolating experience, actually, and we all got competitive on what pram you have got and are you doing cotton nappies? Dare you get the jar out because you are feeding your child jarred food not organic prunes? . . . I was watching other people – perhaps that's what made me think I was obviously inadequate and all the rest of it.' The comparisons women make with other women, even the competitiveness that they feel, is intensified because they are doing much of the day-to-day parenting by themselves. Their partner isn't there to share in the decisions and to reciprocate reassurance.

Women are, of course, sophisticated in how they use these parenting resources. They weigh the writers' advice alongside that of friends and relatives and consider how it fits in with their own outlook and way of going about things. They adapt it to fit their own circumstances. But in considering and sifting the advice, they are also internalising and endorsing the stereotype of the mother that these guides reinforce, accepting the advice as 'expert' and taking on responsibility in the household for selecting and instituting systems. For these reasons, parenting books can become oppressive.

Even those who consciously reject what American sociologist Sharon Hays terms 'intensive mothering'[31] find that there is a parenting school that's been dreamt up just for them, with accompanying merchandise. The 'Bad Mother' or 'slummy mummy' is just another packaged maternal type and those who dreamt it up write humorous books and newspaper columns about their lives.[32] Although offering escape from the confines of 'good' mothering, women find themselves still defined in relation to it: if they are not actively 'good mothers', they must be self-consciously 'bad mothers'. These books and columns are aimed squarely at the middle-class market, the lax mothering judged amusing presumably because the reader is safe in the knowledge that the kids are all right really, in their well-cushioned homes. The middle classes have licence to laugh at their own, supposedly inadequate, mothering. And they are allowed to laugh at working-class mothers (pramfaces, Chav mums, Vicky Pollard). If working-class women were given such a platform to laugh at their own perceived fecklessness, the reaction would be a great deal more uneasy.

Interest in our own and others' Schools of Parenting is evident on the websites dedicated to child rearing, where women with children of all ages debate their attitudes and experiences intensively. These forums are billed as an antidote to 'outside' pressures, a democratic forum where posters can swap real life experience and no single opinion is worth more than another. These sites can undoubtedly be an important source of support for women feeling isolated or looking for peer advice on particular problems. Hazel is a tutor and mother of two sons, living in Essex. Her relationship with their father was unhappy and violent, and when the children were at primary school they divorced and he moved abroad. Her family, which had emigrated from Sierra Leone to the UK with Hazel when she was a child, didn't live nearby and she felt very isolated. The forums that she joined were an invaluable source of support. 'Slowly, slowly, I started to go on the internet, on Mumsnet. And I joined a lone-parenting web group also, just to get some kind of help and support from other parents . . . It's amazing the world of information that you can find, if you feel isolated. You find so much and it also gives you the confidence to know that you are not alone. There are other people going through sometimes worse situations than you.' The help that Hazel accessed through these sites inspired her to set up her own website and support group for local lone parents which has now become a core part of her social network.

Jane, a mother of two and teacher from Leeds, also found websites helpful in a time of need, when she suffered post-natal depression after the birth of her second child: 'I used some of the chat forums on Netmums and I found people experiencing exactly the same thing as me, all of whom, like me, seemed convinced that there was something seriously wrong with them. And I read them and thought, "These people are mad, there's nothing wrong with them." And then I thought, "Well maybe I'm mad too!" So I did find that quite supportive, actually. And I hadn't really known about that when I had my first child and I think it is quite a good resource.'

As well as this acute role, it's clear from the contributions and the regularity with which some people post messages that these parenting websites provide valuable ongoing camaraderie and entertainment for their members. They've also adopted campaigning roles, calling for everything from a clamp-down on junk food advertising and sexualised products for children, to improved support for those suffering post-natal depression and miscarriage. This has undoubtedly done a great deal to highlight these important issues. But despite such significant benefits, these sites also unwittingly contribute to a culture that singles out mothers as their children's main carers.

The mother of all UK parenting websites, Mumsnet, is visited by over one million people each month.[33] When it was originally set up in 2000, the founders, Carrie Longton and Justine Roberts, claimed that it wasn't intended solely for mothers at all. The choice of name, then, is curious. 'They chose "Mumsnet", hoping not to alienate dads. They need not have worried,' one *Observer* journalist breezily suggested when Mumsnet had been up and running for a year. 'The site has attracted more than its fair share of men. As Carrie amusingly puts it, "Being a mum goes beyond gender."'[34] But the claim that the site is for both mothers and fathers sits oddly not only with the name but also with the logo, a parody of the 1970s show *Charlie's Angels*, about three ass-kicking female private investigators (remotely directed by their male boss, Charlie). Similar, women-centric signals are sent out by the campaigning pages symbol (Rosie the Riveter declaring 'We Can Do It!'[35]) and the local forum pages ('Meet local mums'[36]). Naive or disingenuous, the 'beyond gender' claim rings hollow. Fathers are allocated a separate Dadsnet section, in which many posters are, in fact, mothers in search of a male point of view. Men, perhaps feeling unwelcome, stay away: a mere 1 per cent of those using Mumsnet are fathers.[37]

The website not only underscores the idea of women as primary parents but also provides a forum in which women become more and more bound up in their role as mothers. No stone of the mother's lot is left unturned on this site. Play-date etiquette, emergency recipe enquiries ('QUICK: have accidentally melted butter . . .'),[38] fractious siblings and school holiday dilemmas are all catered for in its web pages. Mumsnet members spend over one hundred minutes a day on the internet, excluding work use. Eighteen per cent visit the Mumsnet site several times a day, 13 per cent visit it every day and 21 per cent visit it most days.[39] With the children in bed and some quiet in the home, mothers are pouring themselves a drink, firing up their laptops and spending yet more time thinking about their children. Mumsnet and its kind create mummy addicts. Motherhood becomes their entire universe, as women pore over the way they bring up their children and organise their homes.

Wendy works in advertising and is the mother of two children, one of whom is at primary school. Her youngest child is looked after by a childminder on the three days of the week that Wendy works. She lives in London with her husband, who works full time. 'I am not really into Mumsnet and all that. I think of myself as a woman who has got children. I am not a mum – well, I am – but I don't want to be cast as just that on a social networking site or whatever . . . A lot of my friends don't have children . . . [Having children] is so universal that it doesn't necessarily bring you closer . . . I don't necessarily like people more just because they are mums or feel that they can understand. Yes they can understand the school run but how meaningful is that? I looked on Mumsnet a bit about pre-eclampsia, when I got it the second time, but it just panicked me. And the other posters were all, kind of, "Oh Jane, I have got my fingers crossed for you," and they would post up the next day about what had happened. I can't bear it, you know. None of them know each other or anything.'

Despite its campaigning credentials and degree-educated membership,[40] the liveliest debates on the site are about domestic trivia. As one member gushes, 'I am newish on here and what I like is that you can talk about what interests you to others who feel the same. Eg how many of your real-life friends are going to want to talk about details of housekeeping? Not many, that's for sure!!!'[41] Quite. Other sites similarly encourage a fixation on mothering. On Netmums, posters agonise over acceptable children's television programmes ('I have to say I'm not very keen on [*Peppa Pig*] as I think that the programme actually teaches kids bad habits . . . After starting to watch it [my daughter] started raspberry blowing . . .'[42]). Meanwhile at Babycentre, the members of the 'Actively Trying' forum excitedly report in if their pregnancy test has come up BFP (big, fat positive), cross their fingers that it's a 'sticky' one (that they don't miscarry) and send lucky 'babydust' to the other posters.[43]

But it isn't all group hugs on these sites. Alongside such examples of 'we're all in this together' chummy equality, judgement also exists. 'No one knows anyone's kids, so you don't get anyone judging you,' asserted Justine Roberts just shortly after the Mumsnet site had been set up.[44] More recently she reiterated the claim: '[People] are not judged the way they could be in real life.'[45] But this is undermined by some of the content on the site. The anonymity she lauds actually means that Mumsnet, in common with many other internet forums, is used by some posters to criticise others harshly. There are posts proclaiming the superiority of particular parenting styles and waspish comments about others' parenting decisions. These sites may enable a new form of democratic discussion, but they also provide a platform for censure and moral superiority. While members post their concerns about children's cyber bullying, others on these sites are in danger of being bullied themselves.

As befits its solidly middle-class membership,[46] the dynamics and tone on the Mumsnet forums resemble the chat in a girls' sixth-form common room. The in-crowd patrols the site, high-handedly setting out its views and slapping down new girls or those who step out of line. A poster who has just joined the site makes the cardinal error of signing off with kiss signs ('xxx'). One Mean Girl snaps back that this faux pas will make other posters self-combust with fury, 'and as we are all on here neglecting our DC [darling children] and DP/DH [darling partner/darling husband], we just don't have time to clean up that sort of mess.'[47] It seems there's always time to neglect crucial domestic duties in order to make smart-arse comments, though. On another thread, a woman who settles her young baby using 'controlled crying' asks for others' thoughts on the method. She is accused of being 'barbaric' by one respondent, though another is more lenient, magnanimously sanctioning the practice if 'applied FLEXIBLY'.[48] Elsewhere a poster seeks opinions on whether or not it's safe to leave a baby in a hotel room asleep, with a monitor, and attend a party downstairs. She is immediately 'flamed' and the example of the McCanns invoked by one respondent. 'Not a chance. It's how it works when you have children, I'm afraid,' someone else sanctimoniously opines.[49] Fear-mongering and fury combine to put this poster in her place.

For all the talk of 2010 being the year of the 'Mumsnet election' and its campaigns on issues such as formula milk marketing and maternal mortality, the site's significance as a mainstream political force is questionable. During the 2010 General Election, the high profile of Mumsnet notwithstanding, 'family friendly' policies languished near the bottom of the political agenda and David Cameron's first Coalition Cabinet, in which women barely got a look in,[50] saw the equalities portfolio tacked onto the main job of its most likely looking female member (Theresa May, who we might imagine already had her hands full as Home Secretary). It suits politicians and the media to collude in the idea that, in taking part in a Mumsnet webchat, you get a rough ride. The media can then report on politicians getting 'handbagged' in the witches' coven, and the politicians get the chance to look fearless and show their human side by talking weaning. Meanwhile the Mumsnet questioners are puffed up about holding politicians to account on issues including the biscuits and nappies they favour and acres of media coverage is generated for the site.[51] Like the good-looking school-mate of an older brother, the politicians swan in, pat the excitable Mumsnet girls on the head, flirt with them for their own amusement, and leave. You are 'cool and fab', Ed Miliband, the then Environment Secretary, told Mumsnet on the day of his webchat on the site.[52] 'I can feel that global warming from here,'[53] giggled Mumsnet in response, allowing itself to be patronised and pigeonholed.

Despite the support these sites can offer, the campaigns they run and the agenda-setting claims made for them, many of their threads contain chatter to no end, huge speech bubbles with nothing inside them. Here the personal is . . . just personal, with little sense of a collective cause. Having vented their spleen online overnight the mummy addicts wake ready to start their duties afresh the next day. Content with the jaw-jaw, they fail to join the dots between their experience and that of the other online posters. The emphasis on individual experiences and feelings *as* individual experiences and feelings without consistent reference to the social, economic or political context within which they occur risks portraying women alone as responsible for overcoming the problems they discuss with insufficient demands being made of government or the other institutions and forces that frame their lives.[54] Despite the potential of the internet as a tool for change, too often it is just another means by which mothers are sucked into a damaging vortex of self-absorption, impossible standards and excessive scrutiny.

One of the greatest deprivations for a new mother is the loss of anonymity as she is exposed to the intervention and judgement of others. To walk down the street with your child is to risk unsolicited tips and instruction. I have lost count of the number of times people have told me what I should be doing in order to stop my child crying, sneezing, pulling his socks off or whatever form of apparently unacceptable behaviour he is indulging in at the time. When he was a baby, people thought nothing of shaking the pram, lifting him out of it and taking him from my arms – all without permission being asked or granted. A friend, as a new mother, was stalked during a visit to a museum by a woman quizzing her on her breastfeeding intentions. On one occasion I was walking with another friend and her children when we were stopped by a passer-by. 'As a child lawyer,' announced the woman, presenting her indisputable credentials, 'I advise you to keep your daughter closer to you, to prevent her being snatched.' The unwelcome advisers are full of their own righteousness as self-appointed guardians of the child's welfare.

The effect of this oppressive monitoring is a form of self-censorship. In *Making Sense of Motherhood*, her study of the transition to life as a mother, the sociologist Tina Miller details how a number of the women she interviewed restricted the amount of time they spent outside the home with their young babies because they feared being exposed as inadequate mothers. She also notes that in later, follow-up interviews, some of the mothers came clean about the strain of their very early mothering experiences, having felt the need to present them in a more positive light at the time.[55] New mothers feel monitored, judged and under pressure to live up to an illusory maternal ideal.

Several women that I spoke to in writing this book volunteered that they thought they were depressed in the months after the birth of their children. This was a result of the isolation and standard-setting they were exposed to, combined with chronic exhaustion, relentless grind and loss of autonomy. Those who sought medical treatment were variously prescribed antidepressants, a course of Cognitive Behavioural Therapy and even acupuncture. I worry that diagnosing depression pathologises an often rational response to an extreme situation. As Olive, a mother of two, points out, 'If you are labelled with post-natal depression, then you feel like you are a bad mother because you can't cope with it. I was depressed. I had every reason to be depressed. The doctor said, "I think you are a bit depressed." I am exhausted, I have no job, I have no life, I am stuck at home with this crying baby and these pointless domestic tasks to do . . . You go nuts just walking around with these books, thinking, "Can he have butternut squash?" . . . Wouldn't you be depressed?!'

Anti-depressants play an important role in helping to tide people over difficult times in their lives. But there is a danger that we are trying to medicate away the symptoms of a far greater issue rather than addressing ourselves to it as a society. The mental strain experienced by so many new mothers is a social problem not a medical one – it requires collective changes, not just individual treatment. Within five weeks of having a baby, women are three times more likely to suffer the onset of depression than women who have not recently given birth.[56] Given how common motherhood is, it is reasonable to assume that the great majority of these women are not more likely to be predisposed to mental illness than any other part of the population. We are inattentive to these signs of systemic discontent at our peril. Female postnatal depression is more likely among women who feel that their partners are providing insufficient support, including with childcare.[57] Under our system of parental leave women are left alone with their utterly needy babies day after day for months, as around them people tell them how fortunate they are and how happy they must be, all the while dispensing unwarranted advice. This is a cruel set-up. The injury to women's mental health denotes their despair at the situation in which they find themselves.

Beyond this critical early period we continue to feel compelled to act out the role of the good mother in public and to make a display of our contentment and fitness in that role. We find ourselves ending each remark to our child with a term of endearment – 'Not far to go now, darling!'; 'What shall we buy for dinner, sweetie?' – exaggeratedly poised to come to the rescue as they tackle the most challenging playground equipment, and gently but clearly chiding bad manners, all in a bid to demonstrate to onlookers what loving, conscientious and right-minded mothers we are. When the performance falters and we utter a cross word, or our child misbehaves, we feel the disapproving eyes of others upon us and become hot with shame.

Every day mothers are made to feel inadequate because, in being passed the buck of full responsibility for their children, they alone are fingered by the parenting industry and given an impossible list of standards to meet. No wonder they lose faith in their ability to grow into their role. Instead, they end up scrabbling around for a magic bullet, becoming self-absorbed and self-critical in their own mothering, while laying into the way other women bring up their children to alleviate their stress. After all, as they've found out from bitter experience, everyone else is at it. If from the outset fathers were able to participate equally in the lives of their children, the responsibility and scrutiny would be shared. Each parent would bolster and encourage the efforts of the other.

They would both feel more assured in their parenting and better able to withstand the demands and judgement of others. The isolation and self-doubt experienced by many mothers would give way to greater confidence in a fully shared enterprise.

4

A Job For Life

I think most of the PAs in the industry are still female and most agencies are still dominated by men, but there are a lot of industries like that. It's not because there is still the same amount of sexism; women are given the same chances as men, but for some reason there do seem to be more men in the top jobs. Melanie, twenty-five-year-old PA, speaking to *The Times*[1]

What could be the cause of the apparently mysterious lack of senior women identified by Melanie? As she observes (in a newspaper feature on the advertising industry), there's a legislative level playing field for women in the UK workplace these days. Yet women are failing to make it to the top at anything like the rate achieved by their male peers. Although the proportion of women in senior positions at work has more than trebled since 1990,[2] this progress is stalling, with only very small increases in the number of women holding top posts in many employment sectors and substantial decreases in some others.[3] The Equality and Human Rights Commission has reported that women occupy only 10 per cent of the most senior posts in business and a quarter of such posts in the public and voluntary sector, for example.[4] How come women are left behind as men race each other to the summit?

The experiences of Ella and Elaine may point to the answer. Ella is a full-time mother of three children living in Belfast. She went back to work both times after having her first two children, but when her third baby was born, she felt the childcare costs would become prohibitive and so left her job. She and her husband now live on his full-time salary from a job in IT. Her youngest child starts school in two years' time and she's thinking of trying to get another job then, something part time that gives her money and some adult interaction but is flexible enough to fit round school hours and holidays. 'I could always try to work in a call centre . . . or at Tesco's stacking the shelves, which is all right up to a certain point, and the latest thought I had was maybe doing an NVQ to become a classroom assistant . . . but that will cost money . . . so I will have to look into it.' Ella has two degrees and speaks three European languages. 'I think I am realistic. I am thirty-five years old. Yes, I have two degrees but I haven't had so much work experience. I haven't had a career. Obviously when you are younger and you are pregnant you are not thinking, "There goes my career." And then I got pregnant again eight months after the first child . . . I cannot take on a full-time job any longer and I cannot take on a job where you have to give so much of yourself. We cannot be so selfish any longer . . . I think it is impossible if you have three children and you want to be fair to them.'

In contrast, Elaine has always worked while bringing up her three children. She had her first child, a daughter, when she was seventeen, and initially took shop and catering jobs while her mother looked after her children. She always found work that would fit around their needs and the help her mother was able to give her. When her mother became ill and was no longer able to care for the children, Elaine decided to become a child-minder. 'It allows me to earn some money and stay at home with the kids because I didn't want to give them to anybody else to look after. It's worked out really nicely . . . Sometimes I think it would be a lot easier to go out to work than be at home looking after children, a lot easier . . . But I like the idea that I can be with my own children as well. And the children I look after are adorable.' Her two eldest children have now grown up and she has an eighteen-month-old son with her partner of the last twelve years. After he was born Elaine worried that if she didn't return to her job quickly the parents she worked for would find other childminders. 'They were phoning up to say, "How are you feeling? It's not really working out with the grandparents we asked down to help out."' Elaine returned to work when her son was two weeks old. 'I had planned three weeks . . . but I said, "You can come back a week early, although I won't be taking them to clubs and things because I'm still healing." But after that we just got back into the routine. I just got on with it.' Like other women working in childcare, Elaine is at the sharp end of dealing with the pressure that all mothers in paid work find themselves under.

From the full-time mother looking for a job after a break of three years, to the full-time childminder who goes back to work when her child is two weeks old, millions of women attempt to negotiate domestic and working life, most trying to run the two in tandem. Whether they work outside the home full time or part time or not at all, they carry the ultimate responsibility for the hands-on care of their children and all their decisions about work are made with this in mind, in a way that their partners' decisions are not. For large numbers of women in paid employment, limited and costly childcare facilities, school days and holidays that are ill-matched to the world of work, and fathers who toil in inflexible jobs with some of the longest working hours in Europe mean that it's left to them to reconcile work and family life. UK working hours are topped only by Poland and Latvia within the European Union and male employees, including fathers, work the longest hours of all.[5] Research carried out by the charity 4Children has found that it is the long working day, together with financial hardship, that puts the greatest strain on family life.[6] At the same time, the results of a government survey of parents show that one in five families struggles to meet childcare costs, about a third of parents believe there are too few childcare places in their area and a similar proportion has difficulty finding affordable holiday care.[7] The time we spend at work in this country, and the expensive, piecemeal nature of childcare options, makes life logistically very difficult for parents.

Helen has witnessed first-hand the constraints mothers face in Melanie's industry. Now a full-time mother, she worked for an advertising agency before having children. 'There is a kudos around spending a really long time in the office, even if you are not actually doing anything. So if you leave before seven at night you are frowned upon, you are seen as not working hard enough. And then you are up at four in the morning producing stuff for a pitch – and that's expected of people. So if they are not able or willing to do that people think there's no point in thinking about them for a promotion.'

Unable to compete in the UK's culture of presenteeism, mothers are left out in the cold. For all the media hot air about 'working mums' and over-excited claims about supposed 'mummy wars' between those with paid jobs and those who look after their children full time, most women's decisions about work are straightforward. Women who look after their children full time do so either because they want to, seeing it as the best option for their family and themselves, or because they believe it makes better financial sense than going out to work and paying for childcare. But around 70 per cent of mothers in couples and just over half of lone mothers are in paid work.[8] For vast numbers of women there is no question of whether or not they do this. Housing and living costs mean they need to do so. And they like working.[9] Women want to put energy and commitment into their family *and* into their jobs, to spend time with their kids but also to get the affirmation, sense of purpose and achievement that paid work can bring. And once mothers have a working role beyond the home, the wider activities of the outside world open up to them: early evenings spent meeting friends or seeing a film, catching up on the newspapers on the bus journey home, a swim at the leisure centre at lunchtime. Talk of work–life balance is meaningless: work is an important part of most women's lives and a gateway to friendships, social networks and the wider community. For many, it is every bit as central to their identity as motherhood.

Linda is a single mother of two children from Swindon. She found a part-time job as a fitness instructor after the birth of her second child. 'That time at work was extremely important to me, to be something other than just a parent. I really didn't want to just be defined as a mother . . . I had pride in my work and it was something I could do and had confidence in myself about . . . And I think it's an adult world: there's something about losing your adult identity that I would find hard . . . I think what started to happen is that I looked forward to going to work but I also looked forward to my time at home. So it actually became the perfect combination. I think to be with children all the time is too much . . . that's not who I am. You don't stop being who you are [when you become a mother] – you add to it.'

Maggie, a photographer and mother of three, works on a part-time freelance basis. She too sees work as essential to her sense of self – as well as a welcome change from family life. 'There's nothing more exhausting than a day at home with three kids . . . It is easier to be at work – it's easier to negotiate adult to adult . . . It's just that whole invisibility which is crucifying. I quite like busy periods at work – it's self-affirming to feel that people need you to do things. Whereas at home nobody really acknowledges that you are needed . . . I think so much of it is to do with your public standing, isn't it? For loads of women work is just a crappy grind so perhaps that aspect of your life and identity wouldn't be something that you want to cling to or how you get your self-realisation. But just to be part of a team, to go out to lunch everyday and have the structure and the routine.'

As Maggie indicates, most jobs have a positive effect on our sense of well-being. They are central to our individual identity, our role in society and status, meeting our psychosocial needs and, of course, providing us with money.[10] And work has to provide women with tangible financial and psychological benefits because making it fit in with looking after our children, perhaps even achieving the 'perfect combination' that Linda is fortunate enough to have, is a struggle. The feminist movement of the 1970s secured equal rights legislation for women in the workplace. But, as discussed in Chapter 1, women are still held back from achieving their potential because the unequal division of domestic tasks means that they have to balance paid work against family commitments to a degree that men do not. In some cases, these domestic pressures are then used against women by reactionary employers.

On paper it all looks so easy: a paid period of maternity leave – check; up to twelve months off – check; returning to work at the same level – check; the right to request flexible working on return – check, check, check. But despite all these rights, having children is still bad for a woman's career, damaging pay and prospects. Some 57 per cent of women with children under five in the UK are in paid work compared to around 90 per cent of fathers;[11] a child's age makes no difference to a father's employment rate, whereas it does for women.[12] The instances of women downgrading their careers once they've had children, though decreasing over recent decades, is still significant at 14 per cent.[13] Even women who return to work full time experience a steep increase in the gap between their pay and that of men and women without dependent children.[14] And 2.8 million women work in part-time jobs that under-utilise their skills,[15] as Ella is contemplating. The fact that mothers in couples in full-time paid work still end up being responsible for most of the domestic chores demonstrates the inequalities that endure in our society.[16]

Having looked after her child largely alone since its birth, the mother automatically takes charge of arranging care when she returns to work: the carer is deemed to be her substitute, and so primarily her responsibility.[17] Karen, an academic and mother of one, explains, 'I was very aware that I was doing it all myself but I guess it came down to what was practical. I was at home with my son and so therefore I had the resources and the time to be able to identify local childcare in a way that my husband doesn't. And also I just felt that I knew him better . . . We were very much a package, everywhere I went, he went. And so I felt much more attuned to what was best for him and to kind of vet the suitability of childcare that was available.' The foundational role of the mother reaches its logical next stage.

Many couples talk in terms of the money that the mother will earn as needing to justify the expense of any paid childcare. Rather than considering themselves to have joint caring responsibility for a child, a joint income and a mutual interest in paying for childcare in order to continue both their careers, parents begin to talk about whether it's 'worth' the mother returning to work, weighing up her individual earnings against the cost of care. Childcare days are regarded as freeing the mother of domestic responsibility in order to go to work, rather than enabling both parents do so.

Mary works part time in the media and has two children. Her husband is a freelancer, working full time when he has a contract, with periods of time off in between jobs. She says, 'I would say that I am ninety-nine per cent involved in the childcare and he is one per cent involved and that's not an exaggeration . . . It's not on his radar at all . . . At the moment my husband isn't working, and the nanny is still coming in so he has these lovely days where he potters about and does his own thing. She comes when I need to leave for work and when we are both working it tends to have to be me that gets back in time for her to go home. I'm the one who is racing back to the house.'

Even mothers with more proactive partners still think of child-care as enabling them alone to go back to the workplace. Siân works part time as a teacher in Bristol, her husband has a full-time job in the public sector working flexible hours so that he is better able to share in the weekday care of their daughter. When they are both at work she is looked after by either Siân's mother-in-law or a childminder. 'I feel all the childcare is put into place so I can go to work. I feel as though if either of us were going to stay at home it would be me, therefore childcare is allowing me to work . . . It was something that I assumed and I couldn't tell you why. There is no logic in it . . . I think, if there is an issue with childcare, it's my fault. Whereas what I should actually say is, "Well, how can *we* resolve this?"'

Relatives, schools and nurseries reciprocate this attitude, treating the mother as their primary contact. Kate is an arts manager with two school-aged children. She says, 'The whole structure is set up to go to the mother first. The school has both our contact numbers but they will always ring me first; they make that choice to phone the mother first and it's the same with the doctors.' This is echoed by Bev, a mother of three from Northumberland, who worked part time as a solicitor when her first two children were young before becoming self-employed. She recalls, 'If the children were ill, the nursery rang me and it was always assumed that you will leave work and look after them. And I sort of went along with that because I was working part time and you are earning less but at the same time I thought, "How annoying is that that [my husband] doesn't go home?!" But . . . then I was always the link with the nursery . . . So all those things conspire against you.'

A large proportion of women with dependent children, like Bev, seek part-time work, reckoning this is the best way to spend time with their children and continue with their careers.[18] In shocking contrast, only 4 per cent of men with dependent children work part time,[19] and they are much more likely than women to work part time because they cannot find a full-time job.[20] Nearly all part-time workers who do shorter hours in order to fit work around home life are women,[21] and women make up three quarters of the part-time workforce.[22] Mothers are in the workplace for fewer hours than they might be if the childcare were more equally shared with their partner. It's then their wage that falls, along with their promotion prospects, as a result.[23]

Mothers with part-time jobs are four times less likely than mothers in full-time employment to work in senior or professional posts.[24] For women seeking a new role after having a baby, part-time work outside the public sector provides thin pickings, with a heavy concentration of poorly paid, low-skilled jobs (for example in the service sector, working for contractors or agencies). As well as the frustration this causes, some women in very low-paid work are left with the prospect of doing more than one job in order to scrape together enough money to get by.[25] It is also a disaster on a wider economic level: it's estimated that women working in roles for which they are over-qualified costs over eleven billion pounds a year in lost output to the UK economy.[26]

One significant step forward for parents, and other employees, is that flexible work (including part-time working but also flexible full-time work such as flexi-time, compressed hours, working from home and staggered start and finish times) is now widely available in the UK. Over 90 per cent of employees are estimated to have access to at least one type of flexible work, most commonly part-time hours.[27] The spread of new ways of working, greatly stimulated by technological advances and in part forced on companies by the recession of 2008/9, signals that the momentum behind flexible working is growing.[28] Decent flexible working should form an important part of any plan to move towards greater shared parenting.

But there is a gulf between what is available in theory and what happens in practice. A 2009 Equality and Human Rights Commission report noted that sixty per cent of UK workplaces received no requests for flexible working in 2006,[29] suggesting that a gap has emerged between genuinely flexible employers who encourage and agree to these requests and others who might make passing reference to it in their Human Resources blurb but don't follow this through. In the research by the charity 4Children, 55 per cent of respondents wished for more flexibility from their employer.[30] As I examine in more detail in the following chapter, fathers are still reluctant to ask for flexible working. Mothers with young children are three times more likely to make such a request than fathers,[31] and less than 20 per cent of men work flexibly.[32] Fathers tend to take up flexible working because that's the work pattern that they inherit in their job rather than because they proactively seek it out.[33] Men are also more likely than women to ask for flexible working for reasons other than caring responsibilities, such as returning to education.[34] For all its benefits, in the case of fathers this does nothing to relieve the care burden on mothers. So flexible working, and part-time working in particular, is perceived as primarily for mothers rather than a sensible way for all employees to combine work with the other calls on their time. As a result, women are penalised in their pay, choice of jobs and career progression in a way that would not be the case if flexible working were the norm. Only 10 per cent of women who move from full-time to part-time work after having children return to the same employer, and the part-time wage gap has not narrowed since the right to request flexible working was introduced in 2003,[35] indicating that a significant and stubborn prejudice against part-time work in particular still prevails. It is shocking enough that progress in tackling the pay gap between men and women for full-time workers, which has slowly narrowed since the mid 1970s,[36] nonetheless still stands at an average of 9 per cent.[37] But, even more disgracefully, over the same time period, the gap for part-time workers – a full 36 per cent – has stubbornly refused to shift.[38]

One of the main reasons for the narrowing of the full-time pay gap in recent years has been that young women's earnings have overtaken those of young men, reflecting their higher attainment in education and training. In 2011, women in their twenties in full-time work earned 3.6 per cent more on average than men of the same age. But for women over the age of twenty-nine the gap reverses and widens: women in their forties earn almost 16% less than their male peers.[39] It is no coincidence that twenty-nine is also the age at which women typically have their first child. As most couples decide that the father should remain working full-time while the mother becomes the main carer, the pay gap for women takes hold and then deepens. Even before having children, women tend to work in lower paid sectors than men.[40] Yet in fact, moving between full-time and part-time work and taking time away from work in order to care for family, make up 36 per cent of the pay gap – a far bigger proportion than occupational segregation at 10 per cent.[41] The pay gap for mothers is severe and long lasting, only beginning to narrow once the youngest child turns twenty.[42] And the lower a mother's level of education, the worse the earnings penalty over her lifetime.[43] It's motherhood that really does for women. The mother's responsibility for childcare entrenches her low pay. Trapped in a self-defeating cycle, she returns to work on the understanding that she also keeps the home fires burning. As a consequence her partner continues to build his earning advantage.

Despite the impression given by the anti-flexible-working lobby, an employee's right to request flexible working can be turned down if 'there are good business reasons for doing so'.[44] Extending the right to request flexible working to all, as the government has said it wishes to do, is important symbolically in not privileging one employee's personal circumstances over another. In reality, it is likely to have little effect: mothers will remain the primary users while significant resistance to flexible working still exists and while women still take greatest responsibility for the care of their children.

In comparison to the rest of the workforce (sprightly youngsters, women without dependent children, men), mothers, with their sudden absences for sick children and talk of employment rights, are a nuisance. It's not difficult to spot an employee or applicant who might be, or become, a mother. According to a 2005 investigation by the Equal Opportunities Commission, 30,000 women each year lose their jobs because they are pregnant. They are dismissed, made redundant, or, most commonly, forced out of their jobs, for example by being asked to carry out unsuitable work.[45] And the recent economic crisis has led to a notable rise in such cases, claim campaigners and lawyers.[46]

Prejudice against pregnant workers can take other forms: more than one in ten mothers believe that they are treated unfairly at work as a result of their pregnancy, including receiving negative comments from employers and colleagues.[47] Clare is a mother of one from Swansea. She works in internet development for a FTSE 100 company. She recalls the conversation in which she told her manager that she was pregnant: 'My boss was never really understanding. When I told him I was pregnant the first thing he said was, "Fucking hell!" and that continued for about five or ten minutes, telling me what a nightmare it was.'

Those that return to work after maternity leave soon find that their stock has fallen. The 2007 Equalities Review concluded that mothers with children under the age of eleven, together with disabled people and Bangladeshi and Pakistani women, are the group most discriminated against in the UK workforce.[48] Our existing work culture is such that managers want employees who are able to prioritise their work above all else and dislike it when this state of affairs is threatened. Despite the theoretical avail-ability of modern flexible working methods and nods to a balance between work and family life, the default and preferred model that many managers operate within is one of standard work hours spent in the workplace, so that employees can be seen and called into a meeting at a moment's notice any time between nine o'clock in the morning and five o'clock in the afternoon. The assumption – if it is considered at all – is that some other invisible figure is taking care of the end of the school day. Commitment must be absolute, nothing other than the ghastly '110 per cent' will do.

In this environment, daring to have a baby and take time off to look after it is viewed as subversive. In 2009 Tina Knight,

Chairwoman of Women into Business, an organisation representing small enterprises, participated in a discussion about parental leave on BBC Radio 4's *Woman's Hour*. She raised objections to the cost incurred by having to replace women on maternity leave and was reminded by another participant, Dame Margaret Prosser, Deputy Chair of the Equality and Human Rights Commission, that employers are reimbursed for Statutory Maternity Pay by the government.[49] At this point Tina Knight erupted, 'It's not the cost! It's the personnel being missing from your business!'[50] The inconvenience of procreation is apparently too much for Ms Knight, impatient at the time it takes to bear and nurture little future workers and consumers, not to mention the fact that they will then require picking up from school, occupying in the holidays and tending to when sick.

Tina Knight is not alone in her indignation. In an article for the *Daily Mail*, Alexandra Shulman, the editor of British *Vogue*, wrote, 'What I don't understand is the idea that [women returning from maternity leave] should be able to keep exactly the same job, with all the advantages that entails, and work less for it.'[51] It is not quite correct to say that mothers are 'able to keep exactly the same job'. In fact, maternity legislation allows for circumstances in which a mother can be moved to a different job but on the same terms and conditions as she previously enjoyed.[52] Shulman also omits to mention the significant fact that if women are returning to work part time they will be paid less than a full-time wage. And if they are returning full time, then what's her problem? That women might actually stick to full-time hours rather than give in to the dominant culture of 'full-time plus' presenteeism? Mothers, she writes in exasperation, 'want to investigate four-day weeks, flexi-time, jobshares, and they often then have another baby and are entitled to take another year off.'[53] For Shulman and her ilk, it seems it is the legislation and those who use it that are at fault, rather than rigid employer attitudes or the fact that fathers aren't encouraged to share sufficiently in the care of their children. 'Criticism of the situation is very much the view that dares not speak its name,'[54] says the taboo-breaking Shulman, in the middle of her extensive article on the matter. In fact, Shulman's is just one in a chorus of drearily belligerent voices that have objected to the extent of flexible working and equality legislation. Rather than examining why it is mainly women who try to fit family and work together, or challenging their own practices, employers take the easy option and blame women themselves. In difficult economic times, employee mothers are the cat everyone lines up to kick. Employers pit mothers and others against each other, telling the non-mothers how well they are doing picking up the pieces dropped by feckless women dashing out the door to do the school run. In her article Shulman berates mothers, 'making paper snowflakes with your four year-old while a younger and undoubtedly worse paid and probably childless fellow employee is trying to solve a problem that needs to be dealt with now.'[55] Their bosses having created a highly competitive atmosphere and with job insecurity rife, employees work longer and longer hours to prove themselves. While their colleagues burn the midnight oil in the workplace, mothers resume work at home when their children are in bed.

At least Shulman is honest in her opinions. Other employers now publicly boast so-called family-friendly policies, but these can be little more than an image-enhancing gloss rather than a genuine culture shift. Frieda remembers the response to her enquiry about part-time working at one interview. "They said, "We pride ourselves on our flexible-working policy, but we expect you to work full time initially and we could review it after six months."' This double speak typifies the attitude of many employers, who feel pressure to declare themselves responsive to the needs of employees, but in practice do the bare minimum – or worse, pick off their female employees. When she joined her company Clare was impressed by its claims of 'family-friendly' working, only to get a rude awakening. She went back to work on a full-time basis after six months' maternity leave but, having received such an unprofessional reaction to the news of her pregnancy, found her boss no more reasonable on her return. 'I have been told in no uncertain terms that I am expected to make up my six-month "holiday" . . . I am expected at my desk at seven in the morning and I am still expected to be there at seven, eight o'clock at night and it's been relentless . . . One of the girls who was pregnant at the same time as me has come back semi part time, she works school hours now because she has just had her second child, and I have been told that she has screwed her career and she now will just be left to plod along . . . My boss was talking about this other lady and he was, like, "That wouldn't fly with me. There is no way you would be getting away with stuff like that." But it's not "getting away with it." Jesus! What do they think? If you reduce your hours they are not paying you the same rate. It's not like suddenly you think, "Well, I'll knock ten hours off my week." I think in the current climate, you don't want to rock the boat. Half of you wants to say, "Screw you!" and then there's the other half of you that thinks, "I have got to keep a job."'

As it stands, despite legislative advances, women are still confronted with a stark choice: career or family. For Clare the price for keeping her pre-maternity job was to continue to work full time and barely see her young child during the week. Other women watch their careers go south as they try to work part time. Emma works in the housing sector in Cardiff. After maternity leave she returned to her job three days a week. However, she soon realised that she was in her old post in name only, as all her previous management responsibilities had been transferred to other staff. 'Everything that I had done had been taken off me, the level of the work wasn't commensurate with the grade, I was just a very well-paid admin person . . . My boss said, "But on paper you are still a manager." That's all well and good, but I don't live my life on paper.' Emma felt that in practice she had been demoted and began looking for another job. She has since found one at another organisation, working at the level she was previously used to, but has had to take the job on a full-time basis. She has swapped one sacrifice for another.

Mothers who work in women-dominated, professional occupations and return to the same employer after maternity leave have the best chance of maintaining their careers, even if they return to work part time.[56] The public sector with its early adoption of flexible working and largely female workforce is a good example of this.[57] However, even the public sector falls short of nirvana. Fran is the mother of one child and is expecting another. Before becoming a parent she worked as a manager in the Human Resources department of an NHS trust in the Midlands. Returning from her first maternity leave period she asked to come back to work three days a week but felt that this request was dismissed without serious consideration. 'The very, very first conversation I had with [my boss] where I said I really would like to come back, but I would like to come back part time, she said, "OK, my gut feeling is that is not going to work." And I think from that moment on the writing was on the wall really. We went through the process because she obviously knew she had to do that, but actually I think her mind was made up.'

The irony of this dogmatic approach from within the HR department is not lost on Fran. 'We spent so much time accommodating people working flexibly and working shift patterns and all that sort of thing . . . But people are always really good about doing what is right by the book in a textbook case but when it is a bit closer to home, it goes out of the window sometimes . . .' The upshot of this inflexibility was that Fran resigned: 'You know my P45 came in the post and I didn't have anywhere to take it, it had to be filed away and that was a first for me . . . So it has been a big shift and I think it has made me re-focus on my identity and what defines who I am.' Fran feels that she has made the right decision for her family but, nonetheless, the expertise she brought to her former job and the satisfaction it gave her are now lost.

Women such as Fran have the option to appeal their cases,

and even take their employer to a tribunal, but the downsides are significant. Tribunals only have the power to check that procedures have been followed correctly when a right to request has been made. They can't look at the business case for refusing a request. The process is also stressful, potentially costly and marks you out as a troublemaker among current and prospective employers. As Fran says, 'A lot of people have said to me, "You should have pushed harder, you should have challenged it," and obviously from an HR perspective I understand the legal protection and I think, "Yes, people are probably right, I have got a really good case." But, equally, what would I actually want to achieve? Because the last thing I would want is to force myself into a situation where . . . the person who really needs to be behind it, isn't behind it and that goodwill isn't quite there. I think you are doomed to failure then, aren't you? . . . And I think the NHS is bizarrely quite a small place sometimes and when I was resigning I was just very conscious that I would like to go back into the NHS one day and I didn't want to lose any goodwill. I didn't want to have any kind of reputation for myself. I just thought, "Maybe it's just better to be the bigger person and go gracefully."' Treated unfairly by their employers, women feel that they have no option but to put up with it or walk away. Given the consequent need to recruit and train new staff, employers lose out too. Calculations by PricewaterhouseCoopers show that the cost of replacing a good employee is equivalent to that person's yearly salary and that heavy turnover costs UK employers £42 billion a year once factors such as interviewing time, administration and induction are taken into account.[58]

Women with managers who are actually sympathetic to the requirements of family life feel fortunate. Becky is an administrator and mother of one from Durham. She was looking for another job when she became pregnant but decided to stay where she was because her manager supported flexible working and she got an agreement to work a three-day week after maternity leave. She says, 'When I found out I was pregnant all sorts of other things become important, like flexible working, maternity benefits, the ability to sit in a post that is quite comfortable for a while . . . My boss has kids herself, she often works from home, she's not got a problem with us working from home. If I'm half an hour late it doesn't matter as long as the work gets done and you don't take the piss. She feels that it works in her favour and she's probably right because it means that people work over their lunch hour, or answer emails from home if need be, because you know that you will get the favour repaid whenever you need it . . . I am very lucky. I have to remember when I'm moaning on about not really liking my job there are so many worse situations that I could be in . . . It's that ongoing compromise that I'm still getting my head around. I want to be fulfilled in my career and succeed, not in a material sense but for something that I really believe in, and have job fulfilment. But even if I loved my job, if I had a boss that threatened to sack me if I was five minutes late that then suddenly becomes so much more important because children become ill or sometimes it's difficult to get out of the house and all those things. And it will only get worse as my child goes to school. So those things become important . . . To give that flexibility up it would have to be absolutely the right job for a lot more money than I'm on currently. And that is really frustrating.'

Becky feels 'very lucky' to have returned to an understanding employer with a decent part-time job at the same level as before she had children. Given that 6 per cent of the UK workforce is made up of agency workers, those on temporary and fixed-term contracts, or doing seasonal and casual work[59] and that for many women 'flexible working' means trying to make ends meet doing multiple, minimum-wage jobs around school hours, women like Becky are fortunate. Nonetheless, jobs such as hers are problematic – rare as hen's teeth, women get stuck in these roles.

To be very over-qualified (like Ella, looking for a shelf-stacking job despite her two degrees and three languages) may feel acutely disheartening and frustrating. But treading water like Becky, though perhaps preferable, is a waste and a disappointment too. This should not be all that women can hope for. Far from giving mothers the much vaunted 'best of both worlds' – moving seamlessly between work and family life – these jobs limit women's potential. Fifteen years on, they find themselves still treading water, sticking it out because their employer turns a blind eye on school Sports Day, and mentally counting down to their retirement. As Becky says, 'I am just a bit lost at the moment . . . I think what frightens me is that I will just carry on, carry on, carry on . . . and then end up at fifty thinking, "Bugger, that was not what I planned."'

While their partners are free to skip along professional stepping stones, mothers are like trapped flies, dolefully buzzing round a jam jar, pent in and pent up. This is the flip side to the 'loyalty' displayed by mothers in the workforce – with so few employers willing in reality to agree to flexible working for decent and senior jobs, they don't have any choice but to stay put. Isla, who has a full-time job as a researcher but was 'devastated' to leave her young children when she returned to work, is scathing about claims that women don't want to work or are happy to take up low-status, low-pay part-time work that fits in with family life. 'And now women don't want to work apparently! Or they like these crap part-time jobs that don't use their brains . . . It's bounced back as, "Well, this is what women are choosing because they want to fit in with their families." And my answer is, "No, this is what they take because this is what the structure allows. A structure that doesn't allow women to work on a level playing field, that blames women for taking any maternity leave whatsoever, that doesn't have any built-in family friendliness in a lot of these institutional structures. This is the best choice that women in the UK could make."'

Given the prospect of taking one of these 'crap part-time jobs', as Isla damningly describes them, it is unsurprising that some women who can make the sums add up, either from benefits or their partner's income, or a combination of both, decide to give up work altogether. This is an option Frieda, who runs a charity, is considering for the future, if she has more children: 'I might think I'd rather not work and be at home with [the children] more than do something shit. Because I've done slightly shit jobs and there's no point for me. I just end up feeling miserable. And at that point I'd feel much more that [full-time motherhood] was a decision that I'd made rather than just, "I've had a baby and it's just turned out this way." So I can see a point where that would be a decision I'd make, but who knows.'

As with Frieda, the likelihood of women giving up their job increases as families grow in size. Only just over half of mothers in couples with three children are in paid work, for example.[60] As the mother's promotion prospects and pay decline while she tries to combine work with her solo bid to spare time for an increasingly demanding family life, so too does the regard for this work within the household. In the end, for some families, losing the mother's part-time job and pay packet just doesn't seem that big a deal: it's not 'worth' her continuing. This, together with the stress of running a job and family life in parallel, means that giving up on paid work seems the logical answer.

Michelle is a full time mother of three young children from Gloucestershire. Her husband works as an IT consultant and is away from home from Monday to Friday. She worked as a specialist paediatric nurse before starting her family but found it impossible to continue her job once she became a mother. 'You think, "I am going to have a baby, have a year off, go back, pick up where I left off." It's not like that. I mean, you don't think about having subsequent children . . . I went back part time, they advertised for a job share. The job share never materialised . . . I just felt – in my heart, I just felt torn . . . I could have a newly diagnosed family on the ward on a Wednesday, which was my last day. The ward often wouldn't feel comfortable sending them home if they knew I couldn't visit and follow it up later that week. So they might keep them in longer. That family could have been in hospital for a whole week because they haven't seen the specialist nurse. So I did have to start delegating tasks or just accepting lower standards . . . These are real people, these are real human situations that you just care so desperately about but I just didn't have the emotional elastic to reach that far . . .'

Distress caused by the inability to combine fulfilling work and family life successfully can turn into a rejection of women's career ambitions. Jacqueline Scott, Professor in Empirical Sociology at Cambridge University, suggests that this is one reason why research she's carried out reveals a recent retreat from progressive attitudes to mothers' working – including among women themselves. She found that men and women are less likely now than in the 1990s to think that family life will not suffer if women are in employment.[61] A 2008 Ipsos MORI poll for the *Observer* newspaper supports this sense of regression. Forty per cent of all those questioned agreed that mothers with young children should not go out to work, an increase of 6 per cent from 2003. Thirty per cent agreed with the statement, 'The role of women in society is to be good mothers and wives', and 23 per cent agreed that, 'The man's job is to be the breadwinner and the woman's is to look after the home.' The percentage agreeing with these latter two statements actually increased within the fifteen to twenty-nine age group (to 32 and 30 per cent respectively).[62] The resistance to women moving beyond the home isn't dying out, it is gaining ground among the young, many of whom have probably witnessed the difficulties experienced by their own mothers in combining home and work life. Rather like employers and reactionary media pundits, families end up blaming the mother's work rather than adapting their behaviour and expectations to fit the welcome presence of women in the labour market.

An inequitable division of childcare, and the knock-on effect for women's role in the workplace, matters not only for women's public status and opportunities and the fulfilment that this brings. What women do outside the home also matters to their standing – and power – within it. Gillian lives in Sunderland and worked as a project manager before becoming a mother. She very much wanted to dedicate herself to bringing up her children while they were young and could afford to do this. Before giving up her job, Gillian earned more than her husband. She is now a full-time mother, although she also fits in a few hours of paperwork each week for her husband's business once the children are in bed. 'I'm OK now. I think I've got used to it. But at first not having my own money was very, very difficult. Even when we moved into a new house – you know, my opinion on wallpaper or carpets, I still don't feel that I have as much say in what goes in the house as he does because I'm not paying for it. And there are occasions when we have arguments about things and not in a – well, yes, I suppose – in a nasty way he'll bring that up . . . It has been difficult, especially because I am now working for him – he's also my boss – and I'm doing his menial crap, essentially.'

On becoming mothers, women work as hard as they ever have done, if not harder, but are worse off than before because their domestic work carries no financial reward. Becky also used to earn more than her partner before the birth of their child. 'I don't earn as much as him now because I'm part time. And that was a really big thing for me . . . not having as much of my own free cash . . . that was really hard and I didn't like it at all. I think that is the thing: the balance of power shifts in the relationship.'

As men continue to focus on their careers these divisions intensify. Maggie, a mother of three and freelance photographer explains, 'Before my partner worked on the other side of town, he worked much more locally and everything was much more divided down the middle . . . Now he's got a big staff and endless responsibilities . . . And for the first year of this current job I just kept getting really upset because we kept having these conflicts about [domestic] responsibility. And a few times he would say to me, "Well, what do you want me to do, give up my job?" So there was a part of him that had become non-negotiable suddenly. Part of him is really willing and has found the most flexibility

that he can given all his responsibilities but there was that ulti-
matum of, "OK, so you want me to give up the job?"'

Mothers lose power as their relative earning capacity declines.
But they also lose it because of the obligation they feel towards
their children. The most effective tactic a woman might use to
bring about domestic change would be to refuse to be bound by
this sense of responsibility. But, charged with ensuring a child's
welfare right from the start, few women can countenance walking
away from this. Their lives completely enmeshed, the child is
practically and emotionally dependent upon her. Parental love,
together with an acquired sense of special duty, binds women to
their children. Understandably, then, most mothers are reluctant
to barter their children's welfare. This can leave women open to
exploitation. Linda is a single mother of two children from
Swindon. The father of her first child has moved away from the
area and is no longer in contact. But her younger child spends
half the week with her father, from whom Linda separated while
pregnant. Both Linda and her ex-partner wanted to share equally
in their child's upbringing. Nonetheless, Linda has still found that
she prioritises the childcare in a way he does not: 'It's not always
worked out completely, especially when my daughter was
younger. I still felt like I was doing more of the work or had
more of the responsibility. And sometimes her dad would say,
"I've got this work on so I'm not going to be able to have her."
And also he's changed jobs . . . and he's come to me and said,
"Right, we are going to have to change the days because I'm
doing this." Whereas I would think that I have to get a job that
fits in with my childcare. He would arrange the work first and
expect me to work around that, which I did because if I could I
would, because it was about my daughter. I try not to cause
trouble because I don't want my daughter to be upset.'

Karen is an academic and mother of one son. Her husband and
she have a more usual set-up: she works part time and he works
full time as a solicitor. She explains that although she wants to
progress in her career, her son's welfare is 'My over-riding priority

... you just want to ensure your child's well-being, happiness and emotional balance, that somehow you are achieving that. If I suspect that is not the case then I feel that I am the one to blame and that it is my responsibility to fix it somehow.'

The much talked-about guilt that some mothers in paid work feel about leaving their children in the care of others is a by-product of this sense of responsibility that Karen identifies. Women who arrange full-time care for young children, or after-school clubs and childminder pick-ups for older children, are only doing what generations of men have done: relying on someone else to look after their family while they bring in an income and further their careers. Yet men are not subject to the same disapproval and guilt that women experience in this situation. Sam and her husband both work five days a week while their daughter goes to nursery. 'My husband wishes he could spend more time with her, he would love to spend more time with her, but he has never, ever, ever, felt guilty about going back to work ... I have asked him that question: "Don't you feel awful when you drop her at nursery?" And he really doesn't. So the only thing that I can think of that is different between us is the way family, the media, friends, neighbours talk to us differently because the assumption is that he will be at work and that's fine. They never question that, but the assumption is that perhaps I should at least be at home more of the time and the fact that I am not, I can always feel myself kind of justifying it ... Even his own mum – you know, telling me [our daughter] should only be part time in nursery ... and shouldn't I stay at home with her – would never expect that from her own son. I do think it is totally different.' Were the work of the home shared more equally, this guilt might diminish.

If you can afford it, the decision to leave paid work might appear to make sense, especially if you are part of a couple where there will still be one earner. But economic dependency intensifies when women quit the labour market. Those who look after their children full time often talk about being 'lucky'. But the risks are great. They and their children could be left stranded if their partner – the sole wage earner – loses that income or walks off with it, with potentially harmful long-term consequences for their well-being. Many mothers and their children will, of course, successfully weather a separation and even benefit from the ending of an unhappy relationship. But the odds against them in life are higher. Almost 40 per cent of single-parent families, most of whom are headed by women, live in poverty.[63] Lone mothers come out worst on social and health indices.[64] And some longitudinal data suggest that the children of single parents are at an educational, employment and health disadvantage to others as young adults.[65]

Bronwyn and her husband both decided to take part-time jobs in order to share equally in the upbringing of their children. Bronwyn was on maternity leave with her second child and about to start a new part-time job when her husband told her he had accepted a more senior five-day-a-week job starting immediately. With no relatives nearby and no paid childcare available for her two pre-school children, Bronwyn felt forced to pull out from taking up her new post in order temporarily to look after her sons full time herself. She says, 'On principle I was going to take that part-time job because it was what we had planned . . . but I knew he wouldn't sort out the childcare . . . and there were two little boys in the mix . . . I just feel he had most of the cards once we became parents, which was a shock to me.' This episode contributed to existing unhappiness in the marriage and Bronwyn and her husband split up shortly afterwards. She believes it would be destabilising to put her children into childcare now, while they are dealing with their parents' separation, so is continuing to look after them full time. 'Financially, if you start off even slightly unequal and one of you puts your career to one side, you will never be equal again. To me, if you can afford to, it makes sense to keep up the lower paid career to have equality in the future . . . You have got so much more flexibility if you have got two of you who are equal, and two of you who are on a reasonable salary . . . But now my earning potential is going down . . . it's so uneven now that he had to be the breadwinner . . . I think, you know, don't get unequal and don't put your eggs in one basket.'

Bronwyn is right to be mindful of the importance of maintaining earning power, as an insurance against the unexpected and with a view to a time when children are more independent. For Shanti economic and social autonomy proved crucial to her own – and her daughters' – welfare. Born and educated in Bangladesh, she trained as a computer programmer before she met her husband, who had family in the UK. They had two children and he then persuaded her to move to England with him. Once in the country, he forced her to live in the same house in Yorkshire as the rest of his family from a previous marriage. Shanti says that she was subjected to persistent racist abuse while living there. 'Life was just hell,' she says. Desperate to get out of the house, she managed to get a job for a few hours a week with a local company. The abuse she suffered eventually culminated in a physical attack by her stepson and Shanti ended up in hospital. 'After three years there I was beaten up brutally by my stepson, kicking and all this; I was bleeding through my kidney. The police told me, "If you press charges we can arrest him." But my husband was sitting there, and I didn't have the guts. I said, "No, no, I don't want him to be arrested."'

It was her work colleagues who took her home from hospital and went with her to remove her belongings from her husband's house. 'My best friend from work, she is like an angel . . . She fetched two empty suitcases and she took me from the hospital to my husband's house . . . My husband said, "If she leaves now, it is for good." And she said, "That's fine. She will cope with it. I cannot leave her alone here." An English girl fighting in a foreign house: there she is, very brave,' Shanti says. Other colleagues advised her and her daughters on getting temporary council housing. And it was her job that enabled her to pay for the smart home that she now owns. Shanti herself is sure of one thing:

'Without my job I couldn't have reached where I am today . . . I don't know, I feel sometimes, I would probably have committed suicide. I don't think I could have taken it.'

Shanti's story is particularly shocking. Yet although most women will not have to confront such brutal violence in their domestic lives, cutting off independent earnings and contacts exposes women – and their children – to risk. No matter how much mothers tell themselves that work isn't the be all and end all of life, that the role of homemaker is as important as that of breadwinner, and that children benefit from undivided attention, money still talks. Three out of ten children living in poverty do so in houses where the father works and the mother is on no or a low income (although low wages and bad employment practice mean that two incomes do not always guarantee that a family escapes poverty).[66] If parents split up, the risk of poverty is much greater in those lone-parent households where that parent doesn't work,[67] leaving children vulnerable to the potential misery and severely hampered life chances of an existence on the breadline.

Mandy is the mother of five children. Neither she nor her husband is in paid work. She describes in vivid terms her own family's experience of decades on a low income: 'We were brought up with no money . . . Now I can go to the shop and stretch a tenner like a yard of elastic . . . My grandma was the same. She had breathing problems and couldn't walk two yards but she could swim through a skip like a professional . . . Growing up, I didn't have the Puma trainers, or the Head bag, the things that were in . . . My parents didn't have a car and we didn't have money. I suppose I just looked really scruffy and I didn't have friends at high school . . . And I think maybe my kids suffer the same because they don't have new things.'

Mandy has passed her frugality down to her children. In itself this is sensible, even admirable, but with it comes an almost inevitable paucity of ambition for her children. 'It's good training for when they grow up because more than likely they are going to be on a low income anyway . . . They should live the life they need to get used to and if they do end up going to university and becoming solicitors and doctors, all the better.'

Women may plan to return to the workforce when their children get older but for every year that they are out of work their future earning capacity falls by 4 per cent.[68] Mandy, who hasn't worked since getting an NVQ and then having her first child in her early twenties, over ten years ago, reflects on her own future job prospects. 'I was hoping to go to university and train to become a nurse but then I met my husband and was all loved up and then the babies came. I'm hoping that once I get the littlest one away to school that I can pick it up again. It's what I've always wanted to do. And I don't want to be old and thinking, "I wish . . ." But my expectations have gone down. Even if I can't become a nurse I could work in a hospital as a care assistant or an auxillary. If I can't get to the highest level, and be a nurse, then I would like to say that I've done that.' At least Mandy has time on her side, having started her family relatively young. A woman who takes a break from her career in her mid-thirties doesn't have to be out of the workplace that long before she hits up against ageism when trying to return to work, as well as prejudice about female workers with children.

Although some mothers give up work without a backwards glance, for others it is a decision that, at best, they feel ambivalent about, mindful of the loss it brings. Newspapers talk at high volume about the rise of the breadwinner woman and a recalibration of domestic roles, but these women are the exception. In 2010 the *Sunday Times* featured a headline that screamed, *Breadwinner wives reign in 44% of homes.*[69] Beneath this tabloid shocker lay a more measured analysis: 44 per cent of women earn the same or more than their partners, and of that 44 per cent, it claimed, 19 per cent actually earn more. This is a logical outcome of women's superior educational achievements in recent years. In fact, given their academic success, their earnings relative to men might be expected to be even greater. But, nestled in the middle of the piece sat the most telling paragraph: 'Despite the increasing influence of women in the workplace, overall their pay remains below that of men and continues to fall further behind from the birth of their first baby until their children have left home.'[70] This account of the rise and fall of the working woman broadly tallies with other projections. For example, a 2007 report claimed that by 2030 couples in which the woman is the main earner will roughly double, from 14 per cent to one in four. By 2057, it concluded, women will be 'better qualified and out earning men', before adding, 'in the pre-family stage at least'.[71]

As long as women are propelled into the role of main carer, their careers, earnings and influence within a couple will continue to be compromised. Analysis of longitudinal data demonstrates that rather than simply being determined by earning power, a far more complicated mix of expectations, flexible working opportunities and gender role values influences how parents divide up paid and unpaid work.[72] This in part explains why progress towards equally shared responsibility for domestic work and childcare has stalled.[73] The hope that legislation to secure women's employment rights would set in train a levelling of the playing field at work and in the home has so far failed to come to fruition. This legislation needs to be matched with specific efforts to deliver domestic equality. For a professional woman in her twenties, earning the same or more than her boyfriend, headlines such as that in the *Sunday Times* will make the disappointment to come all the greater. Young women enter the workforce filled with enthusiasm and expectation. We owe it to them to clear the way so that they are fully able to realise their ambitions and abilities.

5

Man Power

'When we had one of our first nights out after our daughter was born, I had to come with a five-point plan about how I was going to improve my performance as a father. It wasn't the most romantic meal we've had.'

Bob, a father of one who has a full-time job as a journalist, ruefully recalls the homework set by his partner, who works in the voluntary sector, in advance of that night. 'I wasn't taking enough responsibility for my daughter's food, and I also don't do the washing. So anyway I had to think of some ways of improving on those points, and I did and I haven't stuck to them and occasionally issues arise. But I think it's hard, it's not the hardest thing in the world, but it's quite hard if you are both quite ambitious and you work quite hard. And you have got good, but not necessarily the most robust, childcare arrangement with no back-up plan. Invariably problems arise . . . I don't think I am lazy . . . I don't think I have got any more waking hours that I could gainfully use. It's not that I watch telly or go out or do any of those things that normal people do.'

It used to be so simple. Men worked outside the home to earn money for their families, women worked inside it, looking after the house and the children. Now everything has become more complicated as mothers have moved into the paid workforce, acquiring wage-earner status, and fathers have been encouraged to be more involved in the care of their children.

Today, the social expectation is for fathers to be 'hands-on dads' as well as breadwinners, certainly more so than their own fathers were. Men now combine work and family life as women do, albeit in different proportions. And it can cause friction in modern families. Bob remembers a comment from a friend: '[He] said, rather depressingly, "Of course you row when you go out. It's the only occasion you ever spend any time with each other."' This brought to mind a fierce argument I had with my husband on a rare evening out, he having left me in a restaurant, our food arriving and then going cold, as he paced outside on the pavement taking an urgent work call. 'I am sick of going to bed with a man who is tapping away on his BlackBerry,' I shrieked melodramatically on his return. A passing woman giggled. 'Sometimes,' my husband replied, 'I feel as if I get nothing right. I'm failing at work and I'm failing at home.' As he unconsciously appropriated the cry of the modern mother, I wondered if this was a perverse sort of equality.

With the second wave of feminism, as women demanded more control over their lives, the involvement of men in caring for their children came under greater scrutiny. At the 1970 Women's Liberation Movement conference in Oxford, delegates made their point about gendered parenting roles by organising a crèche manned by male partners and fathers. Media interest in the crèche was intense and requests for access had to be carefully managed by the organisers. Reporters were no doubt after footage of henpecked men besieged by hyperactive children and were perhaps disappointed by the calm and quietly sardonic individuals they actually encountered. Men looking after children were a huge and potentially entertaining novelty. By the mid 1970s Adrienne Rich noted the 'ripple of interest in "new fatherhood", in the establishing of a basis of proof that men, as well as women, can and should "mother", or for redefinitions of fatherhood which

would require a more active, continuous presence with the child.'[1]
Kramer vs. Kramer, the Oscar-winning 1979 film about a wife who
leaves her workaholic husband and their son, returning fifteen
months later to spark a child custody battle, reflected this new
perspective on fatherhood and brought the issue dramatically to
life. The audience saw Dustin Hoffman, as Ted Kramer, transformed from virtually absent father to doting primary parent.
The scene in which he dodges the New York traffic with his child
in his arms, running to a nearby hospital after a playground acci-
dent, marks his crowning as a caring and actively involved dad.
In the 1980s and 1990s, as women in the UK joined the workforce in large numbers, the 'New Man' was heralded, a father
who not only worked outside the home but was more involved
within it too.

Today, fathers are out and proud. Dads strut the streets,
newborns strapped to their chests. Worthy fathers' research and
support groups such as the Fatherhood Institute, Dad.info and
Fathers Plus have sprung up and flourished, while the altogether
more troubling antics of the militant campaign group Fathers 4
Justice have apparently lost their momentum and ability to shock.
Politicians, from Barack Obama to David Cameron, present them
selves as family men and exhort other fathers to play an active
part in their children's lives.

Fatherhood is a burgeoning academic field.[2] There is now a
sizeable body of research indicating that fathers' close involvement in their children's lives in itself and, most significantly, as
an indicator of nurturing and warm relationships between all
family members, means that children do better in life on almost
every indicator of success. It is directly and indirectly associated
with children's greater academic ability and educational attainment; an absence of psychological and behavioural problems; a
greater sense of self-worth and lower levels of delinquency as
teenagers; and, in adulthood, more satisfactory sexual relationships, lower levels of depression and better self-reported parenting
skills.[3]

Great claims are made for a sea change in the world of parenting. 'Traditional gendered roles of mother as carer and father as breadwinner are dissolving; meaning a generation of families is developing where both Mum and Dad play an active role in childcare,' says Rob Williams, Chief Executive of the Fatherhood Institute.[4] This statement is half true. Fathers are playing a more active role in childcare, and this is welcome, but the gendered division of labour has not fundamentally changed. As we've seen, among most couples with children the father works full time – as the main breadwinner – and the mother combines part-time paid work with doing most of the childcare and domestic work, as the main carer.[5] Fathers who do paid work, like mothers in the same position, feel torn between jobs and family life. Research by the Equality and Human Rights Commission shows that men believe that they should be more actively involved in the day-to-day raising of their children[6] and feel that they don't spend as much time with them as they ought.[7] Like mothers, they are cutting down on social life, leisure activities and sleep to make more time for their families. But unlike mothers they are not cutting down on their paid work hours. Although fathers reduce these hours when they have a newborn child, thereafter they do more paid work than men without children, particularly if they are in a managerial or professional occupation.[8]

Despite the rise in the proportion of women in paid work, and men's stated wish to be more involved in raising their children, the amount of time that mothers and fathers put into family life is still poles apart. As noted in Chapter 1, fathers undoubtedly spend more time now with their children than in the days of the pre-enlightened Ted Kramer, but so do mothers, and therefore a very significant gap between them still remains. Given the unequal division of paid work, it is inevitable that unpaid work will be split unequally too, and vice versa. Fathers might say they aspire to playing an equal caring role but the reality is that this doesn't happen. Adrienne Rich's ripple has failed to become a tidal wave of change in gender roles. The shift in fatherhood and its effect on family life has been overstated.

So why, if men say that they want to spend more time with their children, and this is apparently supported by contemporary social expectations, is it not happening? Government policy and NHS practice has much to do with this, as discussed in Chapter 3. The current vastly unequal default provision of maternity and paternity leave and the exclusive nature of 'woman-centred' health care means that fathers are not given a chance to develop an early, and habit-forming, co-parenting relationship with their children. Bill, a picture editor and father of one from London, is scathing. 'I think the state of paternity leave in this country is rubbish,' he says. 'If people have paternity leave of two weeks . . . it's no bloody use . . . the first month your feet don't touch the floor, you haven't got a clue. You don't know what you are doing, it's a maelstrom of well-wishers and cards, and shit and nappies. You are sleep deprived, your whole world is turned upside down. Emotionally you are a wreck and you are no use at work anyway.'

Although the government has proposed increasing the amount of paternity leave available to fathers, 40 per cent of men don't even take the current meagre fortnight. The majority cite un-affordability as the reason. Paternity leave is paid at a low flat rate, below the minimum wage. Others say that they are ineligible, because they haven't been with their employer long enough to qualify for paternity pay, or won't receive it because they are self-employed.[9] But these are not the only barriers to taking leave. Although some employers are happy for workers to take it and even top up the payments, parents report that in other workplaces it is frowned upon, or even denied to fathers.[10] Some men try to get round these hurdles by combining paternity leave with paid annual leave or sick leave, others take annual leave or sick leave only, but 20 per cent of employed men don't take any time off at all.[11]

Employer resistance was in evidence in 2009, when the then Labour government first proposed that the second half of women's maternity leave period might be voluntarily transferred from the mother to the father. Even though statutory payments would be at the same level as for mothers and would be reimbursed by the government on the same basis, business representatives threw their hands up in the air. 'This is not the time to do it. It's a huge burden to plan for both a male and a female employee being away,' responded the British Chambers of Commerce.[12] A proposal a few months earlier from the Equality and Human Rights Commission to divide maternity and paternity leave more evenly likewise caused consternation: 'We really need a reality check before starting to consider another push on parental leave. These are very difficult times,' said the Federation of Small Businesses.[13]

Employer attitudes towards flexible working for fathers are also poor. The lack of good part-time and flexible jobs with which women are confronted also affects men's efforts to change their working lives. Although two thirds of fathers think the availability of flexible working important when job hunting, the majority work standard hours.[14] Fathers are more likely than mothers to have requests for flexible working turned down.[15] The negative messages being sent out by bosses are so strong that men are concerned about making a request in the first place. They say they would worry about being singled out as uncommitted to their work if they did so and think it would impair their chances of promotion.[16] Fostering a climate of disapproval is a very effective preventative tactic on the part of employers.

Older bosses, who were less involved in home life when their own families were growing up, and for whom the demands of dependent children might be a distant memory, lack empathy with their employees and bring to bear their own, conservative views of how family life should be arranged. Bronwyn, a mother of two children who is now separated from her partner, remembers the time when they both attempted to work part time and share childcare equally: 'I think there are very different ideas, which we were coming across in the early days negotiating with new bosses, of what a good mother and a good father does, almost like there is a moral judgement about it. I won't be wanting to challenge myself at work, I want to be a good mother. Whereas the good father would be wanting to challenge himself . . . So a man publicly saying, "All the fathers in here could be doing it differently," I think is actually quite a threat.'

Karen is an academic and is married to a lawyer. They have one son and she is pregnant with their second child. She comments, 'I think family-friendly policy is just an absolute joke. [My husband's] law firm is headed up by a relic of the eighties, braces and bouffant hairdo and all the rest of it. And his model of family life is a large mansion in the Home Counties filled with the dutiful wife, four children, swimming pool. Lots of holidays, lots of money, lots of material goods, but he is never there. He is probably leaving home at half seven in the morning and he will work later than everyone else so he probably gets home at ten o'clock at night. Never works from home, that's not a policy they advocate either, so he is kind of leading by example: "This is my idea of family. You have a family but it's your wife that deals with it and you provide."'

Attitudes and practices vary from employer to employer but the ability of fathers to take paternity leave and negotiate flexible hours is also related to their economic situation and the sector that they work in. A male doctor in a dual-income household may well be able to withstand the financial penalty of paternity leave paid at the statutory rate. A postman, and sole breadwinner, may not. Fathers in lower socio-economic groups are less likely to take paternity leave.[17] At the same time, paternity leave is linked to a higher level of involvement by fathers in a baby's care at eight to twelve months of age[18] and some of the wide-ranging, long-term benefits to a child of a father's involvement take root at the early stages.[19] The UK's threadbare paternity leave provision deprives fathers of the best start with their children, with all the future advantages this can bring. As such, it entrenches inequality of life chances.

Similarly, the prevalence of flexible working varies from sector to sector. It's more widely available, for example, to those working in the finance, education or health sectors than it is to those working in manufacturing or construction.[20] Negotiating a flexible working agreement depends on bargaining power and highly skilled professionals in well-paid occupations hold the most cards. The lack of leverage for those in lower paid occupations can create strains and hard choices. Ben, a father of three, is currently unemployed and doing basic skills training at his local college. His wife is training to be an early-years carer. He has struggled to find secure work that allows him the time he wants to see his children. 'I was a self-employed plasterer but I dropped back off that because the work was too far away. I was travelling two hours either way a day. I was leaving through the door at six in the morning and I was back in at seven at night. They'd already had their bath. So we knocked that one on the head and I found employment in a factory and it was quite good. It lasted me three years but [business] got a bit slack so I got laid off.' Linda, a mother of two and health worker from Swindon, was herself brought up by her single-parent father. His difficulty in finding flexible employment in the building trade illustrates the severe effects of compromised earning capacity for the whole family. 'The building industry is not very family orientated, so there was no flexible working. I think just after my mum had left we were taken to school by other people but it didn't last and he gave up work. He didn't work all the time that I was a child and we were very poor. We lived in absolute poverty.'

Working in lower paid sectors isn't necessarily the death knell for a balanced work and family life. Historically fathers from lower socio-economic groups have spent a greater amount of time looking after their children than more affluent fathers. This was in part because they were more likely to do shift work and so be at home in the day. Economic necessity also meant that women in these families were more likely to work outside the home, formal childcare was less affordable, and so more of it had to be shared between the mother and the father. The gap has closed more recently as other fathers have made greater efforts to spend time with their children. Research that splits fathers into groups according to their educational attainment shows that the biggest increase in time spent on childcare is among the most educated. Nonetheless, fathers in the lowest attainment group are holding their own,[21] albeit that the sacrifices they may have to make, as Ben found, are greater.

Although much is made of the shift in society's expectations towards fathers being more involved in raising their children, it is weaker than supposed. Those expectations are built around fathers 'opting in' to the care of their children as much as possible. A father's role is seen as taking turns with nappy changes when around the house, playing football in the park with the kids at the weekend, helping with homework in the evening and sharing the ferrying of ten-year-old socialites to Saturday play dates and parties. The baseline expectation is that fathers will still be in full-time paid work, fitting in their childcare around their work commitments.

For mothers the reverse is expected. In fact, the media's enduring interest in men's care for their children – whether at Saturday dads' clubs or as full-time fathers – is proof of this. Fathers who care for their kids are still a story. Decades after the scrum over the crèche staffed by men at the 1970 Women's Liberation Movement conference, 'Fathers caring for children – shock' is a recurrent, and sensationalised, theme in the media. It seizes on stories of a revolution in fatherhood, charting increases in the number of full-time fathers,[22] and the rise of dads' and children's playgroups.[23] A 2010 survey by the insurance company Aviva that claimed that a total of 6 per cent of UK fathers look after their children while their partners go to work, a ten-fold increase in a decade, got widespread coverage. 'It's men who are increasingly left holding the baby', gasped the *Observer* newspaper by way of a headline, despite the fact that its own report included a quote from the Family and Parenting Institute suggesting that the survey didn't chime with its understanding of the trends and should be treated with caution.[24] *GMTV*, another to carry the news, quoted Aviva on its website: 'While generally speaking it's still more usual for men to take the more conventional role of the main income earner, our research shows that this is shifting and more women are becoming the breadwinners. While both roles are equally valuable, nowadays it's *quite likely* [my italics] that women will be heading off to the office while men are changing nappies and doing the school run.'[25] This overstatement wasn't questioned in the *GMTV* report, nor was it questioned by the BBC in its online coverage of the story.[26] Another flurry of coverage in the same year focused on Dads and Little 'Uns play-groups which run in London and Exeter,[27] the interest sparked by analysis of the role of fathers in childcare during the reces-sion. Fathers are expected to get their hands dirty but society does a double-take when they get involved in the day-to-day care of their children.

Society looks for far less from fathers than from mothers, and what it does demand of men is less prescriptive. Approval is comparatively easily won. A father has merely to push a pram down a street or attend a playgroup to be regarded by others as a paragon of caring, modern fatherhood. Even the most generous-spirited of partners might feel exasperated. Isla, a mother of two, works full time as a researcher. Her husband runs his own busi-ness from home. 'Sometimes it is galling because my husband does a lot of what I call the presentation side of [childcare]. He takes the children to clubs, or he'll take one of them to school, and everyone notices him and they say to me, "Oh, you work, don't you? You mustn't see them very much." And I can't say, "Yes, but I get them up and dressed and he only walks them to school", because that's not an appropriate thing to say . . . I think very hands-on dads are quite visible often and it can be annoying because they get credit for doing less . . . And you have to get a bit hardened . . . You have to say, "Yes, he is here a lot", and smile and inwardly note that there is some sort of perception thing where men are more visible when they are doing childcare and that you are just basically invisible.'

Sam, too, has noticed double standards being applied to her and her husband, who both work full time. 'He is kind of the best dad in the world because, if he is working from home, he will take our daughter to nursery. Or, if she is not well, he will take a day off work – you know, we try and do that in turns. So he is kind of a hero and I am left feeling like a bad mum. I think that's what I feel most cheated by. Because I do think that's the way of the world, it still is massively skewed in terms of what the woman and the wife is meant to do, or the mother is meant to do . . . We are expected to be the kind of primary care giver.'

When these relatively low social expectations of men as carers are combined with high expectations of them as full-time earners, it's unsurprising that men continue to see themselves as the main breadwinners. Parental roles become polarised in this process. The arrangement is self-perpetuating: the mother feels that she must cut back her paid work in order to look after the children because the father is working long full-time hours; the father feels he should work these long full time hours because the mother has cut back her paid work. Any intention to do things differently, perhaps even sharing care and paid work equally, falls by the wayside. Institutional structures, cultural norms and inherent beliefs about gender roles prove too strong to resist.[28] In the exhaustion of early parenthood it just seems easier to go native. For professional workers, the childrearing years of their thirties and forties coincide with the peak period for making strides in their careers. As mothers sit that one out, fathers lose themselves in their jobs.

Another significant factor influencing parents' thinking when dividing up paid work and care roles is of course still cash: men earn more than women. But, as we've seen, pay differentials between men and women really kick in as mothers take on primary responsibility for their children's care. We need to recognise that this pay gap is in large part a *consequence* of gendered family roles rather than a valid reason for these roles to be maintained. As the experiences of Becky and Gillian in the previous chapter demonstrate, even in couples where women start out earning more than their partners before they have children, the situation reverses when mothers take on the primary domestic responsibility.

Fathers' feelings about their worker role can be ambivalent. Matt, a full-time programme maker and father of two explains, 'I've often wondered why no one's asked me if I'd like to work three days a week. My wife has just gone back to work three days a week . . . No one has ever suggested that maybe that's something that I should do. Here we are, we've got this income coming in and we've got to fund this lifestyle – what are the rules here? Why does the bloke have to go to work? . . . It was just expected that I would take on that burden by my wife and by me . . . I'm there to be the carthorse and work as much as possible and to exhaust myself in that way because that just seems to be what hunter-gatherer blokes should do . . . It's possible that I could take a much more fundamentally caring role in terms of the children but as a bloke I've always thought that I should be providing for my family. I'm not new man-ish enough to say I'm desperate to take on the childcare and I'm happy to forgo my career for the next five years so that my wife can work five days a week.'

For some men who are the sole earners in families, funding the 'lifestyle' can become a huge pressure. Dave worked in a series of senior jobs while his wife stayed at home raising their son. The stress of maintaining a high standard of living contributed to the eventual break-up of their marriage. 'It put me under a lot of pressure . . . I was very driven to keep earning more money because we couldn't quite keep pace with what we were spending, we were always overdrawn at the end of the month, we had to borrow money and it worried me but I never articulated it very well. I drove myself harder and harder to develop my career and get a bigger job because I felt like that was the deal, that's the lifestyle we had and our friends had this stuff . . . Hamster wheel stuff really. Idiot . . . Things went wrong in our marriage and now I feel it doesn't seem that important to have such a big house.'

Michelle has seen this burden on men in maintaining their side of 'the deal' from another perspective. A full-time mother of three children whose husband works away from home during the week, she is sympathetic to the pressure on him as the sole wage earner: 'I think he is still quite deeply entrenched in the belief that he should be the breadwinner and he is the provider . . . As far as the guys are concerned they are trying to please all of the people all of the time. I think their employers are wanting their pound of flesh now, and you might come home exhausted but you are still expected to do the washing-up, put the kids to bed, and have leisure time at the weekends as a family. I think it's hard.' Men work long hours in their jobs in order to provide for their family, when they might benefit most from being together more.

Nick has made some adjustment to his working hours in order to spend time with his three children. He works a four-day week in IT in the public sector and spends the fifth day looking after his son and daughters. Even so, as the main wage earner with a job that requires a long commute, he feels under pressure. 'I am quite often up and out by seven thirty in the morning or even seven some days. So sometimes I don't even get to see the kids at all. And then in the evenings I try and limit working late to one or two days a week . . . so I am quite often not back until nine p.m. on those days . . . But it would be very difficult to organise our lives differently.'

The paid work of the father is a type of involvement in the care of children and just as necessary. Children cost money. It is not as direct a form of care as shopping for, and making, their dinner, washing their clothes or taking them to the park on the way home from school. Yet it is carried out with an equal sense of responsibility, protection and love. But in not sharing the more banal, yet ultimately very rewarding, work of hands-on involvement, the well-being of children, mothers and fathers themselves is hampered. Men are cast as the some-times distant yet always dependable rock within the family. Bill observes, 'You can't help but take on the mantle of "dad" and before you set off on a car journey you find yourself getting the map out to plan a route and doing oil changes. You almost become a parody of your own dad and you do it in an ironic way. But you also think, "Right I am a dad, and I need to do dad things."'

Yet it is not just force of circumstance that creates this distance between men and their children. They exercise choices that keep them at arm's length from their children's daily lives. They do this by falling in with workplace expectations and staying on the sidelines at home. Although employers are more resistant to male flexible working, men decide not to challenge them. Fathers are three times less likely than mothers to make requests to work flexibly,[29] put off by what it will do to their reputation and their job prospects, this fear no doubt stoked by what they see happening to women who work flexible hours. Even when men do make flexible working requests, they are most likely to be for flexi-time – such as full-time hours compressed into four days, or early start and finish times – rather than part-time working.[30] Some men are drawn into a macho, presentee culture in the workplace, putting their ambitions for their careers and the wish to be seen in the office above time spent with their family. Seventeen per cent of fathers believe that work comes first for them, three times the number of mothers who think this.[31]

Karen thinks back to the time when she was in hospital after the birth of her son. He was in a special care unit for a week and her husband took two weeks' paid holiday to spend time with them. 'The first week, because our son arrived early, my husband had all these loose ends that absolutely had to be tied up and then he wasn't allowed to stay at the hospital so he was – I don't want to make it sound as though he wasn't completely distressed – he was, like, "I will be back to the hospital first thing tomorrow." And then he would turn up at half past nine, which is still first thing, but he had already spent an hour and a half on doing emails, doing his work stuff and then he would leave us at the hospital and then go home and deal with more work things . . . He is a very conscientious person and felt obliged, I suppose . . . But I just thought at the time, "I am not really sure that should be a priority." But we have never mentioned it, I have never really discussed it.' Even Nick, who works a four-day week, believes that he brings a drive and ambition to his work which distinguishes his attitude from that of his partner: 'I have a need to further my career, which is very male, I think . . . I feel like I need to succeed in some way in my career. Whereas my partner, I think, is much more focused on the quality of what she is doing and what she is getting out of it . . . I mean, although I say that I would like to balance my life more, I am quite resistant to the idea . . . partly, I think, to do with feeling like I am on some sort of trajectory.'

Aside from the few who ask to work flexibly, most men attempt to reconcile the demands of work with the demands of home life in informal or ad hoc ways, trying to keep both camps happy while avoiding confrontation or fundamental rethinking of their daily lives. Such 'below the radar' arrangements are used by a substantial number of employees.[32] Typically this might involve a private agreement between a worker and his immediate line manager to leave work early on certain days. Neil, a full-time proofreader, has such an arrangement, in order to pick up his two children from a childminder. 'I don't have an actual agreement to do this but they know my situation and they are happy for me to do this . . . People turn a blind eye. It's a very small department I work in. I don't think it would be feasible if there were lots of people doing it.' In other instances fathers take matters into their own hands and slope off to care for children at home, perhaps sending one or two strategically timed emails or texts to cover their tracks. This is the method favoured by Bob, a full-time journalist, who leaves work early once a week to care for his daughter. 'I sort of bunk off from work on Friday afternoon and hope nobody notices . . . If I can make my daughter go to sleep for a couple of hours I will do a bit more work, or I will work in the evening when my partner comes back, but I am the primary carer on Friday afternoons . . . I do look at my BlackBerry in case I have to pretend I am in the office. But I try not to make or take calls because children get quite quickly distressed if they feel they are being ignored or you have other priorities . . . My workplace would probably be reluctant to formalise it because they might not want to extend the arrangement to everyone . . . I don't think, were it known, I would be in loads of trouble but I think it's probably easier for everyone this way.'

This arrangement is certainly easier for Bob because he doesn't have to formally negotiate it with his bosses, with the aggravation and potential risk to his reputation that might involve. It's also easier for his employers who don't want to create a flexible working precedent for other employees, something to which Neil also alludes. But the problem with this approach, even though it may work on an individual level, is that it doesn't change the work culture. If fathers are making these arrangements on the QT, refusing to voice publicly what they want and pushing for it from their bosses, then bosses are under no pressure to change their thinking. And flexible working for fathers is no nearer to being normalised. Even the most family-orientated male worker risks being intimidated into inaction given this pervasive, closed culture. So employers are free to continue associating flexible working with mothers, brushing off complaints about the consequential pay and promotion penalties, rather than being forced to consider real reform by a united body of male and female employees who want to work flexibly but refuse to be penalised for it. This can infuriate mothers with flexible-work-shy partners, as they alone are 'outed' as having family commitments.

Olive has two children and works part time. Her husband officially works full time but tries to spend a day a week looking after the children. They are both academics. She caustically remarks, 'I have asked my husband many times to tell the college that he is working a four-day week and take a pay cut. He absolutely won't. And it isn't about the money. I think for many men they will not give their workplace any sense that their family commitments affect their work at all. So there is no way he would tell even sympathetic, right-on colleagues that he can't do something work-related because he has to look after the kids . . . The upshot is that his status as a father gives him Brownie points at work "Aaww, he's got a 'dad' side!" – with none of the down side of being a less good employee because you have outside commitments.' Half of all working parents think that their relationship with their children would improve if they could work more flexibly,[33] yet fathers are doing little to bring this about beyond the odd shifty manoeuvre.

This is not just down to finances, fear and ambition. There's another reason why fathers hold back. Despite, when asked, agreeing that they want to spend more time with their children, when it comes to seeing this through they can be more hesitant. Around three quarters of men are happy with the hours that they work, even when they become fathers.[34] A sizeable minority of fathers – 40 per cent – don't agree that their job prevents them from spending the amount of time that they would like with their children.[35] Matt, who has a son at primary school and a toddler, voices these conflicting thoughts as he considers whether or not he'd like to care for his children during the week: 'I don't think I'd enjoy it very much and I very much value the time that I have [at work]. I find childcare quite boring – I love my kids and spending time with them but a whole day looking after a very young child is just boring. I can't do my emails and I can't focus on him in the way that I should do so I end up feeling guilty.' Bob believes this is the dominant view. 'I think most men's idea of what a father's involvement is is probably more civilised than their fathers', so they know they have to change nappies, they want to spend time with their children at weekends, most people I can think of make an effort to come home from work and see their child. But I suspect for most people that is enough.'

Looking after children can be tedious and gruelling. For many men if it's a choice between spending an extra hour in the office or getting back home in time to wrestle tired and irritable offspring into a bath, they will take the former. Time your return right, and instead they will come running to the door, calmed down, scrubbed up and ready for sleep, greeting you like the Railway Children reunited with Father. Then all you have to do is accompany them as they potter off to bed, and give them a kiss as they tell you they love you, Daddy. Michael Gove, the Conservative politician and former journalist, amusingly nailed men's avoidance tactics at this time while a columnist for *The Times*: 'When tiredness sets in, in the hour before bedtime when tears come more easily, there's many a dad I know who finds that urgent work demands his absence, colleagues need to be called, a report submitted, perhaps even a box of tissues has to be purchased before the late-night Tesco off the M3 closes. That period between 6 p.m. and 7 p.m., when the children refuse to take off their clothes, decline to get in the bath, object to having their hair washed, scream at the application of shampoo, shriek when it gets in their eyes, wail when you try to rinse it out, kick when you try to get them out of the tub, pummel you when you try to dry them, run away when you get out the pyjamas, wriggle when you put on the trousers, wee when the breeks are finally on, flail when you try to put on the PJ top, hyperventilate when it's over their head, flop in a faint when the nightclothes are eventually all on, demand the Richard Scarry, discard the Richard Scarry, grab the book you've been reading for the past three years, which they've now outgrown, and which everyone else in their class now regards as babyish, insist that you read it, go into a sustained dry retch when you refuse and then, when you relent, stare into the middle distance and yell for milk is, I think, the worst part of parenting.'[36]

Fathers' reluctance to get involved in the day-to-day graft of childcare is rarely challenged. Men have too little resolve to resist the cultural norms, government policy and employer practice that herd them into a secondary parenting role. In fact, reticent as some men are, these provide them with the perfect alibi. Like socialist firebrands who become more right-wing with age, even noughties new men find that on becoming fathers patriarchy suits them rather well, after all. Maggie isn't fooled: 'There is a really strong residue of entitlement which goes with being a bloke . . . with lots of guys I know it's pretty tokenistic, to be honest.' Mothers, who may well feel the same about the rigours of bath-time and the other routine care of children, have no option but to get on with it. This sense of male entitlement, together with the knowledge that women will always be there to carry on parenting when they just don't fancy it, means that men feel they have licence to keep their distance. Bronwyn, a mother of two who is separated from her husband, says, 'I don't know whether it is true of every male or not, I wouldn't like to say, I suspect it's common to choose to take advantage of a privileged position. And the way men are brought up, it is all about them and it does get you a lot further in the world when you look after number one. But in a sense, if someone else was looking after my children amazingly well, you know, if he had become a stay-at-home dad and was doing a fabulous job – I would probably have stopped thinking about the kids so much because I knew they were being taken care of. And I think, contrary to my expectations, I did turn out to be an OK mum and did quite well at it, so I think he felt he could step away and just look after himself.'

Matt admits that he assumes his wife will take care of the children. Currently between job contracts he plans his time on the basis that the bulk of the weekday childcare will still be shared between his wife, who has a part-time job, and their childminder. 'There's been a lot of tension recently, now that I'm not working. All of a sudden my wife is wondering why on earth I'm not available to do childcare . . . And I'm kind of thinking, "Well, because we haven't discussed it." Maybe I should be but those are the things we are trying to clarify, exactly what my role is in terms of childcare on the days when we don't have a childminder . . . Because left to my own devices I do the crossword, I swan around, I have lunch. I don't desperately want to do more childcare but I can see that I should.'

Carrying on with your life outside the home, building a career and being treated like a hero by your children when you walk through your front door at night is just too good a deal for most men to turn down. And, as time goes by, the thought of spending lots of time with your children becomes more and more unappealing. Michelle observes of her husband, 'I think he is so used to being out of the picture . . . I think he just busies himself, all the time. He thinks "There are other things I could be doing. You know, better things I can be doing, than parenting my children." . . . Even when he is at home, he will be fixing something or sorting the office out or doing some blokey job . . . He has just focused on earning the money and doing things that he has felt good at doing . . . My husband is in the world of work, the world of home is my world. We are in almost two different bubbles apart from the weekends and my Monday-to-Friday routine and his are just so different.'

As Michelle says, men retreat into their comfort zone. Dave, a father of one son from the north-east of England, who has separated from his wife, says, 'I have got friends now who are pathetic with fear when their wife says "I am going away for the weekend, you are looking after the kids."' Fathers know they should be playing a more active role in their children's lives, and at some level wish to do so. They make the right noises about flexible working and spending more time with their children. But often they resist making the sacrifices in status, autonomy and economic power that this would entail. Unlike women, who are forced to throw all their chips up in the air, many men continue to hold on tightly to what they've got, telling themselves that they will put things right with their family at some point in the future. Dan, an engineer from Glasgow and father of a baby girl, thinks about his male group of friends: 'Some of them don't see their children until the weekend. At the weekend they will see them for a wee bit in the morning and they will go to football and maybe see them for a wee bit before they go for their bath, they have very little time with them . . . Some of them are not interested – they are too small, too young, they are not inter-active enough, they can't respond to things – so they keep saying when they are older they will pay more attention, be able to have conversations with them.'

But relationships with our children need to be nurtured from the start. Like learning a foreign language or a new sport, the more practised you become in looking after children the more enjoyable it is. Women get to grips with parenting and their reward is a complex, deep and lasting relationship with their children. They pay a huge price for this, in exhaustion, conflicting commitments and social and economic marginalisa-tion, because parenting isn't fairly shared. But men pay a great price, too, for their limited involvement in family life, missing out on much of the intense joy and satisfaction that children can bring. A qualitative research study with fathers in mainly professional, dual-income households found that they spend only a small proportion of time in sole charge of their chil-dren. The majority of their time together happens at the weekend but this is generally family time that includes mothers.[37] Fathers' individual relationships with their children have fewer opportunities to grow. Stuck in a timewarp, the interaction risks being stunted and remaining infantile.

Many men speak contemptuously of their own fathers and their desire to be more actively involved in their own children's lives. An ICM poll for the Fatherhood Institute in 2010 found that half of the men questioned wished their father had spent more time with them when they were growing up and over a third thought that their father had had little or no positive influence on their upbringing. Almost 40 per cent said they were trying to be closer to their own children.[38] 'My own father had zero input into running the household really,' remarks Neil. But men are not doing enough to sufficiently make up the distance between fathers and mothers in their own lives as parents. Matt says, 'I do exponentially more childcare than my father did and the balance is going that way but it is still not equitable and my wife is the primary carer.' Being around more for their children remains permanently on men's to-do list. Men can feel regret that time with their family is squeezed because of work.[39] But kids grow up fast and *mañana* never comes. Dave looks back on the years bringing up his now adult son: 'I renovated two houses at the same time as holding down big jobs . . . and I have a huge regret, a massive regret . . . because, and this really hurts me actually, I lost weekends I could have been doing things with him . . . There was this time we could have been doing things together.'

In some cases, men's relationships with their children can become so disengaged that, if they separate from the mother, the bond does not withstand the breach. Children are nine times more likely to live with their mother than their father after separation.[40] Although reported contact rates vary according to whether it is the resident or non-resident parent providing the information, and the situation changes over time, between about a fifth and a quarter of non-resident parents never see their children.[41] Non-resident parents are unlikely to pay maintenance to resident parents. Only 30 per cent of main-carer parents receive any maintenance at all.[42] Although some of this is undoubtedly down to systemic problems within the Child Support Agency over the years, the very high level of non-payment also indicates that many fathers who no longer live with their children believe that they can give up any financial responsibility for them. Parents who have no contact with their children are least likely to make child support payments.[43] There can be a variety of reasons for this loss of contact (including logistical and financial constraints that make visits difficult, safety concerns, legal restrictions or a poor relationship between the father and the mother), but for some fathers – and their children – there's a lack of desire to stay in touch.

It's very sad that for some families this is the outcome of a parenting structure that sidelines men. Politicians wring their hands about the fallout caused by disrupted family life and atomised communities, and employers bemoan the lack of application, and interpersonal skills displayed by younger employees. Yet they seem unable – or unwilling – to make the connection between these concerns and their requirement that fathers absent themselves from family life, and from their community, for most of the week.

This polarising structure is so deep-rooted that attitudes towards becoming a parent are understood in a gendered way. 'I expected to feel overcome with joy, while instead I often felt only puzzled. I was expected to feel worried when I often felt indifferent. I was expected to feel fascinated when I actually felt bored . . . Maternal love may be instinctive, but paternal love is learnt behaviour,' says the American writer Michael Lewis about becoming a father.[44] But women, too, experience puzzlement, indifference and boredom. They don't have some magical instinctive ability that sets them apart from men. Fathers are just as emotionally responsive and sensitive to babies as mothers, and the greater the opportunity they have to spend time with their children the more their caring capacity and attachment develops.[45] Like fathers, mothers learn their skills on the job.

Dave agrees with Michael Lewis that new fathers, 'probably feel terribly guilty that they don't feel this huge connection they are meant to'. But he says that they need to persevere: 'It is hard, but that is OK, that is how it is and it will come if you work at it.' Dave had to forge his own responsible relationship with his son immediately from birth because his then wife couldn't leave hospital. Their bond grew from there. 'I can remember some absolutely gorgeous Saturday mornings when my wife had gone out and I had our son in the house, just the two of us all day, and he was just months old and changing his nappy and getting him to sleep on the sofa and just delighting in him and feeding him. I can also remember when he was about five or six taking him on holiday for a week . . . and a wonderful day, the two of us driving there in the car, singing songs . . . My son was in India a few months ago and I spent two weeks with him, just the two of us, and I think it matters. I discovered it was like an onion you have just got to keep peeling. You can't go straight to the core of him. If you sit down and ask him some tough questions about how he is feeling, or what is going on, he just shuts up like a clam. You sit with him for hours and just do some stuff and then peel one layer and then the next layer. It's just magical.'

Dave is one of the lucky few. Most of us build our parenting roles around the fact that women carry and give birth to babies, from then on emphasising mothers above fathers in the lives of their children. This excuses unwilling fathers and excludes the rest. Fathers are more likely than in previous generations to make an effort to get home before their children are in bed, to take them to the park at the weekend and to get involved in home-work, but the overarching responsibility for children still squarely rests with mothers. All fathers should be enabled to play a full and equal role in family life. Men in the UK are not given the opportunity to do this at the moment and some even shy away from it. But this can change. As I will come on to discuss, the experience of other countries shows that men do become more closely involved with their children if actively encouraged to do so. The effect of this on people's lives, and on society as a whole, is profound. The UK has the choice to match the ambition of other countries and allow fathers in to their families' daily lives.

6

The Enemy Within

'I spent a lot of time expecting my husband to fix things, but then I came to realise that he was there in the ways he could be. If he wasn't there, it didn't mean he wasn't a good father or didn't care. I saw it could be my mom or a great baby-sitter who helped. Once I was OK with that, my marriage got better.'

So says Michelle Obama, lawyer, health and education executive, mother of two and wife of the US President, in an interview for *Vogue* magazine.[1] The aptly named 'First Lady' of America – one half of a couple that supposedly symbolises modernity and meritocracy – seems to be advising that capitulation is a solution to domestic inequality. Furious that bath-scrubbing, school paperwork and the household laundry are always down to you? Frustrated that your part-time job is taking you nowhere while your partner is going great guns in the office sixty hours a week? The answer's easy! Take a deep breath, accept things the way they are, and step back in amazement as peace returns to your household. Michelle Obama may live an exceptional life, married to a man with huge ambition and power, but her attitude is commonplace. The path of least resistance runs from Pennsylvania Avenue all the way to the terraced streets of the UK: mothers here are more likely than

fathers to believe that childcare is primarily their responsibility.[2]

So much is gained in becoming a mother. Motherhood opens
us up to intense feelings of love and care that otherwise may
never have been known to us. But we mothers are too ready to
believe that this profound experience comes with unique penalties that we have no choice but to accept. Unequal responsibilities in the home, stagnating careers, financial dependency: we
shrug our shoulders at the price we pay and accept it's 'just the
way it is' rather than looking for more from our partners, our
society or ourselves. We vent our discontent but we do nothing,
too ready to reconcile ourselves to the situation. Like fathers,
mothers, too, have a hand in settling their own fates.

Nicky and her husband live in Cardiff with their young son
and both work full time. '[My husband] will openly admit he
doesn't know where the washing machine is, and cooking and
shopping for food is all down to me,' she says. 'If I nag a lot he
would do it but I can't be bothered. It's easier to just get on with
it.' Celeste, a full-time mother of three from Bristol whose
husband works six days a week, has the same attitude: 'I am not
happy with it but I do accept that's how it goes – that's the norm,
isn't it? Women do the childcare and the men go out to work.'
Rather than asking why this is the 'norm', women resign themselves, claiming that striving for anything better is just too complicated and challenging. Even women who question these standard
family roles fall in with them regardless. Becky is a part-time
administrator from Newcastle who has one son. Although she is
frustrated by the unequal division of responsibilities in her household, finding a way through it seems too difficult to attempt.
'The overriding feeling is just one of having no answers,' she says.
'There is no real answer to this.' Karen, an academic and mother
of one, also holds her hands up, 'I feel a fraud if I am honest. I
am meant to be a feminist but I feel very much that I am taking
up those traditional female roles. And often I don't challenge and
I can't handle the battle. Now and again it will reach a point

where I say, "For God's sake, I can't do everything!" . . . But generally we muddle through, because I think we are too exhausted.' As Karen suggests, fatigue is key to dampening resistance. With so much effort required to keep both home and work life on track, we decide that we have no energy left to confront the complex web of limitations that traps us. We buckle rather than take on the fight. Signing up to our own subordination, we give others no reason to think twice about what is happening.

But mothers' unhappiness has to find some outlet and it is released in a series of self-injurious ways, which end up reinforcing the inequality that is the source of our discontent. In reaction to our loss of social and economic status outside the home, we grip the reins in our domestic life ever more tightly. We collude in distancing the father from the domestic sphere. The home becomes our domain, our power base: we decide that we will exercise control there if nowhere else. Jane, a mother of two and teacher from Leeds, says, 'I remember thinking, "I'm quite powerless, I'm not earning very much money, I'm not part of that whole world of work. So . . . I will be in charge of my sphere and if my sphere is the house then so be it."' Intrusion from the father must be contained. If he is to have a domestic role, it must be on the understanding that he sticks to our rules and standards. Resentful that women are automatically anointed as the primary parent, with the greater effort and sacrifice that involves, mothers lash out. We begin to use the role of expert foisted upon us as a weapon against fathers. The father's backseat domestic role, so effectively established from the start, is perversely reinforced by women themselves as they insist that they will take the lead in the home while the father must follow instructions.

It starts in the first weeks of motherhood. We begin chiding our partner for the way he fastens a nappy or holds a bottle, and this criticism continues down the years as we throw up our hands at the school shoes he buys or his inadequate attention to detail over holiday club arrangements. 'I do want things done in the way I want them done,' admits Mary, a mother of two and media worker from London.

Women are inconsistent, claiming they are frustrated with having to deal with the majority of the domestic burden, yet at the same time unwilling to cede any control over home life. Mary wishes that her partner 'would take some of the responsibility, seeing that it's a shared role, not my role'. Yet at the same time she admits, 'But I probably do add to the problem to some extent myself . . . I don't leave a lot of room for other people to take on those responsibilities.' Tanya, a businesswoman from Cambridge with two children, echoes this. 'Could I relinquish control and allow my husband to do it? The answer is probably not, because I wouldn't necessarily be confident that it would be done to my standards . . . I have done it all this far. So, yes, it's better if I do it.' As time goes by, the likelihood of men volunteering in the home and gaining in competence decreases and perceptions become entrenched: useless, lazy father versus super-competent, selfless mother. Women become invested in their identity as the unsupported domestic drudge and seek to maintain it rather than reverse it. Jane observes, 'Some of it, if I'm completely honest, is almost a bit of a martyr thing going on. I resent it but I'm going to do more and more and more of it, and then I've got even more to resent and then it will be really clear that it's not fair. I actually think there is some of that . . . wanting to make the point.'

Mothers who begrudge their partners' lack of involvement, especially in the gruelling early stages of childrearing, can pull up the drawbridge when it comes to the rewards. Helen, a full-time mother from Oxford, admits that she now feels territorial about her relationship with her daughter. 'There was this long period of time when my partner wasn't interested at all in doing anything and now our daughter is much more fun and she communicates lots, he's more interested in spending time with her. But only when it suits him. So there's a bit of, like, "Actually, you can't do that. You can't ignore her for however many months when you think she's a bit boring and then suddenly decide that you want to spend time with her, but only when it suits you, when the football's not on." . . . I often think of how in other cultures mothers and babies go off and do their own thing and fathers have a much less significant role. And a lot of me feels that that is probably what is natural.' Shellshocked by the realisation that the childrearing will be largely left to us, mothers become brittle and standoffish. The parenting efforts of men are routinely mocked and derided, with snarky comments about their ineptitude. As Frieda, a mother of one from London describes it, 'that kind of rolling of the eyes, "men are all so hopeless, aren't they?" type of shit.' This permitted and infectious caricaturing of men is a coping mechanism for women who have thrown in the towel on equality. A natural alternative to mother's little helper, it gives women a brief hit of superiority, numbing them against the reality of their lot. Mandy is a mother of five from Newcastle. Referring to her husband she says, 'I've got six children not five . . . Half of me wants him to get more involved . . . but the other half wants him to keep out of the way because I can't be bothered with him.' The inadequate advances of the father are rebuffed with criticism, cold shoulders and contempt.

Fathers can feel excluded and back off. 'He frequently won't do things because he is worried about doing them wrongly and would rather get in trouble for not having done it,' says Tanya of her husband. Becky, too, acknowledges that her approach can be off-putting: 'I want to be the person that brings my son up but I don't want to do everything myself. And I think that what can happen between couples is that the woman doesn't really let go enough to let the partner take some responsibility and do stuff. Because my partner will do things in a different way to me, that doesn't mean it's the wrong way. It's just different. Yet it really annoys me. I should really think, "If my son is happy and they are getting on with it then it's fine." . . . I have to be very careful because my partner gets quite upset if I tell him or suggest that he's not doing something right.'[2]

Some fathers who feel they don't get encouragement from their partners even get depressed,[3] and many men talk of the pressure not to put a foot wrong. Matt, a father of two from London remarks, 'My wife is quite a controlling person . . . She likes things the way she likes them and she gets quite upset if things aren't the way she wants them. So she takes on a lot of the responsibility but resents it at the same time . . . It does add to a dynamic where she is shouting the odds about what needs to be done and is resentful about having to do more than her fair share and I'm pissed off with her for trying to run such a tight ship . . . I'd do [more childcare] if I had to but I tend to think that if I did that I'd still be under orders from my wife, who'd be directing things from the office.' Bob is also discouraged by these contradictory signals of maternal fatigue and territorialism. 'It is considered desirable for me to be more involved, equally involved, with all aspects of childcare but my opinion didn't seem to be respected,' he remarks, referring to a disagreement with his wife about their child's bedtime. 'It can be demoralising as a father if you feel your opinion is not seen as valid, for whatever reason.'

While discouraging fathers who want to be more involved, women risk letting off the hook those men who have little interest in contributing to home life. Some are very happy to play along with the useless-male stereotype. It's the perfect excuse to keep their distance from domestic matters. If doing down fathers takes the edge off women's inequality, that's fine by these men. Their partners are playing into their hands. Father-baiting is the little indulgence women are allowed: they can let off steam while toeing the line and doing the grunt work.

Mothers' irrational response to the entirely rational frustrations they feel serves only to widen the gap between parents. Women are unhappy with the unfair situation in which they find themselves and so are critical of fathers, keeping them at arm's length. Fathers then feel excluded and this further reduces the likelihood of their greater involvement. This in turn reinforces mothers' own unhappiness and so the vicious circle continues. In the middle of this are the children, caught between two parents at stand-off. 'Maternal gatekeeping', as it has been labelled, certainly exists. It encompasses not just criticism and oppressive monitoring of men's efforts but also a need by mothers to have their maternal identity validated (an identity which they believe would be compromised if the father took up more of the domestic work). Belief in traditional gender roles, often latent, can also emerge on becoming a mother.[4] Jane explains, 'Some of it is about thinking that I've got to be successful and if my world is the house I must be successful in the house, so I will make sure that everything is really well organised and that the house is always clean . . . And I do wonder as well if there are things deep down that surface a bit when you find yourself in that role of a mother, thinking, "Actually, this is my responsibility." . . . Because we are all a product of the world we live in, which is still a sexist world I think, aren't we?'

For the one third of women who believe raising children is primarily a mother's responsibility,[5] these values make sense. Kim, a mother of two from Oxford, comments on caring tasks, 'I don't think, "Oh, I wish [my husband] would do that." I just think that that is part of my job and I suppose that's the way we've set things up and it works well. And I suppose that if I ever do think that I do an awful lot, I also know that he is earning the money and I do earn some money but he's by far the main breadwinner and that is also an important job. I realise that although it may not appear as if he does as many little things as I do he does this hugely important thing, which is earning the money.' But women risk losing themselves completely in the world of motherhood as they alone take on responsibility for these 'little things' (in fact the significant work of raising the next generation). Heads buried in maternal duties, distracted by the series of lifestyle and consumer choices that contemporary motherhood offers, even celebrating this work as the ultimate fulfilment of womanhood, mothers fail to challenge the basis on which all this falls to them in the first place.

'Maternal gatekeeping' is a phenomenon that restricts male involvement in family life. But it is rooted in the deeper inequalities that shape our existence. It is an attempt by women to adapt to the social structures within which they have grown up and now must operate as mothers, accommodating themselves to their pre-ordained maternal role. Gatekeeping is not the prime mover for pushing men out of the home: they were on the periphery or absent anyway. But it exacerbates a situation that already exists.

Beyond their own homes, mothers extend their suspicion and exclusion of men to other fathers with whom they come into contact. We take to our hearts the occasional heroic dad manfully doing his best in tragic circumstances: a widower or a husband whose heartless wife walks out on him and the children. Otherwise, women have the knives out for men who get *too* involved in the rearing of their children, treating them with ridicule (hen-pecked wimps), pity (unable to get a 'proper job') or suspicion (possible paedophiles). One mother considers men at playgroups: 'The fact that you've got a child with you who is your daughter or whatever shows that obviously you are not a weirdo trying to weasel your way into the group,' she says, indicating the need to be alert to male weaseling weirdos.

Keen to exercise power where possible, mothers gang together to make life uncomfortable for those men brave enough to attend children's play sessions or to trespass in other parts of the mothers' kingdom. Kieran, a father of two from London, recalls his experience: 'Once, in the early days, when I was on my own with our son, I went to some club in the church hall. And I felt like an idiot, actually . . . I don't know, I was not comfortable at all.' Having mixed socially for most of their lives, suddenly it's like being back at the school disco: men on one side of the room, women on the other. Matt, also a father of two, had a similar experience to Kieran and agrees, 'I was sent to Coventry a bit –

the mums didn't want to know me.' Helen is sympathetic: 'I think it must be awful for men. I think it must be really hard and intimidating. I listen to some of the women and think, "Oh my God." Seriously. Today they were talking to this poor woman who was due to give birth last Thursday. She was surrounded by a gaggle of women who were all sharing their horrific child-birth stories and I thought, "What's wrong with you? How can you do this to this woman? She's about to give birth!" . . . And if I was thinking that, imagine being a bloke sitting there thinking, "My God, how am I meant to access the conversation?"' As well as this unspoken freezing-out of men, fathers can be more explic-itly excluded. Isla remembers her husband's efforts to take their children swimming: 'He was asked to leave the "mother and baby" swimming group . . . Get over it, you know? We don't have segregated swimming normally so why would we have it when there are babies there? It was all just a big palaver.'

Although mothers collectively rage at fathers for not taking on responsibility for their children, those who do are treated warily, ignored or intimidated. Mothers resent childcare as a woman's domain and yet they want to keep it that way, viewing men's active involvement as a land grab. Those men who try to cross the border are unwelcome. Rather than realising that encouraging men to play a fair part in raising their families will pay dividends for both fathers and mothers and, most import-antly, children, mothers hoard the domestic power that they are left with.

It is not only latent, traditional values that come to the surface when women become mothers. Women also start to succumb to, and sympathise with, the dominant male view. They develop Stockholm syndrome, siding with the state, employers and fathers in their marginalisation of women, grateful for any leftovers chucked to them from the male high table. Mothers tell them-selves that they are so lucky to have a partner who sticks on the occasional load of washing, so fortunate to be able to work three days a week in a job that a man wouldn't touch with a barge pole, or so privileged to be at home full time with two children as their public roles and status irreversibly deteriorate. Nicky, a mother of one and a university research manager who works full time, says, 'I have a very flexible job thankfully . . . I am lucky. As long as the work gets done I can work in the evenings or I can work at the weekend if I have to.' Women have been bombarded with claims about the difficulty of flexible working in senior posts to the degree that they have learnt to regard the pragmatic approach that Nicky outlines as a blessing from a particularly beneficent boss rather than the best way for an employer to keep a good member of staff. Louise, a student and mother of two from London, goes along with this: 'Most of the women that I've talked to . . . if they could work part time they really had it made. All the women that are able to negotiate three-day weeks all feel like they are really lucky and know that they are in a very privileged position.' The contemptuously named part-time 'mummy track' is not merely something that women are expected to settle for, they should feel positively grateful for it.

There is another reason why mothers fall in with the current way of doing things: it provides an exit route from the pressures of contemporary life. If the sums add up, women can decide that they just want out of the rat race. Throwing themselves into motherhood allows them to perform a vanishing act from their previous lives. In our early twenties, work can seem exciting: we are making our own money, standing on our own two feet, wowing people with our organisational and teamwork skills, gossiping in the corridor and getting drunk together on Friday nights. By our late twenties or early thirties, as most women begin planning for and having children, the shine has worn off. Perhaps we missed out on a couple of promotions, fell out with our closest colleague, or have been ground down by petty bureaucracy. Or maybe we've become jaded about our line of work, regretful that we didn't take another path but fearful that it is too late and too difficult to start again. This disenchantment with work affects men as well as women but, as society is currently arranged, women have a unique route out: the emergency exit of motherhood. We can stick our jobs on the back burner, switch to the slow lane or give up on them all together. We can shift our focus to a place where we imagine we will be the boss – the home. Our fate will no longer rest in the hands of Human Resources. We will take control of daily existence. We will emancipate ourselves, seizing control of supermarket and park trips. Best of all, we can escape with our heads held high, telling the outside world that we are doing this for the good of our children, nobly sacrificing other aspects of our life for the benefit of our brood. It can seem easier to take up a proscribed role in society than attempt to get out of a rut in a job – or face the fact that we can't. Motherhood presents a tempting opportunity to make a run for it.

Maternal dedication and the cost of childcare provide a perfect alibi. Louise reveals her own decision to leave her hated job in a department store: 'One of the reasons why I felt that I almost had a get-out clause was that childcare was so expensive that it wouldn't have even been worth my while to work . . . I think I was looking for a reason not to go back. I think I was looking for a way to justify it and I think most women do . . . I think if you have a husband it's not easy to say, "Look, you are going to be the main provider from now on."' Just as men fall back on an assumption that women will take responsibility for caring for children, women assume that men will keep the household solvent. Michelle, a full-time mother of three from Gloucestershire, also saw having her second child as a form of escape from a job that she was struggling to combine with motherhood. 'Work was so bad . . . you think that it's a way out, I guess . . . I left as soon as you can start your maternity leave. I was out of there.' She contrasts this with her husband's experience: 'I think that it's quite a hard thing for a guy because there is no career break. For women it's quite nice because you can have this opportunity to retrain and to have some time at home. I mean it's almost luxurious. Whereas for a guy, that's it now. Especially the more children we have had, the more my husband has felt that he wants to provide for them.' Men are forced to carry on, to aim for renewal in their work if they feel it's in the doldrums, while women can duck out. Men might come out the other side and move on upwards again, building on all the advantages they already have. Women, with so much against them as it is, risk permanent exclusion from decent jobs if they extend the break for too long.

In the end, career conundrums and other difficulties threaten to catch women up. 'The vast majority of women that I know, even if they are not working now, are very much looking into how they can get back into work,' admits Louise. Kate, an arts manager, would recognise this problem. She encountered difficulties in finding new work after leaving a job she no longer wanted and moving with her children to join her husband who was working abroad for a year. 'I wasn't enjoying the job I was doing any more and I'd taken it as far as I could . . . And then you put that together with being very, very tired. And then my oldest daughter started school and she didn't settle and we had a horrid first term . . . And I started waking up in the middle of the night worrying about my daughter, and I didn't care about work any more – didn't feel anything about what I was achieving there. And we went through a whole year of this – where she didn't really settle at school. And I thought "We can't carry on, we've got to get this sorted." So that was the major trigger for me. And then on top of that my husband got offered a job abroad . . . so it was kind of a no-brainer [to leave] . . . I think if I hadn't had kids and said I was off then people would have said, "What's wrong?", definitely. The truth is the children weren't *the* reason but they were a factor in the decision. They made it acceptable. But then that also has made it bloody hard to come back.' Kate believes that the discrimination she already faced as a working mother intensified on her return to the job market. Her departure from employment has been interpreted as an implicit admission of failure in combining work and home life. 'At every job interview they ask me how I will juggle it with the children, a question they are not supposed to ask. They ask, "What will you do with your family?" And you know they are not asking that of the male candidates . . . When you publicly step down and say that it's to spend time with your family the one thing that people in the sector know about me is that I have kids . . . And that gives people a reason to write me off. People always act surprised that I'm working and say, "I'm glad to see you are busy," like I'm some sort of invalid. Or they say, "How do you manage with the children?" And I feel like saying, "Oh, I've just stuck them in a box somewhere." Or, "I've sent them off to be adopted, I don't have them any more."'

Whatever her mix of motivations at the time she left her old job, Kate is honest about the fallout from it and the frustration this has caused her. 'If I'd had my time again I would have taken a sabbatical, gone abroad and come back and used my job to get to where I wanted to go to next . . . I should have been far more calculated about it . . . My goal is to be running an organisation again. I'm a bossy cow, I like running things and I'm good at it.' Her tenacity in her recent job search has finally paid off and she has secured a new, senior post.

For many couples with young children allotting themselves distinct roles within the family makes practical and emotional sense in the short term. Again, this is often framed as being an option for the fortunate. Fran is a full-time mother of one who left her job when her boss refused her request to work part time. She says, 'I do obviously have a huge amount of time with [my daughter] now and I do feel extremely lucky to have that time and that is really precious. I know from talking to other friends who are in the position where financially they have no option but to work, how lucky they see me as being.' She adds, 'My husband is happy working full time and really would want to continue on that basis . . . He is also really, really into me being at home full time and he really thinks it's really good for our daughter and I think he is really pleased this is the arrangement that we have come to and it's working for us both.' But in making such decisions women risk paying too little heed to the long-term consequences. For some, any negative effects will not pose a serious problem, or will be judged worthwhile. But for others, like Kate, the cost will be significant and they will look back and wish they had done things differently. In dividing responsibilities within a household it makes sense for mothers to consider how they might feel in the future when their children are more independent, or if they ever get into financial trouble, or want to get their teeth into professional life again.

Research on so-called 'psychologically induced path dependence' in people's life choices demonstrates our tendency to feel stuck in our current role and wary of change, placing much greater value on our present situation compared to what we might gain if we were to attempt something different. Such attitudes and thought processes influence women's decisions about careers and what they will devote energy to in their lives, cementing them in their current roles.[6] Women avoid risk, fail to think in the long term and decide it's best to stick with what they've become used to.

While justifiably criticising the inadequacies of partners, government and employers, mothers duck examining their own innate attitudes and preferences and retreat into domestic roles. Rather than try to fight the forces they are up against, women decide instead to sulk. Women sulk at work and sulk at home, wallowing in martyrdom and indulging in territorialism. When not sulking we submit, unquestioningly buying the male line and even taking the view that it's a ticket out of the stresses of modern life. In each of these ways mothers prop up their inequality, reinforcing stereotypes and preconceptions rather than working to break them down. In doing so we become only more securely imprisoned within the domestic realm. Yet, precisely because this harm is self-inflicted, we can do a great deal ourselves to prevent it, as I will explore later. By challenging our own attitudes we have the power to reverse our descent into unhappiness, charging ourselves to do all that we can to create a life with which we are content.

7

Foreign Policy

For all its rewards, family life in the UK is hard. Recent years have brought an increase in paid maternity leave, the introduction of paid paternity leave, the opportunity to share leave, parents' right to request flexible working, free nursery provision for three- and four-year-olds and the arrival of Children's Centres. Yet, welcome as these changes have been, they do not go anything like far enough. We are still left with an unstable combination of relatively high female employment rates, limited childcare and after-school services, long working hours for fathers, and a yawning pay gap. Mothers are forced to square these circles by confining themselves to whichever part-time jobs they can pick up that will allow them to combine paid work with responsibility for their children. And thus we continue to entrench inequality between men and women and put great strain on families. On top of this, the deep cuts in public spending introduced in 2011 are knocking away key building blocks of women's recent advances. Life is now much more of a struggle for parents and children.

In 2010 the Fatherhood Institute published an international Fairness in Families Index that placed the UK in eighteenth position out of twenty-one nations on issues such as parental leave, time spent by men and women caring for children and the pay gap.[1] It doesn't have to be like this. Across the world, new approaches to family policy are being pioneered with some remarkable successes and instructive failures. We should be inspired by the bold example of other countries to forge our own revolution here.

Support for families – from leave following the birth of a child, to working patterns and childcare provision – tells us a lot about a nation. And constructive lessons don't always come from predictable quarters. Yes, the Nordic states can certainly teach us a thing or two about how to help families: within their social democratic systems, raising children is deemed the responsibility of the whole community. But the liberal, individualistic approach taken by the United States also provides food for thought; as do aspects of policy in our near neighbours, such as the Netherlands. Shared parenting has finally made its way onto the political agenda in the UK, and we would do well to take greater note of these international examples. Domestic equality isn't some distant ideal that must remain forever out of reach. Other countries are making great strides towards it.

Take paid parental leave. While the UK has extended statutory maternity leave, it has steadily built up a divide between (generous) mothers' and (minimal) fathers' default leave entitlements. Recent steps to allow greater flexibility in the division of leave are too weak to counteract this imbalance. Yet it is notable that in many of the Nordic states – countries that have made the most progress towards equality – there has been a move towards evening up set leave allocations for men and women. The majority of leave is now made up of substantial periods of well-paid 'parental leave', with large amounts ring-fenced for both mothers and fathers. Sweden and Norway pioneered experiments in a more equitable system way back in the 1970s, while the UK was still debating whether to introduce statutory maternity leave. Determined that equality between the sexes and collective responsibility for the welfare of children should form the bedrock of their society, they pushed ahead with reform.

Originally, parental leave could be divided between parents as they wished but take-up by men was very low, at 7 per cent in Sweden and 4 per cent in Norway.[2] So first Norway, and then Sweden, introduced a number of weeks of non-transferable leave for either parent. Today in Norway, out of a total of fifty-four weeks' leave, nine weeks are reserved for mothers and six weeks are reserved for fathers, with the rest divided as the couple sees fit. In Sweden parents are given 480 days' leave, and sixty days are earmarked for the mother and sixty for the father. Dubbed the 'use it or lose it' system, this leave has to be taken by the parent for whom it is earmarked or it can't be taken at all. And this radical stance, underpinned by high levels of wage replacement, has really boosted take-up rates. Over 90 per cent of men in Norway now take their quota,[3] and 80 per cent do so in Sweden,[4] with a significant effect on the visibility and acceptance of actively involved fathers. Nathan Hegedus is a journalist and father of a four-year-old daughter and a toddler son who lives with his wife in central Stockholm. He writes about his experience of Swedish fatherhood in his blog, *Dispatches from Daddyland*. He has just returned to work, on slightly reduced hours in his substantive full-time job, after nine months of paternity leave. 'It sort of sneaks up on you because it is so taken for granted that you don't really realise. All of a sudden you notice that there are a lot of men pushing strollers or you go to the open pre-school – a drop-in play place – and there's a lot of guys there . . . And that's what I think is really changing, there has been this cultural shift. Whereas in the past men would have taken their parental leave for summer break – that's the old style way of taking leave, over the summer or at Christmas when people are off anyway – it's now building its own place in society, I think. It's getting more entrenched. It's becoming much more the norm to be a dad who is off in March or mid November or something like that.'

This is a great success, but there is still some disappointment with the extent of change the system has produced. Although take-up of the fathers' quota is good, men use only a little of the leave that can be allocated to either parent.[5] In Sweden this is despite the centre-right government introducing an 'equality bonus' tax credit in 2008 to encourage fifty/fifty take-up between mothers and fathers. Nathan remarks, 'You still have a lot of dads here who don't take parental leave. I think there is a pretty wide range. I gush about Sweden a lot but sometimes I take a step back – within Sweden people don't think the system is that great. Men only take a quarter of the leave when ideally they should take half of it. And there are a lot of guys who don't want to do it and it depends on what sort of job you have.' Take-up is worst among the lowest and highest earners. In both countries, earnings are reimbursed while on leave at a high rate of 80 per cent of salary,[6] though this is capped for top earners. But both the badly off and (in particular) the very well off feel that they can't afford to miss out on the lost proportion of their earnings.[7]

This means that, even with a fathers' quota, the proportion of men taking up large amounts of parental leave is small and compromises the progressive effect on domestic arrangements. Nathan says, 'When everyone is back at work, it's women who do far more childcare and are more likely to work part time . . . So the men go back to work full time and they are better dads when they are home and they are better dads at the weekend and maybe they still do the daycare pick-up . . . I think the men probably are more involved in general but I think it does swing back to women to do a lot of the pick-ups and keeping track of doctors' appointments and staying at home with sick kids.'

As Nathan indicates, in Sweden women still do the great majority of housework and childcare,[8] and they use just below two thirds of the leave days taken by parents to care for sick children.[9] As in the UK, this has an effect on women's job options and employers' attitudes. Even in Sweden, women face discrimination. Employers know that mothers take the bulk of parental leave and this counts against them when it comes to appointments and promotions.[10] So-called 'statistical discrimination' prejudices employers against women workers whether they have children or not. With their work options curtailed, many Swedish women opt for less well paid but more flexible public sector jobs. Three quarters of women work in the public sector and three quarters of men in the private sector[11] and this is reflected in their earnings. Men take more leave in households in which mothers earn a bigger or comparable salary to them – as her earnings will compensate for the reduction in his.[12] But this is unlikely, given women's limited job options – and unfortunate as a Swedish mother's future earnings rise on average by about 7 per cent for every month of leave the father takes.[13] In Sweden as in the UK the cycle of mothers' responsibility for childcare, leading to lower paid jobs, leading to responsibility for childcare, continues.

Nonetheless, the Nordic system does show the importance of combining well-paid leave with the 'use it or lose it' model. Overnight men went from barely using leave to taking it in very large numbers. The daily lives of parents in the early months after their baby's birth have been transformed. Men are beginning to enjoy sharing the care of their newborns. They gain confidence as fathers as never before, while women are able to venture beyond the domestic world. Nathan observes, 'There are a lot of moms who expect it to be their space . . . It can be hard to let the dad in. So paternity leave works well for both parents because the mom just has to go to work, and the dad is left alone and has to discover how to look after his baby. So I think it's brilliant in that sense. I wasn't scared of paternity leave for whatever reason . . . But still there was that sense of, "*I* don't know how to pack the snack bag!" . . . It's really increased my belief in my ability as a parent . . . The guys here on parental leave – it's not like they are super sensitive . . . you've just got a lot of dudes hanging out and there are still all these male codes. And yet they are taking really good care of their twelve-month-old, *really* good care, they are great with them. The men are still men but they are able to take care of children too. And that's the new nurturing sensibility . . . They are creating more space [for themselves] and even if they are not taking the ultimate space that you would want them to, they are just taking on more and more of the childcare.' As Nathan's observations compellingly demonstrate, the introduction of well-paid 'use it or lose it' leave exemplifies the significance of policy in shaping people's behaviour and starting to embed cultural change.

Having looked to the Nordics for inspiration, Germany, too, has reformed its parental leave policy. One of the main motivations was the country's fertility rate, which had been very low since the mid 1970s.[14] By the turn of the millennium, almost one in three women in their late thirties didn't have children.[15] A thirty-six month, low-paid parental leave policy, short school days and, within former West Germany, cultural disapproval of '*Rabenmutter*' or the 'raven mother' who deserts her little chicks to go out to work, drove women into full-time motherhood when they had children. Although men could choose to take some parental leave themselves only 3 per cent ever did so.[16] Faced with a choice of economic independence and fulfilment at work or the unknown, enclosed world of motherhood, many women rejected having children altogether. Others, who under the German education system spent almost a decade at university before taking a number of years to get established in a career, perhaps found that they had difficulty getting pregnant. Christa works as a project manager and lives in Berlin with her husband and young child. 'It's changed a lot now but when I studied it was totally common, and you couldn't really do it any other way, to study for eight or nine years. You had to do one Masters degree and then two subsidiary subjects and they were all in different places . . . I'm a typical representative of that time. I finished my degree when I was twenty-nine years old . . . The problem, though, is that when you start your first job and you want to be really sensible about your career, you need at least a few years to settle yourself in your work before you can drop out for even just one year. Anyone who just got their degree at twenty-nine and then had two young children straight away would never, ever, in Germany get a career. So that means that you are perhaps thirty-five before you even consider having children and, of course, it can then be too late. We had real trouble. That situation is very typical among my generation.' In 2006 Ursula von der Leyen, the then Families Minister under Chancellor Merkel, commented, 'In Germany, we've made a childless lifestyle almost a prerequisite for a good career and the ability to take on a position of leadership.'[17]

So Germany looked north for inspiration, seeing this as a chance to boost its fertility rate and to reconcile two very different pre-unification approaches to family life (in which East Germany had a tradition of state childcare provision, whereas West German mothers were expected to stay at home with their children). In 2003 the government pledged four billion euros over four years to extend the school day and introduced legislation to expand childcare services at a cost of one and a half billion euros a year from 2005.[18] Christa has just returned to Germany after living in the UK for a number of years. One of the reasons that drew her back was the country's push on affordable childcare provision. 'I always thought it was very elitist in London. To have enough total household income to pay for childcare usually meant that you had at least one high-earning parent or it had to be two full-time incomes. If you were working part time, or self-employed, or in a not so well paid profession you would barely bring in enough to cover the nursery. The cost of the childcare was probably the most important factor in our returning to Germany.'

In 2005, the German government also introduced a version of the parental quota system combined with high levels of wage replacement. In addition to fourteen weeks' maternity leave,[19] twelve months of parental leave paid at two thirds of earnings (with a cap) can now be used by either the mother or the father. But there is an added incentive for fathers: the paid leave entitlement will be extended by two months if the father himself takes up this extra period. In effect, this is a watered-down quota: a two-month add-on that only the father can take but which doesn't form part of the core leave provision. This has still had a marked effect although weaker provision has produced weaker results when compared to Norway and Sweden. Just under a fifth of fathers took leave in 2009,[20] a significant jump compared to

3 per cent under the previous system. But as in the Nordic states, high take-up is linked to the education and earning power of the mother and most men tend only to take time set aside for them.[21] Again pay differentials are tightly bound up with couples' decision-making[22] (the pay gap between men and women is 22 per cent in Germany[23]), in a way that is self-perpetuating.

Although a great improvement on the past, and one that is producing significant change for some families, the signs are that this innovation hasn't yet done enough to turn Germany's population trends around. The birth rate has continued to fall[24] and there is still cultural resistance to the concept of the 'working mother' (using after-school clubs, for instance, is still 'frowned upon' in some quarters Christa says). So the Merkel government is coming under pressure to justify its family policies, and their cost, while also dealing with the socio-economic fallout from an ageing population. Yet Christa believes that the government will stick with these policies for the long haul: 'In Berlin, a big city state with social problems, they are very, very keen on early-years education. And they are just learning that for children from deprived backgrounds in particular it's very beneficial. They say we'd rather spend the money now than have the social problems later. The cost of dealing with social problems among teenagers and young adults is so much greater than dealing with very young children. And for me, as a middle-class parent, I benefit from these services too, even though they are not primarily conceived for me.'

The lesson from Germany's old, scrapped parental leave policies is clear: voluntary division of leave paid at a low flat rate means poor take-up by fathers. It's disappointing that the UK has headed off in a similar direction, with up to six months' leave on low or no pay transferable to fathers. Fathers will simply not take up this leave in large numbers. The UK government has proposed introducing a new system of more flexible parental leave.[25] But the international evidence is clear: allowing parents to divide up leave between them isn't sufficient to overcome the institutional, financial and cultural bias towards women doing the majority of caring.

Even a 'use it or lose it' fathers' quota – a major advance on current UK law – isn't necessarily enough to change behaviour beyond the early months. The father's quota needs to be integral to the leave period, not additional to it; well paid, in order to replace lost earnings, and, crucially, of a decent length in proportion to the rest of the leave, so as to bring real cultural change.

In these respects, it's instructive to look at what's happening in Iceland. With its tiny population (about 300,000), not to mention the financial collapse it suffered in 2008, Iceland is in many ways an exceptional country. Nonetheless, what it has achieved in recent years for parents has been remarkable. Late to the game compared to its fellow Nordic states, it's learnt from what's happened elsewhere and improved on their approach. Since 2003, mothers and fathers have been entitled to a total of nine months of paid parental leave (or 'birth leave' as it is called) when a child is born. This is paid at between 75 and 80 per cent of earnings depending on salary, with a cap (introduced in 2004) for high earners. Leave can be used on a part-time basis and the period extended, and it can be taken in consecutive or non-consecutive periods of not less than two weeks each. Three months of leave is reserved for mothers, three for fathers and the remaining three months can be divided as the couple decides. Leave can be taken by a couple at the same time or separately. The father's quota is the longest in the world. Unlike in Norway and Sweden, where the ring-fencing of leave for fathers met with some resistance from mothers, who felt that 'their' leave was being taken away from them, all parents in Iceland benefited from this legislation and it was widely welcomed.

Prior to the reforms, barely any men in Iceland took leave. Astonishingly, fewer than eighteen fathers received State Social Security Institute payments each year from 1993 to 1998, about 0.3 per cent of the number of mothers who did so.[26] Now eighty-eight fathers for every 100 mothers take leave, using an average of 100 days compared to 185 days for women.[27] Oddný Sturludóttir is a City Councillor and Head of the City Board of Education that oversees Reykjavik's pre-schools and elementary schools. She is also a single mother of two children and has experienced the effects of these policy changes on a personal and professional level. She says of the new birth leave arrangements, 'It's made a huge difference. Staying at home with a very small child is amazing but with all the breastfeeding and the mother carrying the child to term, the tendency in the past was for the mother to think, "This is my territory, it's our business as women, and it's very hard for you men to understand: you can join in later as a playmate." That's no longer the case. With the father of my daughter, she was born in May and in the following January I began working again and he took over the care. And for him it was a totally different world from what he was used to. As soon as women leave the house, men get more confident, they have their own relationship with their child. The mother isn't always "the specialist" any more. It was amazing how their relationship became strong without me being around, you know, being bossy and knowing all the rules . . . We were in this together. We were very fifty / fifty. Sharing all the laundry, and cooking, and changing diapers and stuff.'

For Eyjólfur, an accountant and father of three currently spending ten months on part-time paternity leave with his youngest child, the ability to share in this early care has had profoundly beneficial consequences for his family. 'One of the reasons I'm taking leave is that my wife got post-natal depression with the first child but less with the second because I was at home a lot more that time. So we are just going to make sure it doesn't happen again . . . I think it's made all the difference for her. It's not much fun being home alone for eight hours a day with a baby . . . It seems normal now that I am taking ten months of paternity leave, no one has raised questions or anything . . . I am really happy that I can get the opportunity to stay at home. Just a few decades ago this was unheard of.' The difference that Iceland's parental leave policy makes isn't just found in individual homes, it's also seen on the streets. Oddný notes, 'All the kid-friendly cafés, they are filled with fathers on parental leave – on Monday at two in the afternoon. It's not only after work. We feel it's very visible everywhere.'

In Iceland, as in Sweden and Norway, most fathers take the leave reserved for them but after that, their take-up tails off. Only 21 per cent of men take any of the weeks that either parent can take up, whereas 93 per cent of mothers use all or some of this period.[28] Across these three Nordic countries the period of leave that can be shared appears to be viewed as primarily there for the mother's taking as a de facto extension of maternity leave. Standard views of family roles, higher wages for men and pressure from unprogressive workplaces inform decision-making here as elsewhere. Mothers talk of encountering disapproval for not taking the full shared leave period themselves: a 'good' mother would want to take the maximum amount of time at home with her child.[29] However, because the overall amount of parental leave is shorter and the ring-fenced periods longer in Iceland than in other countries, the differences in the amounts of leave taken by mothers and fathers are greatly lessened and parents are out of the workplace for relatively short periods of time. Thus paid and unpaid work roles become less entrenched and the stage is set for ongoing change in cultural attitudes.

In her professional capacity, Oddný Sturludóttir has learnt of a significant development in men's involvement with their children's education: 'We have one hundred pre-schools in Reykjavik and what I hear from pre-school head teachers, with twenty or thirty years of experience in the field, is that there has definitely been a radical change when it comes to the biannual parents' meetings. Before it was very uncommon for dads to come in, it was dominated by mothers. But now there are many more fathers. And they say it's because these men have been at home for three months and they bond with their kids at a very early age and they have a different connection with their children to that between fathers and children in the past. They just know their children so much better than used to be the case.' Within his own family, Eyjólfur believes that he and his wife share responsibility for their children in a way that marks a change from previous generations. 'We try to split everything evenly: doctors' appointments, school visits and all that. It wouldn't be fair if it was left to my wife to do it.' For him, the key to shared responsibility is to build it up from birth. 'Our baby, because I'm home now, he's happy with either one of us changing the diapers or holding him; anything like that, he's absolutely fine with it. Because I've always been here since he was born he just doesn't mind. It has to be right from birth. It is so difficult to try to do it later than that.'

Change to parental leave has been coupled with provision of after-school services and childcare for young children. In Reykjavik, for example, every young child has a place provided for them at pre-school. Oddný says, 'This is always a political decision. You need political courage to make these things work . . . In 1994 we had a female mayor in Reykjavik, a well-known feminist. She was the leader of a coalition made up of four parties and they won the majority in the city council. And they worked together and they set the agenda. They said, "We are going to increase dramatically the money that goes into building pre-schools in the city." We call it the pre-school revolution. At the same time they decided that elementary school hours should be extended, so they were not half-days only. So they built a lot of elementary schools too . . . And now every kid from about the age of two can stay at pre-school the whole day, in a safe, professional environment . . . It enables every parent to enjoy a working life knowing their kids are well cared for.'

This radical legislation is already paying off. In 2009 and 2010 Iceland topped the World Economic Forum's Global Gender Gap Report, outstripping every other country on the fair division of resources between men and women, such as educational attainment, health outcomes, economic participation and political empowerment.[30] Iceland has the highest proportion of women in employment in an OECD survey of thirty countries, at 81.6 per cent, way above the OECD average of 56.8 per cent. Almost

84 per cent of women with young children are in paid work and the majority of women have full-time jobs.[31] Although the pay gap is 16 per cent despite almost five decades of equal pay legislation,[32] in one fifth of families the mother earns more than the father, up from 16 per cent at the time the new parental leave legislation came in.[33] Oddný comments of Iceland's childcare and parental leave policies, 'This has had a huge effect on equality for women: to know that their kids are cared for throughout the day while they are at work . . . is so important. For women this has meant that you are not a worse staff member than the male next to you because you can do the same hours. And now dads also have to go to their boss and say, "I need to take three months off to look after my baby." So it means it has balanced things out between men and women.'

This progress is even more notable if we consider where Iceland started. Paid parental leave provision was patchy. Mothers and fathers fell into segregated roles: in 1997 only 57 per cent of mothers had gone back to paid work thirteen months after having a child, while the average work hours of fathers were increasing.[34] Businesses openly discriminated against women: a 1994 poll revealed that over a quarter of managers thought having children would have a negative impact on a woman's career, whereas none of them thought that it would have the same effect for a man. The poll cited one firm in which an HR manager automatically discounted job applications from women with young children at home. All the respondents in the firm agreed that this was sensible.[35] Now, in contrast, 86 per cent of women and 73 per cent of men feel that there has been a positive attitude from their employer towards their parental leave.[36] Oddný sees this as part of a broader, progressive shift among employers. 'Some companies are great – they say, "We want to do good for families." For example there might be a rule that they don't hold a meeting after four in the afternoon . . . And it's totally respected that you have to stand up at four o'clock and leave. And there are days that you have to take off because your child is sick or the school is closed for an internal planning day . . . I don't want to say all companies now are family friendly, certainly not. But companies are realising the good it does them. For example, in PR terms, companies get a good or bad reputation on family-friendliness. And people might be more inclined to buy things or get a service from a company that has good policies. The companies should sense that this is valuable, not only for their staff's quality of life but for their reputation.'

Iceland isn't entirely transformed. Chauvinist attitudes still survive and, as a result of its economic crisis that began in 2008, the state has had to make adjustments to its parental leave policy.[37] Currently the nine months' total parental leave can be spread over thirty-six months, rather than eighteen months as before. Most significantly, the government has had to reduce the maximum level of leave payment, which is reviewed annually, from a high of ISK 535,000 per month in 2008, down to ISK 300,000 per month in 2010 (just below the average income for 2009 of ISK 334,000).[38] As a result, many more fathers are claiming the maximum payment (up from 8 per cent of fathers in 2008 to 46 per cent in 2010),[39] because their income is at that level or exceeds it, and there are concerns that this will reduce take-up by fathers who stand to lose significant income while on parental leave. No doubt aware of the huge influence remuneration has on people's behaviour, the government insists that this reduction in the maximum payment is just a temporary measure.[40] Oddný for one hopes that it will keep this promise. As she says, 'It is very important that [our progress] continues and it worries me a lot that the recession has made this more difficult and caused a backlash . . . It just takes us back ten years, with fathers saying, "My job is more important because I'm the man."' However, she can see some positive outcomes, too. 'We had a crazy situation in Iceland ending in the financial collapse . . . The stress wasn't healthy for anyone. People just worked and worked and it was money, money, money and everything was so materialistic . . . After the collapse certain values have changed. The pre-school head teachers say that parents go to pick up their kids earlier, they spend more time talking to the staff and other parents. And the teachers at the elementary school after-school clubs say the same too. Research shows that children and teenagers are happier and more relaxed than before the collapse. Parents show more respect towards education and are happier with the school system. And work hours have also changed, either because people are re-prioritising their lives or capitalising on the fact that businesses have cut back hours . . . So they work four out of five days a week, or leave work at three thirty rather than five thirty in the afternoon.'

Despite its economic upheaval, Iceland has made huge strides towards equality in a relatively short space of time by facing up to its problems, deciding on a radical and fair course of action, and making a concerted effort to put this in place. As Oddný Sturludóttir says of her country's 'pre-school revolution', 'This will not happen by itself . . . You will never achieve this unless you have policy makers saying this is not only a pre-school or after-school programme, this is a tool for change: welfare for kids, possibilities for women, and for the good of families . . . The pre-school system that we have is relatively cheap, it's for everyone. Parents pay 13 to 15 per cent of the cost of the place per child, the rest comes from taxes. We have a very strong tradition that we all help out.'

It might seem unlikely that the United States could rival the Nordic countries for lessons in family policy. The USA has the distinction of being the only country in the developed world with no paid parental leave provided by the Federal Government. National legislation allows for a period of three months' unpaid leave. However, because US law excludes small businesses and those who have worked for an employer for less than twelve months, 40 per cent of workers are ineligible even for this limited leave.[41] But there is something striking about the US approach: it takes a strictly neutral stance towards mothers' and fathers' rights and roles. Both parents are entitled to this three months' unpaid leave on the birth of a child. The policy is evenhanded, if mean. In practice, of course, it is unlikely that many households could afford for both parents to be away from their jobs, unpaid, for three months. Cultural norms and wage differentials between men and women mean that mothers stay at home to care for babies. Half of mothers manage to put together a mix of sick days, holiday, disability leave and paid maternity leave to finance a period at home with their child. The rest take unpaid leave.[42] Nearly 90 per cent of fathers take some time off when their child is born, but for the majority, this is just a week or less.[43]

Yet there are some advantages to this stingy system: the period of maternity leave during which women are completely detached from the labour market is short. It's partly as a result of this that, despite the lack of state provision for parents, the United States appears between the middle and top third of global league tables for sex equality.[44] Life is difficult for working parents in America, which is why a third of mothers don't have a paid job.[45] Employment rates for US and UK mothers are roughly the same,[46] and the American family's dilemma very much reflects our own: for many parents it is not possible to combine working and childcare, so a notable proportion, invariably women, quit. But those American mothers who do stay in paid work at least suffer less discrimination than elsewhere. A short maternity leave period, equal in length to men's leave, means that employing or promoting a woman isn't seen as a particularly 'high risk' decision for employers. And minimal interruption to careers helps keep them on an upward trajectory.[47]

So, do these advantages outweigh the lack of state provision for families? Nathan Hegedus is in a good position to judge. Although he has been based in Sweden for the past three years, he moved there from his native USA, where he lived in a suburb of New York with his Swedish wife until his first child was a year old. 'In the States, it's all about what you can build on your own, or what you have automatically . . . In Sweden it's not like we have an amazing support network but the society just naturally provides it for you . . . In America I actually did take paternity leave. I may have been the first man in my company to do so but I took six weeks off when my daughter was born and then six more weeks spread out over her first year . . . The year was up and everyone had been very supportive but . . . I think at some point in the United States you do have to get back to the grind. You live near your family and you have people take care of your kids and they help to make it work or you work some great free-lance life or you have cheap immigrant childcare. There are lots of ways in America that people make it work and I suppose they see it as successful . . . The strength of the American system is that you do have immense flexibility to tailor your own family schedule. And of course you have to have a good job and you have to have money and you have to have a great support network or something. And you are also left to fall if it doesn't work . . . You can build your own life as long as the mom wants to stay at home. Or I could quit my job. But these are stark choices.'

Faced with these stark 'choices', Nathan and his wife decided to move to her home country of Sweden. 'It just seemed like we would have this unsatisfying, grinding existence, which a lot of Americans just take for granted. There is a sense that you are just meant to suck it up and put up with it. Now that I've lived in Sweden I don't understand why people do that.'

The American system is hard. It allows for too short a time off with a newborn child and leaves parents to fend for themselves. Either you muster the resources alone to stay on the hamster wheel or you fall off. It doesn't recognise the interest that the whole of society has in raising happy, healthy and, in the future, employable children. As such, it is not a model to be imitated elsewhere. But it provides two valuable lessons: if you want equality of opportunity in work and equal attitudes to men and women among employers, don't keep women out of the labour market for long periods, and equalise entitlements between men and women as far as you can.

In a country that has chosen not to differentiate between mothers and fathers in its leave provision, an active equal parenting movement exists. Organisations such as the Third Path Institute and EquallySharedParenting.com (the latter run by a husband and wife, Marc and Amy Vachon, who do just that), promote and campaign for a split between responsibility for earning a living and caring for children among couples. The fact that these organisations exist is proof that such a model of family life is far from the norm in the US – the case still has to be made – but they do indicate that there is an awareness of equally shared parenting as a feasible family model. However, Nathan says that he sees no wider determination to change. 'I get puzzled why there is not more political will . . . Now that I've moved to Sweden I realise, parents are everyone, we are this huge block of people, if everyone had the political will it wouldn't take a whole lot to get the system changed . . . There does not seem to be this political will to structurally change things in the States . . . It doesn't have to be a Swedish system. America's a different country. I'm not saying that every country should have Swedish-style parental leave, though I actually think they should and could. But . . . you could do something that would still fit the American culture of freedom and flexibility and profit . . . I don't know, I mean it's getting harder and harder as a middle-class American to make it work. It's just this grind and you end up paying outrageous amounts of money to put your kid in crappy daycare. You work two jobs and I've no idea why people put up with it but I don't sense that there is some impending revolution. I'm newly converted to it and it's like, "People, wake up!"'

In the context of the USA's neutral legislative approach to mothers and fathers, it is disappointing to witness the path that Australia has taken on parental leave. Up until 2011, like the USA, it had no statutory paid parental leave (although the government did pay out a 'baby bonus' to those eligible and families were entitled to twelve months' unpaid leave that, apart from six weeks reserved for the mother, could be shared between men and women as they wished). Some employers did provide their own paid parental leave schemes, meaning that around half of parents were entitled to some paid leave.[48] Australia has a strong tradition of the male breadwinner family. Paid maternity leave has for a long time been actively resisted, deemed an unjustifiable subsidy of a personal choice that discriminated against full-time mothers. Tessa, who lives in Sydney and looks after her son full time, says this attitude still exists. 'I think there's quite a lot of hostility towards it. People think, "Why should I pay for someone else's lifestyle choices? It's your baby, why should I pay for it?" They don't really see the greater good of it.' Despite this, in 2009 Kevin Rudd's Labor government announced its intention to introduce eighteen weeks' parental leave paid at the level of the minimum wage. The announcement was made on Mother's Day: the leave was to be for women only. Although this leave can be transferred by the mother to the father, there is no paid paternity provision at all.[49]

Men in Australia work some of the longest hours of the OECD countries and fathers of young children are especially likely to work overtime.[50] Tessa detects a mood among fathers in Australia to move on from this traditional model of family life. 'Australia has a culture of working quite long hours and it's usually women who take time off to look after children. It's a blokey society – it's not really culturally accepted for men to do it. I think it would be quite detrimental to their careers, as much as it now is for women . . . But I think it's definitely changing. Fathers are quite hands-on. All the dads I know are pretty fifty/fifty when they are around.' Nevertheless, she says that her husband, who works full time in media planning, would very much like to spend more time with his son but feels constrained. 'I know that my husband really struggles. He's lucky that he's been with the same employer for a long time and put in the long hours before we had our son but now he leaves at six o'clock in the evening so that he can be home by six thirty and it feels like a lot of pressure because he doesn't get everything done. And he's probably viewed as less committed to the job, even though he does a lot at home and he's always on his BlackBerry in the evening . . . My husband would really love to work just four days a week but it's not really an option financially or in terms of the work culture.'

This is something that Trudy, the mother of one son, who is pregnant with her second child, and works part time as a doctor in Sydney, would recognise. Her partner also works long full-time hours as an investment banker. 'He would definitely like to change his work patterns but he just hasn't been able to find another job yet. He works too hard and feels that he doesn't have enough time to see his son.' She looks back with regret on her own decision to return to work when her son was coming up to eight months old. 'I think I went back to work a bit early. That was my choice – I said how long I wanted off. And then when I said that I wanted to come back part time I didn't feel that I could say I want to come back part time *and* I want to take another six months off. I thought it would be asking too much and I felt bad; I shouldn't have felt bad, but I did. My employer had done a lot for me, I just felt that I owed it to them not to mess them around. So I ended up going back a bit early and I was desperately unhappy the first two months. I felt that I'd shortchanged my son and wouldn't have the chance to be around for him at that stage again. So with this baby I am going to take a year . . . If my husband had been able to take some leave when I went back that would have been brilliant. He would have loved that. He wants nothing more than to take time off with our son. I think it's really hard to be a dad now. You are expected to be involved with the children but you are still expected to have the traditional work role.' Having started from a neutral, if unpaid, base, Australian legislation has gone backwards in singling out women as the default primary carers and failing to enable men, through paid, ring-fenced paternity leave, to take on more responsibility for their children.

What these countries teach us, in their different ways, is the importance of some big policy choices: ring-fence core parental leave for mothers and fathers after the birth of a child, pay parents at a high rate during that leave, encourage mothers and fathers to take comparable lengths of leave, and ensure that neither parent feels forced to take too much time out of the workplace, by facilitating combined leave and part-time work.

Another key issue about which the UK can learn much from other countries is how to promote genuinely flexible working. The Netherlands is perhaps the leading country in Europe for flexibility at work. Dutch parents are encouraged through government policy to practise a 1.5 jobs model of working – that is they both do part-time jobs, adding up to 1.5 jobs in total – and to share the childcare between them. The Netherlands has the highest rate of part-time working among both women and men of any member of the EU or the OECD.[51] All employees who have worked for an organisation for one year or more have the right to decrease, or increase, their working hours. This applies to parents and non-parents: a short-hours culture is encouraged for all Dutch workers. Employers with less than ten employees are exempt and an employer can refuse to grant the request if it seriously goes against the interests of the company. Part-time working can be kick-started on parental leave, when a reduction in work hours can be combined with parental leave payments in part compensation for loss of earnings.

Other European countries also have bold attitudes towards working shorter hours. Sweden, France, Belgium and Germany all give parents the right to work part time, rather than merely the right to request flexible hours. With the exception of Sweden, part-time working is open to all, not just parents. In some of these countries this is accompanied by a right to return to full-time work or increase hours at a later stage. By making part-time working a right in this way, it helps address men's fear of being marked out as uncommitted if they want to work flexibly. When they shift to part-time working, they are exercising their rights rather than asking for special dispensation.

The more all employees – and not just mothers – take up flexible working, the more likely that high quality jobs will be available on a flexible basis; that the stigma and resentment attached to part-time work will ease; and that everyone, from those with all types of caring responsibilities, to those who want time to pursue other interests in the week, will be able to do so. Perhaps this helps to explain why staff retention is so much better in these countries than in the UK. France and Germany, for example, have a 5 per cent resignation rate, compared with 10 per cent in the UK.[52]

In the Netherlands, as elsewhere, childcare and after-school services are essential to ensuring that parents of young children are able to work. Nurseries take children from a few months old in order to enable parents to go back to work part time within their period of leave. This provides critical support to parents as they seek to balance work and family life.

The provision of extensive, affordable childcare reaches its apogee in Sweden. Early childhood education and care is an entitlement from twelve months of age and costs are pegged to a family's income. Paid parental leave lasts up to fourteen months, so very few children are in childcare before their first birthday but 70 per cent are in daycare between the ages of one and two years and 97 per cent are in daycare from three to five years of age.[53] This means that mothers' employment in the labour market is high, at between 72 per cent and 81 per cent depending upon the age of the children, and most women work full time.[54] The nursery, school and work day are well coordinated. Nathan observes, 'It's very accepted to move your work shifts . . . Even if you are both working one hundred per cent, one parent doesn't start work till nine thirty and the other one starts work at seven thirty so they can do the pick-up. And you keep your children in state-funded care until five in the afternoon . . . I don't hear people talking about "the juggle" like they do in the States. It's busy and people get stressed but there's not that practical "How is this going to work?" concern . . . The safety net isn't going to let your kid get stuck every day for a few hours. There's going to be some sort of solution . . . People work hard and they work more than one hundred per cent in a lot of cases but there is just a more reasonable sense of the work day . . . They don't expect you to be there at seven thirty in the evening.'

But although Swedish childcare is considered important in enabling women to work, and so promote equality between the sexes, it also exists because it is believed to benefit children ahead of their entry into pre-school classes at the age of six. Over more than thirty years Sweden has prioritised childcare and has established an exemplary system. The majority of childcare staff members are degree-educated and work with highly trained childminders. Six per cent of staff and 20 per cent of managers are men.[55] Children learn about the world around them and national norms and values through play. Once children enter school and until the age of twelve, local authorities are required to provide them with 'wrap-around' educational and recreational care at the beginning and end of the school day, and throughout the day in the holidays. All these care services are affordable for families, with a ceiling set on fees and the cost of provision subsidised by central government. The common view in Sweden is that formal care of this kind is good for children as well as for parents, rather than somewhere to park kids during the working day as the more sceptical in the UK view our own childcare.

However, Sweden is a class apart from most other countries. Elsewhere, such as in southern Europe, there is an equally firm view that young children should be looked after at home – by the mother. In these countries, lack of government-funded care, combined with inflexible working patterns and conservative views of gender roles, mean that younger working women are all too aware of the sacrifices they will have to make if they have a family. And, as in Germany, these women are not standing for it. Instead, they are leaving contemplating childbearing until a relatively late age, or deciding to give it a miss altogether. Ironically, in these countries where family is paramount, women feel discouraged from having children. Italy, the archetypal family-orientated country in Europe, has the highest birth rate among women over forty in the western world and a persistently low fertility rate.[56] The fertility rate is also a cause for concern in countries such as Spain, Portugal and Greece. But even among these countries there are signs that governments are slowly waking up to the expectations of modern women. So, for example, the Spanish government, alarmed by low fertility and female employment rates, increased childcare provision for pre-school children in the last decade.

Public policy influences private behaviour whether or not it is explicitly intended to do so. Take-up of parental leave by fathers shot up in Iceland once the well-paid 'use it or lose it' father's quota was introduced. The same effect is apparent in Norway and Sweden. Female employment went down in Germany when the government brought in a thirty-six-month parental leave period at a flat rate of pay.[57] American women, with little government support, are forced into either inflexible full-time paid work or full-time childcare. Part-time working rights in the Netherlands help secure very high employment rates for women; the same is true of extensive, affordable good quality childcare in the Nordic states, where daycare and early learning help to narrow gaps in children's life chances.

So, in those countries that have pursued the goal of equally shared parenting, what have been the effects for their societies as a whole? One overarching cultural change is that men are enabled, and expected, to play an active role in the day-to-day lives of their children. When Sweden pioneered parental leave in the 1970s, those few fathers that took time off paid work were dubbed 'velvet dads'. Now, in the Nordic states, such ridicule is long gone. Full involvement in the life of your children is part of what makes you a man rather than a threat to it. Pram pushing as a signifier of change raises its head again, but with a significant difference from when it is invoked in the UK. A newspaper in Iceland reports, 'It is now common to see the father pushing the stroller along the town's walking paths, *even in the middle of the day on a weekday* [my italics]. Something that wasn't seen a few years ago, but times change and so do the dads.'[58] In this regard, Iceland is streets ahead of countries outside the Nordic states.

The flip side of men doing more childcare is that women spend more time in paid work. Countries that aim to provide relatively equitable parental leave, offer wide availability of good quality, affordable early-years and after-school care and promote flexible working practices have higher female employment rates. So, for example, the percentage of women with young children who are in the workforce in Iceland, Norway and Sweden far exceeds the OECD average and is a great deal higher than in Spain, Greece and Italy, where flexible working and childcare provision are less widespread.[59] The UK sits between these two extremes, with a greater preponderance of part-time female employment than in the Nordic states.[60] Since Iceland introduced its new parental leave system and increased childcare provision, both the gap between the numbers of mothers and fathers returning to work after parental leave and the hours that they work have narrowed.[61]

In addition, Icelandic women's attitude to work has reportedly 'changed completely' since the 1990s. Whereas formerly women's declared interest in management positions or promotions decreased after they had children and men's interest increased, there is now no difference when these life events are factored in.[62] Progress on the gap in pay, rather than the gap in expectations, is slower: only over time as paid and unpaid work roles are more evenly shared can this really be tackled.[63] This demonstrates, yet again, the strong link between pay levels and caring responsibilities.

In the domestic sphere, research in Sweden has shown that fathers' take-up of parental leave is linked to lower rates of separation and divorce.[64] Swedish men who take parental leave are less likely to split up from their partners than those who do not. They are also more likely to share general responsibility for looking after their children with their partners.[65] This latter correlation is mirrored in Iceland. There, fathers who take three or more months of parental leave are significantly more likely to be involved in the day-to-day care of their children when they are three years old.[66] Inevitably there will be an element of self-selection here: men who want to be closely involved in their children's lives and are committed to their partners are probably more likely to take parental leave, particularly in countries where this won't significantly disadvantage families financially. Nonetheless, it seems reasonable to say that parental leave, along with other factors, increases the chances of a father having a deeper, more sustained engagement with home life. A father's period of parental leave may well foster a commitment to his family and partner, as well as reflect it. For the mother's part, having a partner who understands what looking after a child, day in and day out, entails may strengthen the relationship.

Equality in the home also affects the birth rate: a key concern for countries with declining populations. A woman is more inclined to have another child if she knows that she can count on her husband to play his part.[67] Fertility levels have increased in Iceland following its pursuit of an equally shared parenting agenda, and the trend continued upwards in 2009.[68] As other developed countries worry about their fertility rate, Iceland's is the highest among the Nordic states, and Europe as a whole, and well above the OECD average of 1.63,[69] having risen from 1.93 children per woman in 2002[70] to 2.05 in 2005.[71] It is one of only four countries in an OECD survey to have a fertility rate sufficient to sustain its population (the UK is not among these four)[72] and the number of births in Iceland is set to keep on rising.[73] The fertility rate is important not only for a country's economy but also for what it tells us about attitudes towards childrearing. It seems that couples who split work inside and outside the home, and in particular childcare, are more likely to have more children together. Icelandic men are doing an increasing proportion of unpaid work in the home and taking time off work more often when children are ill.[74] Iceland's rising fertility rate suggests that the new parental leave legislation is fundamentally changing the organisation of family life, making it more equally shared, and so more enjoyable to the extent that couples are having more children. Research with Swedish couples also shows that those who share family responsibilities are more likely to have a second child.[75]

Public policy can affect fertility rates in other ways. The ready availability[76] and affordability[77] of childcare increases the number of children families have. So too does the flexibility of employment practice. Analysis of European Community Household Panel data shows that women working in the public sector, where there is typically greater stability and flexibility, have more children than their counterparts in the private sector. In fact, women choose to work in the public sector precisely because of this compatibility with family life.[78] Given the importance of formal childcare provision and flexible working practices to boosting the birth rate, it is not surprising that within Europe the Nordic states have the healthiest fertility rates and the Southern Mediterranean countries have the lowest.[79]

And the effect on the lives of these children – these products of increased fertility rates – is positive too. The World Health Organization, with its fervour for breastfeeding, has reason to be pleased. Nearly three quarters of mothers still do some breastfeeding at six months in Sweden, compared with 29 per cent in the UK.[80] In Iceland, following the parenting and childcare reforms, 74 per cent of children were being breastfed for more than six months,[81] even though 36 per cent of women are back at work at that point.[82] Partner presence and support have been found to have a significant influence on a mother's decision to breastfeed.[83] This would indicate that the high take-up and continuation rates for breastfeeding in Sweden and Iceland are perhaps due to fathers having a substantial period of leave. It may also be that the great flexibility afforded by the system helps in Iceland. A mother has the option to increase her hours back at work slowly and gradually and thereby to keep up her breastfeeding if she wishes. As Oddný Sturludóttir comments, 'A friend of mine is pregnant at the moment. She is going to stay at home for three months and then for the remaining six months she and her partner are both going to work part time, splitting the day between them, so that she can breastfeed for longer and also work for part of the day. This is all negotiable with your employer.'

With the vast majority of mothers in the Nordic states in work, child poverty rates are much lower than the OECD average,[84] despite divorce and separation rates broadly comparable to the UK (which has an above average child poverty rate).[85] Child poverty is linked to divorce and separation in many countries because, following a split, fathers usually don't have custody of their children, and so may disengage from their children's lives – taking their income with them. If the mother is well established in the labour market the effects of this are ameliorated. Additionally, in the Nordic states parents are likely to have joint custody of their children following separation. In Iceland, this is now the norm. In 2005, 73 per cent of divorcing couples agreed joint custody. Among formerly cohabiting couples, the figure is 74 per cent.[86] Oddný Sturludóttir, who herself alternates weeks caring for her children with her former partner and father of her youngest child, observes, 'Fathers in Iceland, year by year, are becoming more confident in their relationships with their children . . . Most couples share custody. It's common that parents have an arrangement where the children stay one week with the mother and the next with the father. This can vary a little but that is the assumption . . . It's good and healthy for children to stay with both parents after they separate.' Hinrik works in IT and is a divorced father of one. He lives in Reykjavik, as does his ex-wife, and their son stays with him on alternate weeks. He shares Oddný's belief that this is best for children. 'For the younger generation things are changing quite a lot. It is considered very normal for fathers to be a big part of their child's life . . . Your parents are your foundation. They are there if anything goes wrong, you can always talk to your parents . . . And also there's a little bit of selfishness, it would be hard not to see him . . . But the same goes for his mother. I would never want sole custody. He needs his mum too.'

Not only is a happy and continuing relationship with both parents clearly of enormous benefit to children on an emotional level, it is also of material benefit to them: they are much less likely to be raised on one income. Encouraging equally shared parenting from the start pays enormous dividends for families and wider society – even when families break up, which may be less likely among couples who share their parenting in any case.

Are there any downsides to this generous provision in countries such as Iceland and the Nordic states? Teresia would argue that there are. Originally from Sweden, she has lived with her British husband in the UK since 2000 and they have two primary-school-aged children. Although she has recently started her own business, she gave up her previous career because she wanted to devote her time to raising her family. She thinks that this decision would have been considered unacceptable in Sweden. 'What's happened there in the last fifteen years is that the woman is now just expected to go back to work full time after a year or eighteen months. No one stays at home. I mean, there would be headlines: "This woman has chosen to be a house-wife: outrageous!" It upsets people almost – you are a traitor to the system . . . It's very extreme and it's got to the point where Swedish women actually refer to themselves as brain-washed. I felt almost as if I was de-programmed when I left. It took me years to be happy with not working. I'd think, "I am not allowed to do this!" . . . In Sweden there seems to be a fear of letting people choose . . . that if you let people go they will immediately slip back into the practices of the nineteen-fifties. Which isn't true.'

Nathan Hegedus agrees that Sweden is a conformist society: 'Absolutely. I mean there just aren't stay-at-home parents here . . . Everyone has this amazing leave but after that the kids just go into daycare. They all do. And even if you were to keep your kid at home they would be totally lonely because there are no other kids out in the middle of the day, only babies . . . Here you have a lot of opportunities but you have to fit into the system. There's a real hard edge to it. It becomes, "OK, your time is up – back to work." . . . Swedish society is pretty straight down the line and people believe in the system and contribute to the system and live within it. The good side of it is that it's a very equal society and the bad side of it is that you are not always allowed to stand out or do different things . . . But we saw the other way of doing things in America. And for me as a dad who wanted to take parental leave and not quit my job the Swedish system presents more opportunities.'

Other countries' family policies demonstrate that they really can affect family roles and relationships and the opportunities that women and men have to live rounded, fulfilled lives. Governments that determinedly pursue a shared parenting agenda deliver fundamental improvements to family life. Friðgeir, a software engineer who lives in Reykjavik, is preparing to take a total of three months' paternity leave when his son is born in a few weeks' time. He is optimistic about the long-term future for equality in Iceland and, more immediately, within his own household. 'I think we will do things equally, in bringing up our son. If anything I will hog him and make him a daddy's boy. I do think care falls more on women then men at the moment . . . But I think that at some point we might get to equally shared care. Without the parental leave and everything else being equal you won't get there. Guys are as they are because of their upbringing, and fifty or one hundred years ago we were even more "manly" men than we are now. There is a trend towards everyone being more equal. I think that we are going to see guys and girls caring equally for their children . . . We are not going to achieve this with this generation of parents or even the next one but it's more likely with the one after that.' Hinrik is similarly optimistic. He notes how far Iceland has come since the days when his parents raised him: 'There's definitely been a generational change. My mum mostly took care of us, even though my dad was around a lot. It was more traditional. But at the same time she raised me to do things differently when I grew up. I guess she was of that generation where she knew of all these progressive ideas even though in practice she couldn't manage that for herself . . . The change from my parents' generation to mine has been phenomenal. I think [equal parenting] is very obtainable.'

Brave and determined reform, with a commitment to the long game, can't be dismissed as only possible in small quirky countries such as Iceland or those with a tradition of very generous state support such as Sweden. It's happening in large economic powerhouses, with a similar welfare philosophy to our own, such as Germany, where provision outstrips that in the UK. If it's happening there it can happen anywhere. In the World Economic Forum's Global Competitiveness rankings for 2010–2011, Germany moved up two places to take fifth place, while the United States fell back two places to fourth, overtaken by Sweden, which came in second. The UK was ranked in twelfth place.[87] Of course, there are a whole range of reasons for these positions but generous provision for parents isn't holding the Nordic states or Germany back. We too can decide that the approach we've taken hitherto isn't working and resolve to set off down a new path. It will require clear thinking, an eye to the long term and a determination to face down the doubters and do what is right. For decades, UK politicians have protested that they won't get involved in the private world of the family, while in practice shaping and influencing it in multiple, significant ways. Now, belatedly, the UK has cottoned on to the importance of shared parenting for bringing greater fulfilment to parents, happiness to children and stability to wider society. The experience of other countries demonstrates how systematic and radical we must be to have any chance of delivering a meaningful shared parenting agenda. If we get it right, we can create a truly family-friendly society in Britain.

8

The Birth of Equality

'Everything has to change!' wailed a friend. She spoke in mock despair but also with an exasperation born of bitter experience as we discussed the UK's busted parenting culture. For everything does have to change. Currently, we raise young women to believe that the battle for equality was won back in the day and that whatever they want is out there for the taking, provided they roll up their sleeves. This isn't true: the odds are stacked against women, particularly if they become mothers. But things could be different: it doesn't have to be like this.

The significant progress that women have made in the past fifty years – in education, working life, social status and autonomy – has been won on the understanding that we continue to run a home and raise children, fitting the pieces of the jigsaw together as best we can. This not only makes looking after children laborious as much as fulfilling, but it also prevents us from putting as much energy as we'd like into our jobs and social lives and intellectual and leisure pursuits. We spend our days on parole – all our time must be accounted for. Every hour has to have purpose and output: a lost afternoon is work not done or children not nurtured.

At the same time, fathers are prevented from changing how they live when they have children. Tied to the workplace, they too lead a restricted existence. Amid this our children are deprived of the active involvement of both parents. They suffer the indirect resentment of a mother and the absence of a father. This unhappy situation is enforced in myriad ways, from ill-conceived parental rights to divisive work practices, and roles and identities that parents find impossible to let go.

The net results of our strictly gendered roles are plain for all to see: women whose skills go to waste; a large and persistent pay gap between the sexes; men who feel disconnected from their children's lives; family break-up, and even child poverty. Women are educated to the hilt only to be severely limited in their ability to use their learning if they become mothers. The state loses its return on educational investment. And while we agonise about social breakdown, relationships within families – supposedly society's bedrock – are put under tremendous pressure by the polarisation of men and women's lives.

Looking internationally, we can see that other countries are successfully beginning to tackle these problems through radical change. So to do anything less in the UK is to endorse inequality and to accept that we lack the motivation to do enough about it. If women are truly to live full and rewarding lives, then men must be enabled to share equally in raising children and looking after the home. If we take on the jobs of bringing up our children and earning the family income together, the effort will be shared, the enjoyment enhanced, and the opportunity to pursue other interests increased. Our goal must be for women and men to share all the responsibilities and pleasures of life. As such, our equality is interdependent – fathers must gain more freedom in order for mothers to do so too.

In the course of writing this book, I talked to a mother with one son and another child due imminently. We met at her workplace. She was officially on maternity leave but didn't want to waste a moment at home while she was still able to work. She proudly told me of the long hours she spent in the office, the many foreign trips which took her away from her family for days on end, her husband's role as the main carer and her son's greater emotional attachment to him. She believed that this reversal of standard roles was equality in action. Is there any bottom line for you in terms of your family life? I asked her. She was happy to say that there was not.

The conversation disturbed me and for a while I wasn't able to work out why. Was I guilty of double standards? Did I think that such detachment from family life was worse in a woman than a man? But I knew that I would find such indifference unsettling in a man, too. And then I realised that the reason her attitude left me discomforted, even angry, was because I didn't share her vision of equality between the sexes. It is not about women wrenching powerful, main-earner status from men and marching out the door leaving their partners to vacuum the stairs and make up the school lunchbox. Rather it is about mothers and fathers having the opportunity to participate equally in raising the children they have conceived and combining this with other activities that keep their entire selves alive.

So what will it take to achieve this? From the very start, mothers and fathers need to be treated as parents with equal status and a shared interest in the health and well-being of their children. Men should have the same legal right as women to take paid time off work to attend antenatal classes and medical appointments if they wish. Advice should be addressed to both parents, and reflect each one's interests and concerns. What matters is not only what is written and said, and to whom it is addressed, but also the way that the information is presented. Mothers and fathers should both be depicted in caring roles and advice should be premised on the assumption that each parent will take a day-to-day, hands-on role in raising their children. Antenatal classes should include much more discussion of parenting, and the active involvement of both parents in the tasks of raising children and looking after a home. There are now local examples of antenatal services waking up to this: it's time for the whole of the NHS to do the same. In a welcome move, towards the end of 2011 the Royal College of Midwives published *Reaching Out: Involving*

Fathers in Maternity Care. This aims to give maternity service staff 'insight' into how they 'might best encourage' fathers' involvement from pregnancy through to family life. It is to be hoped that all those working in maternity services take their cue from this sound advice.

As part of this, after the birth itself, a father should be allowed to stay overnight with the mother and their new baby. Some fathers will be unable to do this, not least if the couple has other children to look after. But the option should be provided, in order to signal the vital role each parent has in childrearing and to enable the mother and father to support each other and have every opportunity to become closely attached to their baby in the first few days. Around the country there are some very well-appointed midwife-led wards where parents can stay overnight in individual suites. In our straitened times, a significant extension of such facilities to all maternity wards is unlikely to happen soon. But the need and desire for it is there, and it should be our ambition that the NHS provides these facilities. As Frieda, a mother of one and a former NHS manager herself says, 'I think if that's what people want then you just fucking do it. Obviously it's expensive and . . . you are not going to do it overnight. But if that's the public mood then it's something you should be moving towards . . . It's all that blinkered, "There's not enough space" stuff. There's no one thinking through the emotional side of it, which is: actually, if you've been through a fifty-hour labour followed by an emergency C-section that's when you'd really like your partner, rather than popping it out after four hours in the water.' In the meantime, with this firm goal in mind, maternity wards should improvise with portable beds for fathers, or even just a blanket and a chair. A handful of local pilot projects, such as at the Royal United Hospital in Bath, are experimenting with such 'light touch' options with great success. There fathers are allowed to stay overnight, required to stay fully clothed and asked to go home if they need to shower: it's not the most comfortable provision imaginable but it's a very important start that could be replicated in other hospitals. In children's wards across the UK, mothers and fathers come and go day and night without any visiting restrictions and with access to pull-down beds, communal kitchens and bathrooms, in order to share in the care of their children. So-called 'maternity' services should be just as child-focused and welcoming of both parents, recognising that this is in the interests of the mother, her partner and their baby. Of course, birth does not have to happen in a hospital. For those for whom it is a feasible option, facilitating the involvement of fathers is another reason to encourage home births. Experiencing the birth of their child in their own home will shore up men's feeling of inclusion in the process and their role as an equal parent.

The experience of other countries also shows us that over the coming decades maternity and paternity leave in the UK needs to be reformed completely. As Jane, a mother of two living in Leeds, says, 'I do think that a lot of the patterns of behaviour and inequality stem from the fact that as the woman you are the one that has to be at home and I think if you want to change that it has to come from how you enable men to take a greater share in [leave] really.' Allowing parents to allocate poorly paid leave between them is a start but will not improve the situation for the vast majority.

A much better solution would be to scrap the current uneven mix of leave available to men and women in the first twelve months after birth. Instead there should be thirteen months' paid leave. This would be split into two equal periods, half earmarked for the mother and the other half for the father on a 'use it or lose it' basis. Anything other than a fifty/fifty division of leave condones and perpetuates parental inequality.[1] During this leave, parents' salaries would be fully reimbursed by the government (although with a cap on the highest earners to constrain costs). In the first month, leave should be taken together to allow both parents to share this challenging period. With this one month taken concurrently, thirteen months' shared leave means the baby could be looked after by one or other of its parents throughout its first year. After the first month the mother should be responsible until the child is at least six weeks old; this is in line with International Labour Organisation recommendations on compulsory maternity leave[2] and it protects the health and safety of the mother not to return to work more quickly than this.

But after this period, the majority of the remaining leave should be taken separately by each parent in order to ensure that both become fully experienced in the sole care of the child. Each parent's quota of leave could be taken in one block or in a limited number of smaller blocks of time. After the first six weeks it could be taken on a full-time or part-time basis (or a mix of both), enabling parents to combine work and care over a longer period. Parents could even both return to work part time if they wished, taking care of their child on complementary days of the week.

The leave should apply equally to those adopting children or becoming parents by surrogacy as well as those in same-sex couples. Women who are bringing up children without an involved father right from the start could, if they wanted, nominate a relative – a parent or sibling, for example – to whom at least some of the father's leave entitlement could be transferred, or they could take it on themselves. Self-employed fathers, or those who work on a contract or casual basis, should be able to claim some payment in the same way as mothers with a similar work record now do through their Maternity Allowance. Under its proposed changes to parental leave the Government would move towards this, but this payment needs to be lifted above its current sub-minimum-wage level for both men and women. Given the necessarily radical nature of this new system, it could be phased in to allow government funding and employer planning to be gradually adjusted. But, as Norway and Sweden did in the 1970s, it is crucial that we commit to urgent reform now and stick to it in order to realise the goal of genuinely shared parenting for future generations. While opposition on grounds of cost will undoubtedly be fierce, the long-term benefits for society will more than justify the expenditure, as other countries have found. This is one of the reasons why the 2010 Marmot Review of Health Inequalities in England recommended a full year of paid parental leave.[3]

At the moment our pitifully short and poorly paid paternity leave is so unappealing that many fathers forgo it. Taking on some of the mother's low-paid – or unpaid – leave is no turn-on either. A right to more than six months of fully paid leave is a much greater prize to forsake, particularly when the caring responsibility cannot be passed on to the mother: either the father looks after the child or someone other than one of the parents does it. For the first time men will genuinely engage in striking the balance between work and childcare that is the stuff of women's day-to-day lives. For eligible parents on low incomes, full reimbursal of wages will mean that they can afford to take a number of months out of the workforce to look after their new child in a way that hasn't been possible up until now. Sharing parental leave is particularly important for these families as the close involvement of fathers is linked to the improved educational outcomes crucial to social mobility.[4] With our poor record in this area,[5] the UK would do well to take note of this. From the Nordic experience we know that fathers on very high incomes are the least likely to take parental leave as caps on payments mean a big loss in pay. However, if fathers were unable to transfer their very substantial leave entitlement to the mother, they would be forced to think carefully about how they might manage their finances while caring for their child. With nine months' lead-in time and a healthy budget to play with, this should be possible. Such men are also more likely than others to be in senior, influential positions within their organisations, so may well have success in negotiating further income from their employers, if not from the state. Under these proposals, fathers should also feel less pressure to decline their paternity leave. Managers and work colleagues will find it much more difficult to lean on workers to skip paternity leave when the period at stake is a matter of months rather than weeks and involves sole care of a child.

Linking leave payments to salaries (albeit with a cap) means that the state is paying out more for higher earners, giving rise to worries in some quarters about addressing sex inequality at the expense of socio-economic inequalities. But if we want fathers – across all income groups – to take parental leave, experience shows that they have to be given generous cover against their occupational income. This is reflected in polling among British men: in 2009 four out of five fathers said they would take their two-week paternity leave entitlement if the flat-rate payment was replaced by 90 per cent of full pay.[6] A flat-rate payment to all, or similar model, would mean that many men wouldn't take up their parental leave quota. Ultimately, our chances of greater social equality are increased rather than threatened by moves to promote equality between the sexes. Encouraging fathers to be actively involved in their children's daily lives, and enabling women to play a full role in the labour market, improves children's opportunities in life and reduces the chance that they will grow up in poverty. Employers will inevitably worry about 'losing' male employees to the world of childcare, as they currently do women, but they should also see the benefits. Rather than a mother disappearing from sight for up to twelve months (or forever if she chooses not to come back, so disengaged or overlooked she becomes), she will disappear for about only half that, or less if she returns to work part time before her quota is up.

One of the arguments predictably put forward against cutting back on maternity leave is that it will reduce the ability of mothers to breastfeed their babies. But with over six months' leave on full pay, the mother could exclusively breastfeed in this period if she so wished. Moreover, the likelihood of her breastfeeding will be increased if the father is around for at least the first four weeks. As has been found in Iceland and Sweden, time is less the issue than ongoing support from the father.

Working as a team to care for their children from the very start, a mother and father will together learn how best to raise their children and most effectively combine parenting with all the other responsibilities and interests in their lives. The positive impact on women's sense of emotional well-being during this time would be huge. Sharing childcare would allow more time away from the home and an opportunity to return to it with fresh energy. Indeed, children may also benefit if they are not brought up wholly under the intense, focused attention of the mother: evidence now suggests that having three secure relationships – mother, father and grandparent or other trusted carer – is the most beneficial to a child's social and emotional development.[7] In the long term, a child's experience of care from, and concentrated interaction with, a small band of devoted adults of different ages, sexes and relationships to him or her will inform that child's own thinking and decisions about care responsibilities in the future: shared care and care from men will become accepted as a norm.

Cultural stereotypes will be broken down in other ways, too. Working together, mothers and fathers will be more resilient against the onslaught of advice and marketing from the parenting industry. The peddlers will need to adapt or die: there's no point in emblazoning their packaging solely with smiling mums if it's cheery dads who might be wandering down the supermarket aisles with their seven-month-old. The same holds true for magazines, newspapers, books, department stores and toy and clothes shops. Even social researchers might begin to consider the effect on young children of fathers going to work or the optimal period of paternity leave to allow for a close relationship with a child while keeping a career intact.

By enabling men to position themselves at the centre of the family unit from the start, society can capitalise on birth and early baby-care as an emotional watershed for fathers. It will increase the practical care that men give to their children and their commitment to the family. Looking after a child in itself encourages the father to be more nurturing, developing his sensitivity towards, and attachment to, his child. It eases a man's adjustment to fatherhood, improves his satisfaction with family life and is even thought to reduce aggression.[8] Bill, a father of one from London, is sure that greater involvement of men at this early stage would have a long-term effect, 'I think that a lot of the things that people talk about in society – things like, "Where is the father figure? Where has he disappeared to?" – could be addressed by better paternity leave. So the father then has a chance to bond with the child and has a vested interest and sees the child growing up . . . If they said to me you can have time off on pay, that would be brilliant . . . I think it would lead to less domestic tension, because it is a team effort.' Dave agrees there are profound benefits of shared care to the relationship between father and child: 'I am absolutely convinced that if fathers can be taught the bonding experience in the first hours and weeks, my experience of it is that it made a huge difference . . . You know, I think it's about being there at the birth and for those first few hours and getting up in the night time and doing the night feeds alongside your wife and sharing in all of that. That's when the baby really starts to connect with you and you start to connect with it.'

Ensuring that leave periods are properly paid and ring-fenced for each parent will draw criticism. But this is the only way to guarantee that as wide a range of people as possible take parental leave, with all the positive, far-reaching and long-term benefits this brings. Politicians' pledges to 'encourage' shared parenting mean little without the financial wherewithal to make it happen. Critics may decry 'social engineering' in restructuring our parental leave policies, but it is naive to imply that the current provision doesn't push parents into particular domestic arrangements and forms of care. We are already socially engineering the mother and father into different roles; we just pretend that is not the case. Detractors dismiss the Nordic 'gender quotas' but our own leave system is entirely gendered: pushing mothers into the role of main carer and fathers into that of main earner. While our political rhetoric consists of much talk about choice, genuine freedom for families to devise their own arrangements will only come if we allow parents the option to care equally for a child, and to combine that with fulfilling work. Whatever else the UK does, it has to get this policy right. Without splitting and fully reimbursing leave, so that both parents have the opportunity to try their hand at childcare over a sustained period, forge an intimate connection with their child and reflect on how they want to arrange their family life, all efforts to encourage equally shared parenting will be in vain.

Isla, a mother of two from Manchester who works full time and shares the care of her two children with her husband, is clear that it is only through tackling both parental leave policies and also providing flexible working that women can hope to gain a level playing field with men. 'I cannot see Britain getting out of the rut it's in with attitudes towards women working and the use of women's skills in the workplace, doing jobs that are beneath them and the qualifications that we've paid for . . . It's an absolute waste of their brains and the education they were given. As a society it's not viable to keep going like that and I think one of the only ways to change that attitude is to have shared parental leave. I think you should only allow, say, six months for the mother so that the father is actually forced into taking some paternity leave and if people choose not to take it, it's up to them . . . I can't see how it's economic to have job vacancies and women who can fill those vacancies with high qualifications, under-utilising them. I don't care whether they do part time, job share, full time, whatever, but as long as it is always women's problems, and children are women's problems, and being back in the workplace is women's problems and maternity leave makes you not want to employ women, it just seems to me that it's basically just shoving it in the women's area and makes it seem like a women's issue all the time, and it's not a women's issue.'

Part time, job share, full time, whatever: all UK employees should have a right to flexible working rather than the current weak right to request it. Certainly, the government is correct in wanting to extend this right to request to everyone, not just parents. In theory, this will help remove the 'us and them' stigma that attaches to many, particularly part-time, women in their jobs. But we know from the fact that fathers are more likely to work full time and standard hours,[9] even though they have always shared the same right as mothers, that the situation is more complex than this. For men, the risk of being refused flexibility is deemed too high and the cultural pressure not to ask is too great. Only by normalising flexible working, by making it a right rather than something for which you have to beg permission, will things change. Limiting rights to those who have worked twenty-six weeks or more in a company should also be scrapped, in order to encourage a greater number of flexible job vacancies. And to reflect the fact that parents may want to work longer hours and increase their income as children get older, there should also be a right to return to full-time work or to increase hours, as elsewhere in Europe. At the moment there is no obligation for employers to revise part-time arrangements – meaning parents can be stuck with part-time pay for years after their children have stopped relying on them to shepherd them to and from school. Taking their cue from government, employers must work with all employees to encourage flexible working, proactively talking through the options with them. The most enlightened organisations might even offer all their staff the opportunity of around six months' paid leave at an important point in their life – whether they are parents or not.

Flexible working need not mean part-time working – it can include working from home, compressed hours, early starts or late finishes. It does not inevitably mean a loss in income, which is partly why it is more attractive to men than part-time working alone. Flexible but full-time work may also be more appealing to the private sector, making jobs there more manageable for everyone with caring responsibilities and creating greater parity between private and public sector employment. Increasing flexible working opportunities will encourage more women into the workforce and widen access to decently paid jobs. As such it is essential to increasing household incomes in the poorest families and reducing child poverty.

A culture of flexible working would also open up more senior jobs to parents with caring responsibilities. Some extra out-of-hours work is bound to be necessary in such jobs but most people in high-level positions, with or without children, accept this. Frieda, a mother of one who heads a charity, sees this as a reasonable requirement of her job. 'Obviously some weeks are harder than others and I do spend the nap time on my weekday with my daughter working and I work in the evening sometimes as well. But I would probably do that with whatever job I was doing and however many days I worked. Because that's how I tend to do things. It does feel pretty much OK actually.'

In 2010 the Confederation of British Industry came out in support of enabling parents to share caring responsibilities,[10] marking a significant change from business attitudes in the past. Perhaps employers have realised that to continuously declare the end is nigh – as they did with the introduction of the minimum wage, extensions to maternity leave, paternity leave and the right to request flexible working – is no longer sustainable. We are wise now to their cries of wolf. Perhaps they have also woken up to the fact that allowing male and female employees to share family responsibilities equally spreads the load for workers and managers and is repaid in effort and loyalty. And no doubt they have noted that offering reduced working hours during the recession enabled employers to retain staff yet cut costs: flexibility can benefit both parties. Companies offering flexible working exist across every sector of the UK economy, indicating that there is no barrier to flexibility according to the type of work involved.[11] Those that have embraced it particularly enthusiastically include BT, Sainsbury's, Nationwide, B&Q, the National Grid, KPMG, sections of the NHS and the civil service.[12] Organisations have found not only that it is manageable but that it improves employee relations, commitment and motivation, turnover, recruitment, absenteeism and productivity.[13] Flexible working should be accompanied by measures to reduce our long hours culture, opening up full-time, standard-hours jobs to more people and enabling more parents to pursue full-time work – doing away with the common binary choice of care or career.

A right to part-time working is commonplace in the EU, and businesses, with appropriate safeguards, have adapted and benefited. A right to flexible working in all its forms would go one better. The UK could build on its existing flexible working legislation to become a world leader and every worker and employer could enjoy the positive effects of this. Performance based on competency and outcomes, fitted flexibly together with the rest of our lives, rather than standard work-time hours and location, must become the norm.

This should be complemented by universally available, good quality, and affordable formal childcare – both nurseries and childminders and, later, breakfast, after-school and holiday clubs. Crucially, childcare must be provided for parents immediately they both return to work after the birth of a child, in order to ensure that the transition is seamless. Although the UK government is introducing free nursery provision for disadvantaged two-year-olds, it's unfortunate that this will not be offered to all families and that, along with this policy, the government has removed the obligation on some Children's Centres to provide full-time daycare and to weaken staff qualification requirements.[14] This seems to contradict the government's emphasis on high-quality services, over benefits and tax credits, as the tool for improving children's life chances. In the short term, such formal childcare will enable women to combine work and motherhood while men are adapting their own working practices. But we should guard against a mother's reliance on formal care (as well as support from other relatives or friends) absolving the father of his own caring responsibilities and denying him an opportunity to form his own deep bond with his child. As Frieda remarks, 'It's good for the child to have lots of interaction with both its parents, and society's answer shouldn't just be, "Well, we want everyone to feel that they've got an equal right to work so hand your child over to someone else to enable you to do that."' Formal early-years care frees up parents to do paid work and, if it is of a high quality, provides a stimulating, caring environment for their children. Both these outcomes, in turn, contribute to narrowing inequalities between children and improving the life chances of those from lower socio-economic households.[15] But parents should be encouraged to see such formal settings as a valuable complement to care by them, rather than something that the mother is responsible for in order to allow her to work. In the UK, as in Iceland, fathers should be expected to take an active interest in their children's time at pre-school, and their engagement welcomed. The ability for both parents to work flexibly and be equally involved in the daily care of their children should become a mainstream option, rather than a model for which only the most dogged or privileged can aim.

These reforms should be matched by encouraging children to see parenting as something to be equally shared between men and women. How we organise parenting at home sets an example for our own children and will greatly influence them in their own decisions if they go on to have a family. School also has a role to play, partly through the Personal, Social, Health and Economic (PSHE) curriculum, which includes a focus on the 'roles and responsibilities of parents'.[16] PSHE as a whole has never been made a statutory subject in the school curriculum but learning and thinking about what makes for good parenting is as vital to individual and national well-being as being able to read and do basic mental arithmetic. Careers advice should also be adapted so that children and young adults make choices and plans that take into account the shared cash and care responsibilities of any future family life. Most young teenagers are unlikely to engage very seriously with the prospect of their own parenthood but discussing the basis on which future decisions should be made will influence the context within which they make these choices in years to come. Boys and girls should both grow up with the expectation that adult life will require, and enable, them to play a range of roles – paid worker, parent, community member, self-improver and pleasure seeker. Bronwyn, herself the single mother of two young boys, says, 'I think [schools] should be doing an awful lot with boys and young men, because it's their expectations that are completely unrealistic . . . *Men* think they can have it all, that they can carry on having the full life. Nobody ever says to them they might have to hold back on their career, nobody says they might have to pull back on their social life . . . You can tell fifteen-year-olds, but it's not easy to go back and tell the twenty-five-year-olds, and the thirty-year-olds.'

The teaching profession should also practise what it preaches. Nursery care and primary teaching are female-dominated occupations, reinforcing the sense that it is women who are responsible for children. Women make up almost the entire childcare workforce in the UK.[17] This is of concern to the government, which says it wants to see 'a greater gender balance in the early years workforce'.[18] Low wages and poor status discourage men from entering this line of work. In order to encourage them into the field, and to recognise the vital, rewarding yet exhausting work done by everyone in this sector, the government must enhance its prestige by offering higher levels of training and pay. Such investment would in turn encourage more parents to see the value of formal childcare, creating a service to which increasing numbers of people would feel committed. Most parents, particularly single mothers, want more male childcare workers.[19] If this were to happen, children would see with their own eyes that their care is the work of men and women, complementing the message that they should also be hearing from their own parents.

Encouraging a healthy mix of men and women in work settings should not end there. Internationally, policy and practice to support parents in combining family responsibilities with the rest of life tends first to happen when there are high numbers of women in power.[20] Frequently this representation has come about because of the adoption of voluntary or compulsory quotas for women in parliament.[21] The UK should adopt quotas in local and national government elections. Many instinctively recoil from such 'preferential treatment'. Yet this is to ignore the informal positive discrimination from which men currently benefit, from having more time to dedicate to their careers because they are less home-bound, to being favoured by other men who recruit in their own image. At least quotas mean that we can privilege certain candidates openly and for a justifiable end, which is more than can be said for the old boys' network. Quotas won't so much push out deserving men as give deserving women a fighting chance. This will strengthen the gene pool at a senior level so that stronger candidates of both sexes get to the top. Those in influential positions are unrepresentative of the community at large – a fact that has not gone unnoticed by commentators on the current clutch of main Party leaders, who sport matching Y chromosomes as well as CVs. The country seems to be in agreement that there is a problem: if so, we need to take pro-active steps against it.

A softly, softly approach will achieve nothing. The number of women at Westminster – at a little over a fifth of MPs after the 2010 election – is still wholly inadequate. Even this small proportion was only achieved because the Labour Party instituted all-women shortlists for the 1997 general election and ended up with many more women on its benches, embarrassing the Conservatives into doing something too. Quotas may risk identikit women joining these identikit men, a grim army of groupthink Ken and Barbies. But introducing quotas alongside measures to enable men and women to share childcare and paid work, and manage their time more flexibly, would free up people of all backgrounds to pursue public lives. This really would broaden and strengthen the make-up of our institutions.

In quotas as in much else, the UK lags behind its European neighbours. The one advantage of this is that we can learn from the experience of those countries that have gone before us. If we are serious about encouraging shared parenting to a degree that is meaningful, we can draw ample lessons internationally about how best to achieve it. We can combine the well-funded parental leave of the Nordic states with the gender neutrality of the USA. We can take the best of Swedish provision while remaining true to our national preference for exercising personal choice. Our system could be based on genuine choice for all rather than on declared or hidden dogma. For once perhaps the UK could decide to revolutionise its parenting policy and set the pace for other countries, rather than be left standing.

Yet changes in public policy and employer practice can only take us so far: mothers and fathers need to be open to these new possibilities in order for them to take root. Parents put up little fight as they are dragooned into standard gender roles, going along with what everybody else is doing and with what's affirmed by the prevailing culture. Worse, they take up defensive, territorial positions in these roles, staking out their turf as primary parent or main breadwinner and refusing to budge. Women who say that they would rather be left to look after their kids without fathers interfering are as much of an indictment of the current situation as fathers joking with colleagues that they couldn't wait to get back to work after paternity leave. Men and women need to be inspired by the possibility of a more enjoyable parenting experience to abandon their hackneyed, self defeating attitudes. As Bill pithily puts it, 'Mum has got to let go and Dad has got to do it properly and not just say, "What do you mean she has not been fed?! She's had a crisp!" It's working together as a team . . . sharing it so that more people enjoy it, not seeing it as a chore or like a job but as a way of life. I think that way is the path.' Fran, a mother of one, agrees. 'I am very conscious of trying really, really hard not to fall into that trap of going, "Do it like that, do it like that," when [my husband] is here. I don't know whether he would say I get that right all the time, but I do try. Because I have watched other couples and I just cringe . . . I think the woman is not helping herself at all by undermining or challenging somebody's different way of doing things.'

There is much that we can do even before we get the UK-wide structural change that must come. As Nathan Hegedus points out, parents are a large and powerful force. Working together constructively there is a great deal that we can achieve. Within couples parents can stop to think through, seriously, their care arrangements rather than being swept along by norms; they can choose to be honest about what they expect from each other rather than seething with silent resentment; mothers can refrain from criticising fathers' parenting or from playing the martyr; fathers can be resolute in asking to work flexibly and in covering half the days their children are sick and half the school holidays; both can ensure that they are equally practised at the whole range of parenting tasks. Parents can take a more relaxed view of their own parenting, realising that good enough *is* good enough; they can hold back from judgement of others; and they can refrain from wallowing in guilt about wanting a life outside the home – or not. They can get involved, as families, in their community, supporting others as they wish to be supported themselves and demonstrating the social value of parenting and investment in children.

More broadly, parents can use their consumer power to reject mumsy baby products and gendered children's clothes and toys; protest against sexist advertising, publications and programming; and boycott non-family-friendly firms. Parents can lobby MPs on maternity and paternity leave provision; lobby their local maternity ward about fathers staying overnight; lobby their school to provide wrap-around care. They can band together in the workplace to ask for greater flexibility, to compare notes on pay, and to support everyone with outside commitments in meeting all the calls on their time. Parents don't have to consent to the current social structures, they can resist them and demand change. In fact, progress on these fronts will hasten that change.

Moving away from the orthodox model is hard: it opens up uncharted territory that exposes us to ourselves and to others. In contrast, sticking with the standard way of doing things is like wearing a pair of old, favourite shoes – comfortingly familiar. Matt, a father of two, explains, 'To create your own model and challenge this archetypal pattern takes a lot of effort and courage and it's easier to just go with the flow and do what everyone else does at the expense of peace of mind and happiness . . . Life is pressurised anyway, so to put the brakes on and ask, "Why are we doing it?" is really difficult . . . Because once you get on that hamster wheel it's just easier to keep going. But I think it's a mistake. When I see relationship failure – which I do a lot – and the resentment and bitterness that builds up between partners: the misunderstanding develops into just being unhappy a lot, I think the kids suffer. I think we have an obligation to be a bit more honest with ourselves. Because I think there's a certain dishonesty in just going with the flow. We have a responsibility to say, "There are some risks involved here if we just keep on going at this." But it's just easier to go at it and blame the other person. That's not particularly honest and I would absolutely include myself in that. I tend to feel resentful and angry and bitter and pissed off and you have to ask yourself whether that's justifiable.'

As Matt observes, most parents don't embrace change because they feel it will take too much effort when they are already frazzled or because, shortsightedly, it suits them not to think about it. Questioning our priorities and contemplating doing things differently are too daunting. Kieran is a father of two who left his staff job as a print journalist for a freelance life in order to more equally share parenting with his partner, who works for a local authority. He is frank: 'Most people don't ask certain searching questions of themselves and they go with what is expected of them. And what is expected of dads is that they go to work and that is expected by their female partners. Personally, I think with every couple that doesn't have a roughly equal split of childcare they are equally responsible for that. It's chosen by their actions.' Parents have to take the long view, keeping in mind their best interests, and those of their children, in the years to come. Rather than unthinkingly sticking with the familiar, we must engage with the full range of options in how we organise our parenting. We must be prepared to step into the unknown: giving up ground and claiming a stake in other areas.

Take shared leave in a child's first year. To begin with, like many women, fathers may well embark on their weeks alone with the baby with great trepidation. But as with most challenges, initial fear will recede as they master a new life. Only the most sunny-minded of mothers greets a day ahead with her young baby with absolute joy, but most get through it and, as the weeks go by, learn to enjoy it as much as they feel frustrated by it, often ricocheting between the two emotions from hour to hour. Men, too, will do the same. Kieran explains, 'For me it's just not an option to not be involved in parenting. Is it hard work? Yes. It is bloody awful. Sure. Utterly draining and exhausting. Is it rewarding? Well, sometimes. When you're awake enough to appreciate it, yes. But my priority is to be a dad. I do not countenance sacrificing being part of my children's life in order to work so therefore work has to work for me.' Lee is a father of one who works part time and is the main carer for his daughter as his wife works full time. He comments, 'Don't get me wrong, there are days when you just want to hide under the sofa but . . . I am still very happy doing it.' Like women, once men get over their initial fear of being with their children, they grow into the role. Kate, a mother of two daughters who occasionally works away from home, observes of her partner, 'My going away has forced him to get on with it . . . It's made him more confident . . . He realises that he can do it and also that he enjoys doing it so now we get, "Can Daddy do my pony tail because he's better at it than you." And you go, "Yeah! Great!"'

But it is not just men who might approach shared leave with nervousness. Women, too, may baulk at having their leave reduced, 'taken away' from them and given to men. We must try to avoid feeling territorial about men's role in our children's lives or over-sensitive to the public praise and encouragement they receive, acknowledging the greater good of men becoming confident in their fathering. This is true in the long term, as shared parenting pays dividends for years to come, and it is also true in the short term as we return to jobs with our working lives more intact than if there had been a prolonged absence.

For those who through force of will or circumstance are already able to share the parenting equally, the common understanding and emotional well-being it provokes is profound. Bev has three children. Her youngest child was born at the same time that her husband was made redundant so they shared the care of their newborn. She comments, 'My husband said, "You have no idea until you do it full time and you do it yourself – you can't clean, you can't cook a meal!" And I'm going, "Er, yes!" And he said, "Every father needs to have done it, not just for a weekend and not just for a week but relentlessly to understand what people are going through."' Monica, a mother of two who shares the weekday childcare with her husband, both combining it with paid work, explains the importance to her of sharing both roles: 'On maternity leave I would be sitting in a park at four o'clock thinking, "God, how many more hours will I be on my own with an eight-month-old baby, just really doing my head in?" But when I went back to work and my partner began sharing the care, he experienced that for himself and I felt that he really understood what it was like and I am sure he tried to understand. And I would be at work calling him up saying, "I need another hour here." So I was starting to experience what it was like when he was trying to finish something off and I wanted him to come home. For me, living each other's experiences really helped us to empathise.' Fran, whose husband for a while looked after their child one day a week, says, 'I think the fact that he had that time when he was the main carer, albeit it just for one day a week, it made a massive difference to how he really saw things through my eyes and I think he really appreciates how draining and how intensive it can be . . . Friends and family have commented since about how close he seems with our daughter, and how hands-on he is and how capable he is with her and it definitely has had a lasting impact.'

Men who enjoy an active part in their children's upbringing

benefit the neighbourhoods in which they live, too. They can play a greater role in daytime community life: lending a hand on school trips, calling in on an elderly neighbour, even helping to maintain social order on the streets. The community can reciprocate by doing more for parents. Rather than viewing child-rearing as a private concern, we should each understand our stake in raising happy children, and the importance for us all of supporting fathers in family life. The behavioural, educational and psychological benefits to children of growing up within a nurturing environment in which both the mother and the father are intimately involved in their daily lives[22] means that neighbourhoods will be better places. Businesses, too, will gain from employing well-adjusted, educated young adults with their valuable soft skills. And governments reap rewards from educated workers who pay tax, rather than costing the state time and money in crime and anti-social behaviour.

At its most mainstream this interdependence might be expressed in an extended family living with or close to each other, a neighbour picking up a child from school, a local business sponsoring a children's football team, or the government providing decent holiday clubs. But it can reach more imaginative heights in groups of unrelated people – of all ages, with children and without – living together and pooling resources. The notion of communal living is not some embarrassing throw-back to the Age of Aquarius, but a modern and fulfilling form of family life, enabling generations to care for each other in an emotionally, financially and environmentally beneficial way. Yet whether we live together with fifteen other people or more conventionally, we should all think of ourselves as living communally – with an eye to each other's interests as well as our own, understanding that the two aren't mutually exclusive.

Aside from communal living, other domestic set-ups also provide inspiration. Comparative studies have found that lesbian couples with children share both paid and unpaid work more equitably than heterosexual couples,[23] with the non-biological mother less likely than comparably qualified heterosexual fathers to work outside the home full time.[24] Among men, gay and bisexual fathers are more than twice as likely as heterosexual fathers to say they have primary responsibility for their children. Research with gay fathers suggests they take on a greater share of domestic tasks than straight men and are more actively involved in looking after their children.[25] This is not to say that gay men and lesbians have got it all sussed. They are vulnerable to jealousies and tiredness, and logistical and financial pressures along with everybody else. But households operating outside of the heterosexual convention, and so less bound and influenced by traditional social and gender norms, appear more able to develop arrangements based on ideals and fulfilment rather than historic inevitability. In so doing they allow heterosexual parents a glimpse of what might be possible in their own lives.

Sharing the care of children throughout their dependent years, and moving between the public and domestic spheres as equals, may seem daunting and difficult. In practice it requires reciprocity, energy and patience – probably more so than clearly dividing the jobs of cash and care. There may be more daily negotiation but there is also the underlying satisfaction in a joint enterprise. And it is worth reminding ourselves of how this effort is repaid. The benefits of equally shared parenting do not just pay dividends for women, although this has been my guiding concern throughout this book. Others benefit too. Fathers form meaningful relationships with their children of significant long-term benefit to both; children learn that both mothers and fathers can provide care; couple relationships are more likely to last; and mothers and fathers spread their bets, so the family isn't dependent on the father for income or on the mother for care, if either of them leaves, dies or is unable to provide one of these functions for any other reason.

If changes in the home are promoted by the government and actively supported through flexible working and more high-quality, affordable childcare, a narrowing of life chances will emerge. Rates of child poverty will fall and young children of all backgrounds will benefit from the stimulation and learning inherent in good, formal childcare at this early, life-defining stage. Greater family stability and happier children will mean less crime and disorder on our streets and a richer, stronger life within our communities. A rise in the fertility rate – a likely outcome of making family life easier – will help to alleviate care and financial resources requirements for our ageing society. Although the prospect of eliminating the pay gap between men and women altogether remains very far off (women's ability to bear children is likely always to put them at a disadvantage in some employers' eyes), steps to reduce the difference in working patterns between women and men should have some impact, which in turn will influence the decisions about roles that families make. With more women in paid work and able to maintain their positions in the occupations for which they are qualified, the government will finally be paid back for its investment in their education, rather than spending billions on benefit payouts and losing tax revenue.

The majority party in the UK Coalition Government, the Conservatives, pledged to make this country 'the most family friendly in Europe'.[26] Their Coalition agreement with the Liberal Democrats includes a commitment to 'encourage shared parenting from the earliest stages of pregnancy'.[27] It's clear what is needed to achieve this and the active and committed role that the government, and through it, employers, schools and other agencies must play. It goes far beyond flexible parental leave and widening the right to request flexible working. It runs completely counter to the government's severe cuts in public spending. The Deputy Prime Minister, Nick Clegg, has spoken of wishing Britain to be, 'a place every family wants their children to grow up in'. As he says, 'if we are not in government to do this, what are we here to do?'[28] Yet the government has cut back support for childcare and reduced financial help for families. In this environment it is mothers who make career sacrifices over fathers, and so the cycle of segregated roles persists, with everyone losing out in the process.

I'm tired of hearing the loud and dreary chorus that insists that policies such as shared, decently paid parental leave or good quality, widely available childcare are unaffordable or unrealistic. The cost of our current parental leave policies as a percentage of GDP is 0.15 per cent.[29] In contrast, Norway spends 0.47 per cent and Sweden 0.67 per cent.[30] UK parents have been ground down to expect and demand too little and policy makers don't feel under sufficient pressure to improve the situation. But equal opportunities for women and men aren't a luxury. The eminent sociologist Professor Gosta Esping-Anderson estimates that funding the best parental leave and universal high quality child and elderly care would cost roughly the equivalent of 5 per cent of GDP.[31] At the same time Goldman Sachs has calculated that closing the gap between women and men's participation in the workforce would increase GDP in the UK by 8 per cent.[32] All of this would reduce the burden on the state, enhance child, family and social well-being and encourage long-term, sustainable prosperity as a nation. Investment to get parenting right from the get-go is money well spent. Other nations have shown that real change is possible and their economies have not suffered as a result. The clever countries realise that equality between the sexes isn't something to aspire to at a point in the far distant future when we have a healthy, stable economy; it's crucial to *delivering* that healthy, stable economy in the first place. Now the UK needs to be bold and act with conviction, having the courage to admit that our current policy direction is the wrong one and must change.

For decades women have struggled to hold together family life and remain part of the world outside the home. For each generation the tensions between the two become greater as pressure about what constitutes 'good' motherhood bears down increasingly heavily while professional, social and intellectual horizons for women also expand. Worryingly there are now indications that, as happened in Germany, some professional women in the UK may be rejecting motherhood, viewing it as incompatible with their careers.[33] All of us – government, employers, members of the community, fathers and mothers themselves – must now work to release women from this bind. Men and women must come out of their corners, meeting in the middle to share all the responsibilities and pleasures of life. Together we can create a more equal society of which we can all be proud.

Afterword

On the Threshold

My son is now just three years old. Already he is a little maniac on his scooter, racing fearlessly off into the distance. With a cry of 'Look at me!', he demands that I bear witness to his fledgling independence. His blond hair flaps behind him in the breeze, a junior easy rider.

As he and the rest of his generation hurtle towards the future, what does it hold? When I spoke to Sam, working hard to keep her career on track and financially afloat while also raising the young daughter to whom she was devoted, she feared that nothing would have changed for parents by the time our children are adults themselves. If Sam is right, in thirty years' time mothers will still find themselves making awkward excuses as they sprint from work to collect their children from school. And fathers will continue to work long days in their jobs, returning home to briefly glimpse their offspring heading off to bed.

But there is an alternative. One in which mothers and fathers each have a life outside the home while also looking forward to their turn at the school gates and then catching up on that day's playground drama while flipping fish-fingers and checking home-work. This alternative – of genuinely shared parenting – is not some abstract, unattainable ideal. It is real and within reach.

It won't suit all couples to share equally in the life of the home and life out in 'the world'. But many of the mothers and fathers that I spoke to do want this. They want to spend time with their children, to combine work and home life, to call on care from others to ease the pressures on them and to create more free space in their lives. That option should be open to everyone, allowing a genuine choice about how we organise our families.

We have tested the contemporary family model to destruction and it isn't working. Women will continue to be brought up and educated as peers with men. They will continue to set their sights on the same ambitions and expect the same opportunites. Now we have to fix our family and working lives, completing the revolution that we started so many years ago.

There is a great deal at stake. Sharing the effort and rewards of raising our children and striving in the world will benefit not only mothers and fathers but also our sons and daughters and the wider community. The impact will be cumulative as, over the years, families and neighbourhoods become more closely bonded. This isn't simply a prospectus for equality between the sexes but an opportunity to enhance the happiness and well-being of society as a whole.

Even in the course of writing this book my experience of motherhood has changed. My son and I have each felt our way to a more independent existence. He has begun to discover his place in the outside world, while I have re-established mine. Though I have reclaimed parts of my former life, everything is, of course, completely different. I love my son. I don't want my old life back. But I also know that being a parent in the UK is tougher than it should be. Like so many other fathers and mothers in this country, my husband and I spend each day attempting to allot sufficient time to our son, our work, each other and ourselves. Heads down – busy, busy, busy – it can feel like a very individual quest. But were we to look up, we would see that every other parent is doing the same. This is the struggle that defines life for this generation of parents as the mothers and fathers featured in this book have expressed so well. As a collective voice we can campaign for change from others and resolve to change ourselves. The social good – including the good of our own young, vulnerable offspring – requires a down-payment of personal effort and commitment. We will all be repaid, with interest, in the end.

I hope that future generations of mothers will be able to push open their front doors, crossing fathers on the threshold, as they both move freely between their private and public roles. I hope that men and women will each take their children's hands, leading them together through to adult life. And I hope that they will look back at the not too distant past in this country and wonder that things were ever this way.

In the park my son scoots round in circles. I wave and he casually waves back, revelling in his liberty. From the moment we first hold our children, we slowly let them go. Now the time has also come to free ourselves.

Acknowledgements

There are many people whom I wish to thank for their help in writing this book. First of all, Jo Kavenna, who, as we talked one afternoon while I was on maternity leave, realised that there were the makings of a book in what I was saying, even before I did. Her support has been invaluable and unstinting ever since. Thanks also to Barnes Martin for his aid in getting this project off the starting blocks.

I am very grateful to my agent, Zoe Waldie, and to Liz Foley, Briony Everroad, Kate Bland, Ruth Warburton, Penny Liechti, Victoria Murray-Browner, Lisa Gooding and the rest of the team at Random House for their belief in the book and for their enthusiasm, advice and professionalism along the way. Thank you, too, to all those who have given me the benefit of their expertise on parenthood and family policy, or advance copies of books and papers, notably Rosalind Bragg, Adrienne Burgess, Majella Kilkey, Tina Miller, Roger Olley, Sam Pringle, Katherine Rake, Oddný Sturludóttir and Oriel Sullivan.

Thank you to Kim Barnes, Richard Beecham, Sara Beecham, Emma Bell, the Bengali Women's Support Group in South Yorkshire, Anna Brown, Sophie Challis, Melinda Chandler, Liesel Evans, Eliane Glaser, Jean Goodier, Anna Lucas, Will Maclean, Andy Miller, Jodie Reed, Jo Riordan, the staff at the Riverside

Community Health Project in Newcastle upon Tyne, Chris Rybczynski and Suzanne Thompson for all their help in many forms. My appreciation, too, to the staff at Coin Street Family and Children's Centre for taking such good care of my son when my husband and I are working. Thanks also to my friends in the world of broadcasting for teaching me the importance of voices; and to the 'voices' in this book – the mothers and fathers who so kindly agreed to talk to me and spoke with such honesty and eloquence about their experiences of parenthood: I am very grateful to you all.

I am deeply thankful to Nicky Busch for her comments on my manuscript and, most of all, her companionship and insights in the hours we've spent together with our children. I am hugely grateful to my parents, John and Pat Asher, and to Lynda Pearce and Guy Schofield, for their devotion and support in caring for their grandson. Above all, I am indebted to Nick for his love, patience and wisdom during the writing of this book, not to mention over the past fifteen years.

Further Reading

Some of the books listed below have been referred to earlier or cited in the endnotes, others have not. I don't include individual essays, papers, reports or articles in this list but all those I have drawn from are referenced in the endnotes.

Almond, B. (2010) *The Monster Within. The Hidden Side of Motherhood.* Berkeley: University of California Press.

Astbury, J. (1996) *Crazy for You. The Making of Women's Madness.* Oxford: Oxford University Press.

Badinter, E. (1981) *The Myth of Motherhood. An Historical View of the Maternal Instinct.* London: Souvenir Press.

Banyard, K. (2010) *The Equality Illusion.* London: Faber and Faber.

Benn, M. (1998) *Madonna and Child. Towards a New Politics of Motherhood.* London: Jonathan Cape.

Bridgeman, K., Keating, I I. and Lind, C. (eds.) (2008) *Responsibility, Law and the Family.* Aldershot: Ashgate.

Bristow, J. (2009) *Standing up to Supernanny.* Exeter: Imprint Academic.

Burgess, A. (1997) *Fatherhood Reclaimed. The Making of the Modern Father.* London: Vermillion.

Collier, R. and Sheldon, S. (2008) *Fragmenting Fatherhood. A Socio-Legal Study.* Oxford: Hart Publishing.

Crittenden, A. (2001) *The Price of Motherhood. Why the Most Important Job in the Word Is Still the Least Valued.* New York: Henry Holt and Company.

Cusk, R. (2008) *A Life's Work. On Becoming a Mother.* London: Faber and Faber.

Dinnerstein, D. (1987) *The Rocking of the Cradle and the Ruling of the World.* London: The Women's Press.

Douglas, S. J. and Michaels, M. W. (2005) *The Mommy Myth. The Idealization of Motherhood and How It Has Undermined All Women*. New York: Free Press.

Esping-Anderson, G. (2009) *The Incomplete Revolution. Adapting to Women's New Roles*. Cambridge: Polity Press.

Figes, K. (2008) *Life After Birth*. London: Virago.

Figes, K. (2010) *Couples. The Truth*. London: Virago.

Fineman, M. A. (1991) *The Illusion of Equality. The Rhetoric and Reality of Divorce Reform*. Chicago: University of Chicago Press.

Flouri, E. (2005) *Fathering and Child Outcomes*. Chichester: John Wiley & Sons.

Friedan, B. (1992) *The Feminine Mystique*. London: Penguin Books.

Gatrell, C. (2005) *Hard Labour. The Sociology of Parenthood*. Maidenhead: Open University Press.

Gavron, H. (1970) *The Captive Wife*. Harmondsworth: Pelican.

George, B. (ed.) (2009) *The Book of Dads. Essays on the Joys, Perils and Humiliations of Fatherhood*. New York: Harper Perennial.

Hanauer, C. (ed.) (2002) *The Bitch in the House. 26 Women Tell the Truth about Sex, Solitude, Work, Motherhood and Marriage*. London: Penguin.

Hardyment, C. (2007) *Dream Babies. Childcare Advice from John Locke to Gina Ford*. London: Frances Lincoln.

Hays, S. (1996) *The Cultural Contradictions of Motherhood*. New Haven: Yale University Press.

Hills, J., Sefton, T. and Stewart, K. (2009) *Towards a More Equal Society? Poverty, Inequality and Policy Since 1997*. Bristol: Policy Press.

Hochschild, A. R. with Machung, A. (2003) *The Second Shift*. New York: Penguin.

Hodgkinson, T. (2009) *The Idle Parent. Why Less Means More When Raising Kids*. London: Hamish Hamilton.

Hrdy, S. B. (2000) *Mother Nature. Maternal Instincts and the Shaping of the Species*. London: Vintage.

Hrdy, S. B. (2009) *Mothers and Others. The Evolutionary Origins of Mutual Understanding*. Cambridge, Mass: The Belknap Press of Harvard University Press.

Hunt, S. A. (ed.) (2009) *Family Trends. British Families Since the 1950s*. London: Family and Parenting Institute.

Kamerman, S. B. and Moss, P. (eds.) (2009) *The Politics of Parental Leave Policies. Children, Parenting, Gender and the Labour Market*. Bristol: Policy Press.

Kelly, M. (1999) *Post-Partum Document*. Berkeley: University of California Press.

Klett-Davies, M. (2007) *Going It Alone? Lone Motherhood in Late Modernity*. Aldershot: Ashgate.

Lamb. M. E. (2010) (ed.) *The Role of the Father in Child Development*. Fifth Edition. New Jersey: John Wiley.

Mahony, N., Newman J. and Burnett, C. (eds.) (2010) *Rethinking the Public. Innovations in Research, Theory and Politics*. Bristol: Policy Press.

McRobbie, A. (2009) *The Aftermath of Feminism. Gender, Culture and Social Change*. London: Sage.

Millar, F. (2009) *The Secret Life of the Working Mother. Juggling Work, Kids and Sanity*. London: Ebury.

Miller, T. (2005) *Making Sense of Motherhood. A Narrative Approach*. Cambridge: Cambridge University Press.

Miller, T. (2010) *Making Sense of Fatherhood. Gender, Caring and Work*. Cambridge: Cambridge University Press.

Oakley, A. (1979) *Becoming a Mother*. Oxford: Martin Robertson.

Oakley, A. (2005) *The Ann Oakley Reader*. Bristol: Policy Press.

Power, N. (2009) *One Dimensional Woman*. Hampshire: Zero Books.

Redfern, C. and Aune K. (2010) *Reclaiming the F Word. The New Feminist Movement*. London: Zed Books.

Rich, A. (1997) *Of Woman Born. Motherhood as Experience and Institution*. London: Virago.

Richards, A. (2008) *Opting In. Having a Child Without Losing Yourself*. New York: Farrar, Straus and Giroux.

Rowbotham, S. (2010) *Dreamers of a New Day. Women who Invented the Twentieth Century*. London: Verso.

Scott, J., Dex, S. and Joshi, H. (eds.) (2008) *Women and Employment. Changing Lives and New Challenges*. Cheltenham: Edward Elgar.

Scott, J., Crompton, C. and Lyonette, C. (eds.) (2010) *Gender Inequalities in the 21st Century. New Barriers and Continuing Constraints*. Cheltenham: Edward Elgar.

Waldfogel, J. (2006) *What Children Need*. Cambridge, Mass.: Harvard University Press.

Wilkinson, R. and Pickett, K. (2010) *The Spirit Level. Why Equality is Better for Everyone*. London: Penguin.

Wolf, N. (2002) *Misconceptions*. London: Vintage.

Notes

Introduction

1   *The Coalition: Our Programme for Government*. The Cabinet Office, London, May 2010.

1 'All I Did was Have a Baby'

1   71 per cent compared to 66 per cent in 2009 and 73 per cent compared to 68 per cent in 2010 (provisional). Source: Participation in education, training and employment by 16–18 year olds in England. London: Office for National Statistics, 30 June 2011.

2   Women were awarded 53 per cent of all National Vocational Qualifications and Scottish Vocational Qualifications in 2007/2008. Office for National Statistics, London, 2009.

3   51 per cent of women in England aged 17–30 participated in higher education in the UK for the first time in 2008/9 (final); 52 per cent did so in 2009/10 (provisional). The equivalent figure for men was 40 per cent and 41 per cent respectively. Higher Education Initial Participation Rates, Department for Business, Innovation and Skills, London, 31 March 2010.

4   Based on median hourly earnings. 2011 Annual Survey of Hours and Earnings. Office for National Statistics, London, 23 November 2011.

5   Kelan, E., Gratton, L., Mah, A. and Walker, L. (2009) *The Reflexive Generation: Young Professionals' Perspectives on Work, Career and Gender*. London: London Business School. This

research reveals that 'many people from this generation have the firm belief that equality between men and women has been achieved and will no longer be an issue for them.'

6   89 per cent of married or co-habiting fathers, 71 per cent of married or co-habiting mothers and 57 per cent of lone parents (nine out of ten of whom are mothers) with dependent children are in paid employment. *Work and Worklessness Among Households 2010*. Office for National Statistics, London, September 2010.

7   Hunt, S. A. (ed.) (2009) *Family Trends: British Families Since the 1950s*. London: Family and Parenting Institute. Citing Lewis, J. L., Campbell, M. and Huerta, C. (2008) 'Patterns of Paid and Unpaid Work in Western Europe: Gender, Commodification, Preferences and the Implications for Policy', *Journal of European and Social Policy*, 18 (1), 21–37.

8   Ellison, G., Barker, A. and Kulasuriya T. (2009) *Work and Care: a Study of Modern Parents*. London: Equality and Human Rights Commission research report 15.

9   Statistics based on analysis of UK individuals' completed time diaries carried out by Dr Oriel Sullivan, Deputy Director, Centre for Time Use Research, University of Oxford. Research presented to British Sociological Association, 7 April 2010. 'Parents spend treble the amount of time on childcare now than in 1975, research shows', British Sociological Association press release, 7 April 2010. These figures are for primary childcare activities only (such as washing, dressing and reading to children) and not childcare as a secondary activity (for example, cleaning, cooking or shopping with children present). Child-related travel is also not included.

10   Women in the UK do between 166 and 191 minutes of domestic work a day (depending on educational achievement), compared to between 101 and 118 minutes a day for men. Statistics for 2000 presented by Dr Oriel Sullivan, University of Oxford, to the British Sociological Association, April 2010, op. cit.

11   Kan, M. Y., Sullivan, O. and Gershuny, J. (2011) 'Gender Convergence in Domestic Work: Discerning the Effects of Interactional and Institutional Barriers from Large-Scale Data', *Sociology*, April 2011 45: 234–251.

12   Rich, A. (1997) *Of Woman Born: Motherhood as Experience and Institution*. London: Virago. First published in the USA by W. W. Norton and Company, Inc. in 1976.

13   Men do 333 minutes of paid work per day and 148 minutes of unpaid work. Women do 202 minutes per day of paid work, and 280 of unpaid work. Statistics for the UK based on individuals' completed time diaries, 2000–4. Gershuny, J. I. and Kan, M. Y. (in press) 'Half-way to Gender Equality in Work? Evidence from the Multinational Time Use Study'. In J. Scott (ed.) *Gendered Lives*. Cheltenham: Edward Elgar.

14   Harkness, S. (2008) 'The Household Division of Labour: Changes in Families' Allocation of Paid and Unpaid Work'. In Scott, J., Dex, S. and Joshi, H. (eds.) (2008) *Women and Employment. Changing Lives and New Challenges*. Cheltenham: Edward Elgar.

15   Harkness, S. (2008) 'The Household Division of Labour: Changes in Families' Allocation of Paid and Unpaid Work'. op. cit.

16   Miller, T. (2010) *Making Sense of Fatherhood: Gender, Caring and Work*. Cambridge: Cambridge University Press.

17   *Becoming Parents Together*. The Tavistock Centre, London 2009.

18   Studies show a small but consistent decline in relationship satisfaction in the early years after a couple has their first child (although for a sizeable minority it increases). The more a couple's lifestyle and activites diverge after having a child, the greater the disenchantment. For review see: Cowan, P. and Cowan, C. (2003) 'Normative Family Transitions, Normal Family Process, and Healthy Child Development', in Walsh, F. (2003) *Normal Family Processes: Growing Diversity and Complexity*. Third Edition. New York: The Guildford Press.

19   Kiernan, K. (2005) *Non Residential Fatherhood and Child Involvement: Evidence from the Millennium Cohort Study, London*. London: Centre for Analysis of Social Exclusion, London School of Economics.

20   Hunt, S. A. (ed.) (2009) *Family Trends: British Families Since the 1950s*, op. cit.

21   Bradford Wilcox, W. and Nock, Steven L. (2006) 'What's Love Got To Do With It? Equality, Equity, Commitment and Women's Marital Quality', *Social Forces*, 84 (3).

22 Sigle-Rushton, W. (2010) 'Men's Unpaid Work and Divorce: Reassessing Specialization and Trade in British Families', *Feminist Economics*, Volume 16 (2).

23 Friedan, B. (1992) *The Feminine Mystique*. London: Penguin Books. First published in 1963 by W. W. Norton in the USA and Victor Gollancz in the UK.

24 Rich, A. (1977) *Of Woman Born: Motherhood as Experience and Institution*, op. cit.

25 At the beginning of the twentieth century about five million women were in the paid workforce in the UK. This number increased temporarily during the two world wars. But from the 1960s onwards there was a permanent rise in the number of women in paid employment. In the early 1970s 56 per cent of women were in paid employment, increasing to 72 per cent by 1998. See for review Busch, N. (2010) *A Migrant Division of Labour in the Global City? Commodified In-home Childcare in London 2004–2010*. Unpublished Ph.D. thesis, Birkbeck College, University of London.

26 *Male and Female Participation and Progression in Higher Education*. Higher Education Policy Institute, Oxford, 2009.

27 The proportion of women higher education students rose from 33 per cent in 1970/71 to 57 per cent in 2006/7 and there has been a greater number of female students than males every year since 1995/96. Source: Office for National Statistics data cited in Hunt, S. A. (ed.) (2009) *Family Trends: British Families Since the 1950s*, op. cit.

28 Men and women are equally likely to be in employment before having children. Woodroffe, J. (2009) *Not Having It All: How Motherhood Reduces Women's Pay and Employment Prospects*. London: Fawcett Society.

29 Oakley, A. (2005) *The Ann Oakley Reader*. Bristol: Policy Press.

30 Ibid.

31 Rich, A. (1997) *Of Woman Born: Motherhood as Experience and Institution*, op. cit.

32 Gavron, H. (1970) *The Captive Wife*. Harmondsworth: Pelican. First published in 1966 by Routledge & Kegan Paul, London.

33 'Courage, mothers. While dads push buggies, the revolution still rolls on', Madeleine Bunting, the *Guardian*, 15 November 2009.

34   Wolf, N. (2002) *Misconceptions*. London: Vintage.

35   Cusk, R. (2008) *A Life's Work: On Becoming a Mother*.London: Faber and Faber. First published in London in 2001 by Fourth Estate.

36   The mean age for women giving birth in England and Wales was 29.4 years in 2009: the highest on record. The fertility rate for women aged thirty and under decreased in 2009 compared to 2008, whereas the fertility rate for those aged thirty-five and over increased. The highest percentage increase was in women aged forty years of age and over. Office for National Statistics, London, July 2010.

37   In 1980 just over 40 per cent of women with dependent children were in paid employment. It is now almost 70 per cent. Scott, J., Dex, S., Joshi, H., Purcell, K. and Elias, P. (2008) 'Introduction: Changing Lives and New Challenges' in Scott, J., Dex, S. and Joshi, H. (eds.) (2008) *Women and Employment: Changing Lives and New Challenges*, op. cit.

38   *Distributional analysis of tax and benefit changes*. Presentation at the Institute for Fiscal Studies 2010 Spending Review briefing, London, 21 October 2010. Also *How could the government perform a gender impact assessment of tax and benefit changes?* Institute for Fiscal Studies, London, June 2011. And *What does yesterday's news mean for living standards?* Institute for Fiscal Studies presentation on the Autumn Statement, London, 16 November 2011.

39   65 per cent of public sector workers are women and 40 per cent of employed women work in public sector occupations. Figures for 2010 Trades Union Congress, London.

40   Figures for May to July 2011 put the number of women out of work at 1.06 million, the highest since February to April 1988. Labour Market Statistics, Office for National Statistics, London, September 2011.
     See also 'One million women unemployed, a quarter unemployed long-term'. London: Institute for Public Policy Research, 7 August 2011. http://www.ippr.org/press-releases/111/7826/one-million-women-unemployed-a-quarter-unemployed-long-term. Accessed online 31 August 2011.

2 The Baby and the Bath Water

1   The hospital confinement rate rose from 15 per cent to 99 per cent between 1927 and 1977. Gatrell, C. (2005) *Hard Labour: The Sociology of Parenthood*. Maidenhead: Open University Press, citing statistics from Oakley, A. (1981) *From Here to Maternity: Becoming a Mother*. Harmondsworth: Penguin; and Oakley, A. (1984) *The Captured Womb*. Oxford: Blackwell.

2   The maternal mortality rate reduced from 2,920 in 1928 to fewer than 100 per year from 1985 onwards. Statistics for England and Wales, Office of Population, Censuses and Surveys, cited by Royal College of Obstetricians and Gynaecologists, London.

3   *Woman Centred Care*, Position Statement, Royal College of Midwives, London. First published 1996, updated June 2008. Accessed online on 27 August 2010. http://www.rcm.org.uk/college/standards-and-practice/position-statements/.

4   Miller, T. (2005) *Making Sense of Motherhood: A Narrative Approach*. Cambridge: Cambridge University Press.

5   National Health Service Institute for Innovation and Improvement, Coventry.

6   Ibid.

7   The home birth rate in England and Wales was 2.9 per cent in 2008 and 2.7 per cent in 2009. Office for National Statistics, London, November 2010.

8   *Woman Centred Care*, Position Statement, Royal College of Midwives, op. cit.

9   *Involving Fathers in Maternity Care*, National Childbirth Trust Briefing, London, March 2009. Accessed online on 27 August 2010: http://www.nct.org.uk/about-us/what-we-do/policy/keypolicyareasofnct.

10 Venners, S. A., Wang, X., Chen, C., et al. (2004) 'Paternal Smoking and Pregnancy Loss: a Prospective Study Using a Biomarker of Pregnancy', *American Journal of Epidemiology* 159 (10): 993–1001. And Health Education Authority (1999) *Smoking and Pregnancy: a Survey of Knowledge, Attitudes and Behaviour, 1992–1999*. London: Health Education Agency.

11 Teitler, J. O. (2001) 'Father Involvement, Child Health and

Maternal Health Behaviour. Children and Youth Services Review', 23 (4–5): 403–25, cited in *Involving Fathers in Maternity Care*, NCT Briefing, op. cit.

12   *Involving Fathers in Maternity Care*, NCT Briefing, op. cit.

13   *Pregnancy and the birth: for dads*, NHS Choices website, 26 May 2009. http://www.nhs.uk/livewell/pregnancy/pages/newdadpage.aspx. Accessed online on 27 August 2010.

14   37 per cent of first-time mothers in England do not attend antenatal classes or workshops. Source: Redshaw, M., and Heikkila, K. (2010) *Delivered with Care: a National Survey of Women's Experience of Maternity Care in 2010*. National Perinatal Epidemiology Unit, University of Oxford.

15   *Infant Feeding Survey 2005: A Commentary on Feeding Practices in the UK*. Position Statement by the Scientific Advisory Committee on Nutrition, 2008. London: The Stationery Office.

16   77 per cent of women in England who attend antenatal classes are accompanied by their partner. Source: *Delivered with Care: a National Survey of Women's Experience of Maternity Care in 2010*, op cit.

17   *Sure Start Children's Centres Children's Services, January to March 2010*, NHS Southwark and Southwark Council, London.

18   For review: McMillan, A. S., Barlow, J. and Redshaw, M. (2009) *Birth and Beyond: A Review of the Evidence about Antenatal Education*. London: Department of Health.

19   *Fatherhood: the birth and beyond*, NHS Choices website, 6 April 2009.http://www.nhs.uk/planners/pregnancycareplanner/pages/becomingfather.aspx. Accessed online on 27 August 2010.

20   *Pregnancy and the birth: for dads*, NHS Choices website, op. cit.

21   'Supporting your partner' in *The pregnancy care planner*, NHS Choices website, 6 April 2009. http://www.nhs.uk/planners/pregnancycareplanner/pages/supportingpartner.aspx. Accessed online on 27 August 2010.

22   Lewis, G. (ed.) (2007). The Confidential Enquiry into Maternal and Child Health (CEMACH). *Saving Mothers' Lives:*

Reviewing Maternal Deaths to Make Motherhood Safer – 2003–2005. The Seventh Report on Confidential Enquiries into Maternal Deaths in the United Kingdom. London: CEMACH. Maternal death is defined as death during pregnancy or within six weeks of a pregnancy having ended.

23 Taft, A. (2002) *Violence against Women in Pregnancy and After Childbirth: Current Knowledge and Issues in Healthcare Responses.* Issues Paper 6. Sydney: Australian Domestic and Family Violence Clearinghouse.

24 *Domestic Abuse: Pregnancy, Birth, Puerperium.* Position Statement, The Royal College of Midwives, May 2006. Accessed online on 27 August 2010 at http://www.rcm.org.uk/college/standards-and-practice/position-statements/

25 *Involving Fathers in Maternity Care*, NCT Briefing, March 2009, op. cit.

26 *Domestic Abuse in Pregnancy*, Position Paper No. 19a, March 1999. London: The Royal College of Midwives.

27 Ibid.

28 93 per cent of births are in hospital. 3 per cent are in a midwife-led unit or birth centre separate from hospital. Statistics for England. Source: *Delivered with Care: a National Survey of Women's Experience of Maternity Care in 2010*, op cit.

29 Over 90 per cent of fathers in the UK attend the birth of their child. Even among those fathers who live separately from the mother, 45 per cent of them are present at the birth. For review see Fatherhood Institute Research Summary: *Fathers Attending Birth*, September 2007.

30 Kasy White, 'No Really . . . Nothing Prepares You', *Offspring* magazine, National Childbirth Trust, Cheltenham & North Cotswolds branch, Winter 2009.

31 *Towards Better Births: A Review of Maternity Services in England*, Healthcare Commission, 2008.

32 Kramer, M. S. et al. (2007) 'Effect of prolonged and exclusive breastfeeding on risk of allergy and asthma: cluster randomised trial', *British Medical Journal*, 11 September 2007. Kramer, M. S. et al. (2009) 'A Randomized Breast-feeding Promotion Intervention Did Not Reduce Child Obesity in

Belarus,' *The Journal of Nutrition*, 139, (2), 417S–421S, February. Gale, C. R. et al. (2010) 'Breastfeeding, the use of docosa-hexaenoic acid-fortified formulas in infancy and neuropsychological function in childhood', *Archives of Disease in Childhood*, 95, 174–9, doi:10.1136/adc.2009.165050.

33   45 per cent of women in the UK exclusively breastfeed at one week, 21 per cent at six weeks and less than 1 per cent at six months. *Infant Feeding Survey 2005: A Commentary on Feeding Practices in the UK*. Position Statement by the Scientific Advisory Committee on Nutrition, 2008, op. cit.

34   *Help!!! Mother & daughter just returned home*. Homedad.org.uk website.   http://homedad.org.uk/forum/viewtopic.php?f=2&t=1982. Accessed online on 12 February 2010.

35   *Pregnancy and the birth: for dads*. NHS Choices website. op. cit.

36   For review: Waldfogel, J. (2006) *What Children Need*. Cambridge, Mass.: Harvard University Press.

37   Eligible women receive Statutory Maternity Pay of 90 per cent of earnings for the first six weeks followed by £124.88 per week (as at August 2010) – or 90 per cent of earnings if that amounts to less than £124.88 – for thirty-three weeks and the option of taking a further thirteen weeks unpaid. This statutory payment may be supplemented by employers' maternity schemes. Maternity Allowance, paid at a flat rate of £124.88 per week (as at August 2010) or 90 per cent of earnings, if lower, for thirty-nine weeks, is available for those mothers that are ineligible for Statutory Maternity Pay. Adoption leave also lasts up to fifty-two weeks and is paid at the same rate and over the same timescale as Maternity Allowance.

38   Fathers' two weeks' leave (to which eligible adoptive fathers and same-sex partners are also entitled) is paid at this same flat rate of £124.88 per week (as at August 2010) or 90 per cent of earnings, if lower, although again employers may voluntarily increase this.

39   Parents are entitled to up to thirteen weeks' unpaid parental leave each in total (due to increase by another month following 2010 EU legislation) up to a child's fifth birthday, or eighteen weeks' up to the age of eighteen for disabled children. No more than four weeks can be taken in a year. Adoptive parents

and same-sex partners are entitled to this leave. Surrogate parents are entitled to unpaid parental leave only.

40 This includes adoptive fathers. It also applies to same-sex partners.

41 Regulation impact assessment data cited in Equality and Human Rights Commission (2009) *Working Better: Meeting the Changing Needs of Families, Workers and Employers in the 21st Century*. London: EHRC.

42 It is estimated that employee fathers' take-up of their four week reserved leave period would range from 4 to 13 per cent and take-up of the shared leave period would be between 4 and 8 per cent. Consultation on Modern Workplaces. Flexible parental leave: impact assessment. Department for Business, Innovation and Skills, London, May 2011. http://www.bis.gov.uk/assets/biscore/employment-matters/docs/f/11-743-flexible-parental-leave-impact-assessment.pdf. Accessed online 20 September 2011.

43 Equal Opportunities Commission (2005) *Time-use and Childcare*. London: EOC.

44 See for review: Lamb, M. E. (ed.) (2010) *The Role of the Father in Child Development*. Fifth Edition. New Jersey: John Wiley and Sons.

45 *The Coalition: Our Programme for Government*, op. cit.

3 A Word of Advice, Dear

1 40 per cent of women appearing in news stories in the UK are identified as mothers, wives and so on as compared to 19 per cent of men. *Who Makes the News?*, Global Media Monitoring Project, 2010.

2 Institute of Child Health (London) press release 'Children of working mums "have unhealthier lifestyles"', 28 September 2009. See http://www.ich.ucl.ac.uk/pressoffice/pressrelease 00762. Accessed online on 11 November 2010. The media picked this up and ran with it: 'Working Mothers' children unfit' said the BBC's News Online, 28 September 2010. See http://news.bbc.co.uk/1/hi/8278742.stm. Accessed online on 11 July 2010. 'Working mothers have unhealthiest children,

study finds' said the *Guardian*, 29 September 2010. See
http://www.guardian.co.uk/society/2009/sep/29/working-
mothers-child-health. Accessed online on 11 July 2010.
'Children whose mothers work are less healthy' wrote the
Daily Telegraph, 29 September 2010. Seehttp://www.telegraph.
co.uk/health/healthnews//6239564/Children-whose-
mothers-work-are-less-healthy.html. Accessed online 11 July
2010. 'Working mothers beware. Why children of stay at home
mothers have healthier lifestyles' warned the *Daily Mail*, 29
September 2009. See http://www.dailymail.co.uk/health/
article-1216806/Working-mothers-beware-why-children-stay-
home-parents-healthier.html. Accessed online on 11 July 2010.

3   Layard, R. and Dunn, J. (2009) *A Good Childhood: Searching
for Values in a Competitive Age*. London: Penguin/The
Children's Society. (See online for summary: http://www.
childrenssociety.org.uk/all about us/how we do it/the good
childhood inquiry/report summaries/14747.html. Accessed
online on 11 July 2010.) Media coverage of the report resulted
in the following headlines: the *Daily Telegraph* 'The Children's
Society report should trouble us all; Britain needs mothers
to stay at home and tax system should encourage them to
do so', 2 February 2009. See http://www.telegraph.co.uk/
comment/telegraph-view/4438942/The-Children-Society-
report-on-childhood-should-trouble-us-all.html. Accessed
online on 11 July 2010. 'Mum's cash "leading to split
home"' reported the *Mirror*, 2 February 2009. See
http://www.mirror.co.uk/news/top-stories/2009/02/
02/mum-s-cash-leading-to-split-home-115875-21090902/.
Accessed online on 11 July 2010. 'Kids "damaged" by work
mums', the *Sun*, 2 February 2009. See: http://www.
thesun.co.uk./sol/homepage/news/article2195193.ece.
Accessed online on 2 September 2010. The BBC website also
reported the inquiry findings with the headline 'Selfish adults
"damage childhood"', 2 February 2009. Despite this sex-
neutral heading its report included a section subtitled
'Working Mothers' with no mention of the possible role of
fathers. See http://news.bbc.co.uk/1/hi/education/7861762.stm.
Accessed online on 11 July 2010.

4   See *The Mommy Myth: The Idealization of Motherhood and How it Has Undermined All Women* by Professor Susan J. Douglas and Meredith W. Michaels (New York: Free Press, 2005) for a compelling and witty case that fear, fantasy, marketing and politics have combined to produce the 'new momism'. Although written with specific reference to the United States, much of what the writers observe and argue translates all too easily to the UK.

5   See Chapter 1, note 9.

6   De Frain, J. D. (1977) 'Sexism in Parenting Manuals', *The Family Coordinator*, 26 (3), 245–51.

7   42,104 books are listed under 'parenting books', subsection 'health, family, lifestyle' on Amazon.co.uk, as of 24 February 2010.

8   *Buggies – which way should they face?* Talk To Your Baby campaign. See online at: http://www.literacytrust.org.uk/talk_to_your_baby/resources/1578_buggies#background. Accessed online on 2 September 2010.

9   'Are modern buggies bad for babies?', the *Guardian*, 22 November 2008.

10   Ibid

11   Ibid.

12   Ibid.

13   Ibid.

14   *Cost of a Child* annual survey carried out by the Centre for Economics and Business Research for LV= insurance and investment group, 2010.

15   'Childcare is bad for your baby, working parents are warned'. *The Times*, 11 December 2008.

16   *Let's talk controlled crying. Love to hear your thoughts!* Mumsnet thread started 31 May 2007. http://www.mumsnet.com/Talk?topicid=67&threadid=332444&stamp=070706135142. Accessed online on 2 March 2010.

17   Hogg, T. with Blau, M. (2001) *Secrets of the Baby Whisperer: How to Calm, Connect and Communicate with Your Baby*. London: Vermillion.

18   Hogg, T. with Blau, M. (2001) *Secrets of the Baby Whisperer: How to Calm, Connect and Communicate with Your Baby*. op. cit. Hogg,

T. with Blau, M. (2002) *Secrets of the Baby Whisperer for Toddlers*. London: Vermillion. Hogg, T. and Blau, M. (2005) *The Baby Whisperer Solves All Your Problems (By Teaching You How to Ask the Right Questions): Sleeping, Feeding and Behaviour – Beyond the Basics through Infancy and Toddlerdom*. London: Vermillion. Hogg, T. with Blau, M. (2009) *Top Tips from the Baby Whisperer: Sleep*. London: Vermillion. Hogg, T. with Blau, M (2008) *Top Tips from the Baby Whisperer: Secrets to Calm, Connect and Communicate with Your Baby*. London: Vermillion. Hogg, T. with Blau, M (2008) *Top Tips from the Baby Whisperer for Toddlers: Secrets to Raising Happy and Cooperative Toddlers*. London: Vermillion. Hogg, T. with Blau, M (2010) *Top Tips from the Baby Whisperer: Breastfeeding*. London: Vermillion. Hogg, T. with Blau, M. (2010) *Top Tips from the Baby Whisperer: Potty Training*. London: Vermillion.

19   Figure for 2009 in England and Wales, Office for National Statistics, July 2010.

20   62 per cent of mothers with a child aged up to twelve months old say that they do not have a health visitor, or, for those that do, that they would not be happy to call them. The Family Commission (2010) *Starting a Family Revolution: Putting Families in Charge*. London: 4Children.

21   Hogg, T. with Blau, M. (2001) *Secrets of the Baby Whisperer*, op. cit.

22   Ford, G. (2006) *The New Contented Little Baby Book*. London: Vermillion.

23   *Understanding the Continuum Concept*. See online at http://www.continuum-concept-org/ccdefined.html.   Accessed online on 2 September 2010.

24   Hogg, T. with Blau, M. (2001) *Secrets of the Baby Whisperer*, op. cit.

25   Ford, G. (2006) *The New Contented Little Baby Book*, op. cit.

26   *Undersanding the Continuum Concept*, op. cit.

27   Ford, G. (2006) *The New Contented Little Baby Book*, op. cit.

28   Hogg, T. with Blau, M. (2001) *Secrets of the Baby Whisperer*, op. cit.

29   *Undersanding the Continuum Concept*, op. cit.

30   Hogg, T. with Blau, M. (2001) *Secrets of the Baby Whisperer*, op. cit.

31   Hays, S. (1996) *The Cultural Contradictions of Motherhood*. New Haven and London: Yale University Press.

32   See, for example, the 'Slummy Mummy' column in *The Times Magazine* and its spin off book, *The Secret Life of a Slummy Mummy* by Fiona Neill (London: Arrow Books, 2008) or the 'Happy Families' column in the *Telegraph Weekend* section, written by Stephanie Calman, author of *Confessions of a Bad Mother: In the Aisle by the Chill Cabinet No-one Can Hear You Scream*, (London: Pan, 2008).

33   http://www.mumsnet.com/info/aboutus. Accessed online on 8 March 2010.

34   'Kids? Tell me about it . . .', Kate Kellaway, the *Observer*, 25 March 2001.

35   http://www.mumsnet.com/campaigns. Accessed online on 17 October 2010.

36   http://www.mumsnet.com/Local. Accessed online on 17 October 2010.

37   Mumsnet census 2009. http://www.mumsnet.com/info/census-2009. Accessed online on 8 March 2010.

38   http://www.mumsnet.com/Talk/recipes/924115-QUICK-have-accidentally-melted-butter. Accessed online on 8 March 2010.

39   Mumsnet census 2009, op. cit.

40   34 per cent of Mumsnet members are educated to degree level, a further 14 per cent have done post-graduate studies, and a further 27 per cent have a post graduate professional qualification. Mumsnet census 2009, op. cit.

41   'Mumsnet friends vs Real friends', talk thread started 22 February 2010, Mumsnet.com.http://www.mumsnet.com/Talk/am_i_being_unreasonable/916817-MUMSNET-friends-vs-REAL-friends?hideThreadId=916817&hideThreadId=916817. Accessed online on 8 March 2010.

42   *Pepper Pig* (sic), Netmums.com talk thread started 16 January 2010 http://www.netmums.com/coffeehouse/general-coffee-house-chat-514/wine-bar-494/372373-pepper-pig.html#xzzOha061Cc7. Accessed online on 8 March 2010.

43   'omg bfp!' posted on Actively Trying forum, Babycentre.co.uk 11 February 2009. http://community.babycentre.co.uk/post/

a1604215/omg_bfp_but_had_af_last_week?cpg=1&csi=
2007635447&pd=-2. Accessed online on 14 June 2010.

44   'Kids? Tell me about it . . .', Kate Kellaway, op. cit.

45   'Mother knows best – but does Gina Ford know better?'
Alexandra Blair, *The Times*, 29 June 2009. Seehttp://women.
timesonline.co.uk/tol/life_and_style/women/families/article
6586335.ece. Accessed online on 8 March 2010.

46   Most Mumsnet members have an average household income
of £35,000 or more, read a broadsheet newspaper and have
a degree or higher educational qualification. Mumsnet census
2009, op. cit.

47   Mumsnet friends vs Real friends, 22 February 2010, op. cit.

48   'Let's talk controlled crying. Love to hear your thoughts!',
31 May 2007, op. cit.

49   'Am I being unreasonable to consider leaving 5m DD in hotel
room . . .', posted 25 November 2009, Mumsnet.com.
http://www.mumsnet.com/Talk/am_i_being_unreasonabl
e/867747-to-consider-leaving-5m-DD-in-hotel-room-witgh-
monitor?pg=1. Accessed online on 2 March 2010.

50   Only four out of twenty-three members of Cabinet appointed
in May 2010 were women. See Number 10 website, 19 May 2010:
http://www.number10.gov.uk/news/topstorynews/2010/05/
her-majestys-government-49840. Accessed online on 12 July 2010.

51   'Gordon Brown takes a dunking in great biscuit debate', *Daily
Mail*, 19 October 2009. http://www.dailymail.com.uk/
news/article-1221334/Gordon-Brown-gets-dunking-great-
biscuit-debate.html. Accessed online on 2 September 2010.
'The mother of all ambushes: David Cameron subjected to
online inquisition from disgruntled middle class parents
during webchat on Mumsnet', *Daily Mail*, 20 November 2009.
http://www.dailymail.co.uk/news/article-1229411/David-
Cameron-subjected-online-inquisition-disgruntled-
middle-class-parents-webchat-Mumsnet.html. Accessed online
on 2 September 2010.
'Ed Miliband feels wrath of Mumsnet after nappy gaffe',
The Times, 4 December 2009. http://www.timesonline.
co.uk/tol/news/politics/article6944059.ece. Accessed online
on 2 September 2010.

'Mumsnet strikes again as Ed Miliband admits using disposable nappies for son', *Daily Telegraph*, 4 December 2009. http://www.telegraph.co.uk/news/uknews/6721993/-Mumsnet-strikes-again-as-Ed-Miliband-admits-using-disposable-nappies-for-son.html. Accessed online on 2 September 2010.

'Ed Miliband ticked off over disposable nappy choice', BBC website, 4 December 2009. http://news.bbc.co.uk/1/hi/uk politics/8394736.stm. Accessed online on 2 September 2010.

'Ed Miliband in hot water with mums over nappy choice', *Guardian*, 4 December 2009. http://www.gurdian.co.uk/politics/2009/dec/04/ed-miliband-disposable-nappies-mumsnet. Accessed online on 2 September 2010.

'We use disposables: The throwaway nappy remark that earned Ed Miliband a ticking-off from mums' website', *Daily Mail*, 4 December 2009. http://www.dailymail.co.uk/news/article-1233153/How-Ed-Milibands-throwaway-remark-earned-ticking-mothers.html. Accessed online on 2 September 2010.

52   http://www.mumsnet.com/onlinechats/ed-miliband, 3 December 2009. Accessed online on 9 March 2010.

53   Mumsnet Talk Round Up email, 4 December 2009.

54   Gambles, R. (2010) 'Going Public? Articulations of the Personal and Political on Mumsnet.com', in Mahony, N., Newman J. and Burnett, C. (eds.) (2010) *Rethinking the Public: Innovations in Research, Theory and Politics*. Bristol: Policy Press. In her essay, Richenda Gambles gives the example of threads about miscarriage on Mumsnet that encourage posters to 'go public' with their experiences. Despite the fact that Mumsnet, with the help of its members, drew up a suggested code of practice on treatment of miscarriage this is given much less emphasis than sharing personal feelings in these threads.

55   Miller, T. (2005) *Making Sense of Motherhood: A Narrative Approach*. Cambridge: Cambridge University Press.

56   Cox J. L., Murray D., Chapman G. (1993) 'A Controlled Study of the Onset, Duration and Prevalence of Postnatal Depression', *British Journal of Psychiatry*, 163, 27–31.

57   For review see: Fatherhood Institute Research Summary.

Fathers and post-natal depression: Messages from Research. Updated August 2010.

4 A Job For Life

1   'London's Real Mad Men', *The Times*, 31 January 2009. http://women.timesonline.co.uk/tol/life_and_style/women/fashion/article5593218.ece. Accessed online on 30 February 2009.

2   In 1990, 8 per cent of managers in the UK were women. In 2002 it was 29 per cent. Chartered Management Institute report 2009. Cited in Hunt, S. A. (ed.) (2009) *Family Trends: British Families since the 1950s*, op. cit.

3   The Equality and Human Rights Commission's 2011 *Sex and Power* report on gender equality in the UK workplace found that: 'there were more women in top posts in seventeen of the twenty-seven categories compared to [their report of] 2007/8 . . . However, increases have been small in most areas and in many cases the increases are attributable to just one or two women joining senior posts . . . There have been drops in women's participation in ten sectors . . . In three of these cases, falls have been substantial.'

4   The EHRC's report *Sex and Power 2011* showed that women's average representation in UK top jobs was 10.2 per cent in business, 26.1 per cent in the public and voluntary sector, 26.2 per cent in politics and 15.1 per cent in media and culture.

5   Fagan, C., Hegewisch, A. and Pillenger, J. (2006) *Out of Time: Why Britain Needs a New Approach to Working-time Flexibility.* Manchester: University of Manchester/London: Trades Union Congress.

6   The Family Commission (2010) *Starting a Family Revolution: Putting Families in Charge.* London: 4Children.

7   *Childcare and Early Years Survey of Parents 2008.* National Centre for Social Research for the Department for Children, Schools and Families, London. Published July 2009.

8   89 per cent of married or co-habiting fathers, 71 per cent of married or co-habiting mothers and 57 per cent of lone

parents (nine out of ten of whom are mothers) with dependent children are in paid employment. *Work and Worklessness Among Households 2010.* Office for National Statistics, London, September 2010.

9   'Women were split fairly evenly between working for basic essentials and working for social or personal preference', according to Hunt, S. A. (ed.) (2009) *Family Trends*, op cit. (citing the 2009 British Social Attitudes Survey). Although professional and managerial women are more likely to stress self-fulfilment as a reason for returning to paid work and women in lower managerial, administrative and manual jobs emphasise the financial imperative, this latter group does also mention the day-to-day fulfilment their jobs provide. Crompton, R. and Lyonette, C. (2010) 'Family, Class and Gender 'Strategies' in Mothers' Employment'. In Scott, J., Crompton, R. and Lyonette, C. (eds.) (2010) *Gender Inequalities in the 21st Century: New Barriers and Continuing Constraints.* Cheltenham: Edward Elgar.

10 See for review: Waddell, G. and Burton, A. K. (2006) *Is Work Good for your Health and Well-being?* London: The Stationery Office. (Independent review of the scientific evidence for the Department of Work and Pensions.) The report notes, 'there is a strong theoretical case, supported by a great deal of background evidence, that work and paid employment are generally beneficial for physical and mental health and well-being. The major proviso is that that depends on the quality of the job and the social context. Nevertheless, the available evidence is on representative jobs, whatever their quality and defects, and shows that on average they are beneficial for health.'

11 Labour Force Survey, Second Quarter, Office for National Statistics, London (2008) and *Work and Worklessness Among Households 2010.* Office for National Statistics, London, September 2010.

12 57 per cent of women with children under five years old are in work. 69 per cent of those with youngest children aged five to ten years work, and of those with youngest children aged eleven to fifteen, 78 per cent are in paid work. *Labour*

Market and Family Status of People, and Women with Dependent Children. Statistics for UK 2009. Released by the Office for National Statistics, London, November 2010.

13   Dex, S., Bukodi, E. and Josh, H. (2009). *The Ups and Downs of Men's and Women's Careers*. Presentation to the Economic and Social Research Council's Gender Equality Network Seminar, London, December 2009.

14   'Partnered women with no dependent children earn an average nine per cent less than men. For mothers working full-time with two children at home, the gap rises to 21.6 per cent', Woodroffe, J. (2009) *Not Having It All: How Motherhood Reduces Women's Pay and Employment Prospects*, London: Fawcett Society.

15   *Closing the Gender Pay Gap: An update report for TUC's Women's Conference 2008*. Trades Union Congress, 2007.

16   Harkness, S. (2008) 'The household division of labour: changes in families' allocation of paid and unpaid work', in Scott, J., Dex, S. and Joshi, H. (2008) *Women and Employment*. Cheltenham: Edward Elgar.

17   For review see Busch, N. (2010) *A Migrant Division of Labour in the Global City? Commodified In-home Childcare in London 2004–2010*. Unpublished Ph.D. thesis, Birkbeck College, University of London.

18   56 per cent of mothers with dependent children who are in employment work part time. *Labour Market and Family Status of People, and Women with Dependent Children*, op. cit.

19   Labour Force Survey, Second Quarter, 2008, op. cit.

20   25.6 per cent of part-time working men in the UK say they work part time because they could not find a full-time job, compared to 11 per cent of part-time working women. Statistics for July–August 2010. Labour Market Statistics, Office for National Statistics, London, November 2010.

21   97 per cent of all part-time workers who say they work part time for family or domestic reasons are women. Labour Force Survey 2004, cited in Hunt, S. A. (ed.) (2009) *Family Trends: British Families since the 1950s*, op. cit.

22   7.98 million people were in part-time employment in the three months to September 2010 in the UK. 2.045 million of

these were men and 5.93 million were women. Labour Market Statistics, Office for National Statistics, London, November 2010.

23 Woodroffe, J. (2009) *Not Having it All*, op. cit.

24 21 per cent of mothers in full-time paid work have managerial or professional positions, 5.5 per cent of mothers with part-time jobs do so. Figures for 2002. Hunt, S. A. (2009) *Family Trends: British Families since the 1950s*, op. cit.

25 648,000 women have second jobs (statistics for July–September 2010), Labour Market Statistics, Statistical Bulletin, Office for National Statistics, London, November 2010.

26 *Closing the Gender Pay Gap: An update report for TUC's Women's Conference 2008*, op. cit.

27 Part-time hours are available to 73 per cent of all employees, flexi-time to 51 per cent, job sharing to 46 per cent, term-time working to 38 per cent, compressed hours 37 per cent, annualised hours 34 per cent and regular home working 24 per cent. Statistics from the UK Department for Work and Pensions in-house analysis of the British Market Research Bureau Omnibus survey *Caring and Flexible Working* (2008) cited in *Flexible Working: Working for Families, Working for Business*, op. cit.

28 38 per cent of HR professionals in the UK say that flexible working arrangements increased in 2009, as an alternative to redundancies during the global recession. *The State of HR: From Recession to Recovery?* survey, King's College, University of London, 2010.

29 For review see Equality and Human Rights Commission (2009) *Working Better: Meeting the Changing Needs of Families, Workers and Employers in the 21st Century*. London: EHRC.

30 The Family Commission (2010) *Starting a Family Revolution: Putting Families in Charge*, op. cit.

31 'Requests are significantly more common from women than men, with 36 per cent of women with dependent children under the age of six making a request to work flexibly between 2003 and 2005, compared with only 12 per cent of men with dependent children under six', Working Families Policy Paper on Flexible Working, London, 2006.

32   18.9 per cent. Figures for UK for second quarter 2009. Labour Force Survey, Office for National Statistics, London, released March 2010.

33   Equality and Human Rights Commission (2009) *Working Better: Fathers, Family and Work – Contemporary Perspectives.* London: EHRC.

34   Equality and Human Rights Commission (2009) *Working Better: Meeting the Changing Needs of Families, Workers and Employers in the 21st Century,* op. cit.

35   Ibid.

36   Between 1975 and 2007 in the UK the pay gap between men and women for full-time workers decreased from 29 per cent to 17 per cent. Source: New Earnings Survey and Annual Survey of Hours and Earnings. 1975 data taken from Department of Employment (cited by Equal Opportunities Commission (2005) *Then and Now: 30 Years of the Sex Discrimination Act*); 2007 data from Trades Union Congress (2008) *Closing the Gender Pay Gap: an update report for the TUC Women's Conference, 2008*) using the Annual Survey of Hours and Earnings, both cited in Hunt, S. A. (ed.) (2009) *Family Trends: British Families since the 1950s,* op. cit.

37   Figure for 2011 (provisional), when comparing median hourly earnings. 2011 Annual Survey of Hours and Earnings. Office for National Statistics, London, 23 November 2011.

38   Between 1975 and 2007 the gender pay gap for part-time workers in the UK only reduced from 42 per cent to 36 per cent. Source: New Earnings Survey and Annual Survey of Hours and Earnings. 1975 data taken from Department of Employment (cited by Equal Opportunities Commission (2005) *Then and Now: 30 Years of the Sex Discrimination Act*); 2007 data from Trades Union Congress (2008) *Closing the Gender Pay Gap: an update report for the TUC Women's Conference, 2008*, using the Annual Survey of Hours and Earnings, both cited in Hunt, S. A. (ed.) (2009) *Family Trends: British Families since the 1950s,* op. cit.

39   Provisional figures from 2011 Annual Survey of Hours and Earnings. Office for National Statistics, op. cit.

40   Nearly two thirds of women are employed in just twelve occupation groups, including the low-paid five 'Cs' – caring,

cashiering, catering, cleaning and clerical work. In contrast, two thirds of men are employed in twenty-six occupation groups, including more professional and management roles than women. *Shaping a Fairer Future*, Women and Work Commission, London, 2006.

41 Olsen, W. and Walby, S. (2004) *Modelling Gender Pay Gaps*. London: Equal Opportunities Commission.

42 Hills, J. et al. (2010) *An Anatomy of Economic Inequality in the UK*. Report of the National Equality Panel. London: Government Equalities Office.

43 Degree-educated women face a 4 per cent loss of earnings as a result of motherhood, for those with mid-level qualifications the loss is 25 per cent and those with no qualifications 58 per cent. Metcalf, H. (2009) *Pay Gaps Across the Equality Strands: A Review*. Research Report 14. Manchester: EHRC. Cited in Equalities and Human Rights Commission (2010) *How Fair is Britain? Equality, Human Rights and Good Relations in 2010*. First Triennial Review. London: EHRC.

44 'Who can request flexible working?', Directgov–Employment. Accessed online at www.direct.gov.uk/en/employment/employees/FlexibleWorking/DG–10029491, 5 April 2010.

45 Equal Opportunities Commission (2005) *Greater Expectations: EOC's investigation into Pregnancy Discrimination*. London: EOC.

46 'Pregnant? Wait till the boss hears', the *Guardian*, 23 June 2011. http://www.guardian.co.uk/lifeandstyle/2011/jun/23/pregnant-wait-till-boss-hears. Article accessed online, 30 August 2011.

47 La Valle, I., Clery, E. and Huerta, M. C. (2008) *Maternity Rights and Mothers' Employment Decisions*. London: National Centre for Social Research for Department of Work and Pensions.

48 Equalities Review (2007) *Fairness and Freedom: The Final Report of the Equalities Review*. London: Equalities Review.

49 Employers are reimbursed for 92 per cent of statutory maternity pay; or 104.5 per cent if they run a small business to also make up for the administration costs.

50 *Woman's Hour*, BBC Radio 4, 1 February 2010. Accessed online at http://www.bbc.co.uk/radio4/womanshour/03/2010_05_mon.shtml on 12 April 2010.

51 'Year-long maternity leave, flexi hours, four-day weeks . . . why would ANY boss hire a woman?', Alexandra Shulman, *Daily Mail*, 11 November 2009. See online at http://www.dailymail.co.uk/debate/article-1226157/Vogue-editor-Alexandra-Shulman-asks-boss-hire-woman.html. Accessed online on 20 February 2010.

52 *Maternity leave: returning to work*, Directgov.uk. See online at http://www.direct.gov.uk/en/Parents/Moneyandworkentitlements/WorkAndFamilies/Pregnancyandmaternityrights/DG_065153. Accessed online on 5 April 2010.

53 'Year-long maternity leave, flexi hours, four-day weeks . . . why would ANY boss hire a woman?', *Daily Mail*, op. cit.

54 Ibid.

55 Ibid.

56 Dex, S., Bukodi, E. and Joshi, H. (2009) *The Ups and Downs of Men's and Women's Careers*, op. cit. Dex, S., Ward, K. and Joshi, H. (2008) 'Changes in Women's Occupations and Occupational Mobility over 25 Years', in Scott, J., Dex , S. and Joshi, H. (eds.) (2008) *Women and Employment: Changing Lives and New Challenges*. Cheltenham: Edward Elgar.

57 Women make up 65 per cent of the public sector workforce. Trades Union Congress, London. Statistics for 2010.

58 'Failure to retain competent employees costing UK businesses £42 billion a year.' PricewaterhouseCoopers press release, 4 October 2010.

59 Labour Force Survey figures, cited in McDowell, L., Batnitzy, A., Dyer, S. and Dyson, J. (2009) *Difference, Diversity and Discrimination: Migrant Workers in Health and Hospitality*. Presentation to the Economic and Social Research Council Gender Equality Network, London, December 2009.

60 58 per cent of married or cohabiting mothers and 37 per cent of lone mothers with three children are in employment. Figures for 2007 from Kent, K. (2009) 'Households, Families and Work', *Economic and Labour Market Review*, 3 (5), 17–22, cited in Hunt, S. A. (2009) *Family Trends: British Families since the 1950s*, op. cit.

61 In the UK 'In the 1990s . . . more than 50 per cent of women and 51 per cent of men said they believed that family life

would not suffer if a woman went to work. Since then, the figure has fallen – to 46 per cent of women and 42 per cent of men. Fewer people (54.9 per cent of women and 54.1 per cent of men) now take the view that a job is the best way for a woman to be independent than in 1991.' *Gender Equality on the Slide?* Cambridge University Press Release, 6 August 2008. See also Scott, J. 'Changing Gender Role Attitudes' in Scott, J., Dex, S. and Joshi, H. (2008) *Women and Employment: Changing Lives and New Challenges,* op. cit.

62 Exclusive *Observer* poll: Gender Attitudes, the *Observer*, 7 December 2008. http://www.guardian.co.uk/lifeandstyle/2008/dec/07/women-equality-rights-feminism-sexism2. Accessed online on 20 September 2010.

63 37 per cent of single-parent families live in poverty. Yeo, A. (2007) *Experience of Work and Job Retention among Lone Parents: an Evidence Review.* Working Paper. London: Department for Work and Pensions.

64 Kiernan, K. and Pickett, K. E. (2006) 'Marital Status Disparities in Maternal Smoking During Pregnancy, Breastfeeding and Maternal Depression', *Social Science Medicine*, 63 (2), 335–46.

65 Ermisch, J. (2001) 'Births outside Marriage: the Real Story' in *The Edge*, Issue 8, 8–9. Swindon: ESRC.

66 Equality and Human Rights Commission (2009) *Working Better: Meeting the Changing Needs of Families, Workers and Employers in the 21st Century,* op. cit.

67 53 per cent of children in single parent families are poor compared to 25 per cent in couple families. The poverty rate for single-parent families in which the parent works on a part-time basis is 29 per cent. Where the parent works full time, the rate is 21 per cent. Statistics from Gingerbread. Available online at http://www.gingerbread.org.uk/content/365/Gingerbread-Factfile. Accessed online on 24 October 2010.

68 Woodroffe, J. (2009) *Not Having it All,* op. cit. citing Olsen, W. and Walby, S. (2004) *Modelling Gender Pay Gaps.* London: Equal Opportunities Commission.

69 The *Sunday Times*, 31 January 2010.

70 Ibid.

71   *A Century of Saving*, The Future Foundation for National Savings and Investments, London, August 2007.

72   Kan, M. Y. and Gershuny, J. (2010) 'Gender Segregation and Bargaining in Domestic Labour: Evidence from Longitudinal Time-Use Data'. In Scott, J., Crompton, R. and Lyonette, C. (eds.) *Gender Inequalities in the 21st Century*, op. cit.

73   Kan, M. Y., Sullivan, O. and Gershuny, J. (2011) 'Gender Convergence in Domestic Work: Discerning the Effects of Interactional and Institutional Barriers from Large-Scale Data'. Op. cit.

5 Man Power

1   Rich, A (1997) *Of Woman Born: Motherhood as Experience and Institution*, op. cit.

2   More than 700 papers on 'men's family roles' are published in academic journals each year. Lewis, C. and Lamb, M. E. (2007) *Understanding Fatherhood: A Review of Recent Research*. York: Joseph Rowntree Foundation.

3   See for review: Flouri, E. (2005) *Fathering and Child Outcomes*. Chichester: John Wiley and Sons. And Lewis, C. and Lamb, M. E. (2007) *Understanding Fatherhood: A Review of Recent Research*, op. cit. Also Lamb, M. E. (ed.) (2010) *The Role of the Father in Child Development*, 5th edition, op. cit.

4   'Bounty packs for new mums to include material for dads', Fatherhood Institute, 19 January 2010. http://www. fatherhoodinstitute.org/index.php?id=0&cID=1030. Accessed online on 26 April 2010.

5   41 per cent of mothers in couples work part time compared to 31 per cent who work full time. 2008 figures from the Office for National Statistics, London, cited in Hunt, S. A. (ed.) (2009) *Family Trends: British Families since the 1950s*, op. cit.

6   62 per cent of fathers think men should spend more time with their children. Equality and Human Rights Commission (2009) *Working Better: Fathers, Family and Work – Contemporary Perspectives*. London: EHRC.

7   42 per cent of fathers believe they spend too little time with

their children; the figure is 54 per cent for men with children under one year old. Equality and Human Rights Commission (2009) *Working Better: Fathers, Family and Work – Contemporary Perspectives*, op. cit.

8 Biggart, L. and O'Brien, M. (2009) *Father's Working Hours: Parental Analysis from the Third Work-life Balance Employee Survey and Maternity and Paternity Rights and Benefits Survey of Parents*. London: Department for Business, Innovation and Skills.

9 Reported in results of a survey among parents carried out by the campaign group Working Families, in partnership with Netmums and Dad.Info. See *Working Families launches Take Up Top Up Paternity Leave Campaign*, Working Families press release, 20 January 2010. http://www.workingfamilies. org.uk/articles/pdf/news/5. Accessed online on 6 September 2010.

10 Ibid.

11 Dex, S. and Ward, K. (2007) *Parental Care and Employment in Early Childhood*. London: Equal Opportunities Commission.

12 David Frost, director general of the British Chambers of Commerce, quoted in 'Dads to share maternity leave'. *BBC News* website, 15 September 2009, http://news.bbc. co.uk/1/hi/8256302.stm. Accessed online on 6 September 2010.

13 Stephen Alambritis, Federation of Small Businesses, quoted in 'Cut in maternity leave to give fathers more time off', *The Times*, 30 March 2009. http://women.timesonline.co.uk/ tol/life_and_style/women/families/article5999158.ece. Accessed online on 6 September 2010.

14 Equality and Human Rights Commission (2009) *Working Better: Fathers, Family and Work – Contemporary Perspectives*, op. cit.

15 14 per cent of men requesting flexible working are turned down, compared to 10 per cent of women. Men are also twice as likely as women to be unsuccessful if they take their case to a flexible working tribunal. Fagan, C., Hegewisch, A. and Pillenger, J. (2006) *Out of Time: Why Britain Needs a New Approach to Working-time Flexibility*, op. cit.

16   EHRC (2009) *Working Better: Fathers, Family and Work –
      Contemporary Perspectives,* op. cit.

17   Dex, S. and Ward, K. (2007) *Parental Care and Employment in
      Early Childhood,* op. cit.

18   Tanaka, S. and Waldfogel, J. (2007) 'Effects of Parental Leave
      and Work Hours on Fathers' Involvement with their Babies,
      Evidence from the Millennium Cohort Study', in *Community,
      Work & Family,* 10 (4), 409–426.

19   See for review: Lamb, M. E. (ed.) (2010) *The Role of the Father
      in Child Development,* op. cit. And Lewis, C. and Lamb, M. E.
      (2007) *Understanding Fatherhood: A Review of Recent Research,*
      op. cit.

20   EHRC (2009) *Working Better: Fathers, Family and Work –
      Contemporary Perspectives,* op. cit.

21   In 1975 in the UK fathers with no O levels spent an average
      of 8 minutes per day on childcare, those with O level qualifi-
      cations 6 minutes and those with higher qualifications 3
      minutes. In 2000 fathers in the UK with no O levels or GCSE
      qualifications spent an average of 34 minutes per day with
      their children, those with O level or GCSE qualifications 32
      minutes and those with higher qualifications 36 minutes.
      Statistics based on analysis of UK individuals' completed time
      diaries carried out by Dr Oriel Sullivan, Deputy Director,
      Centre for Time Use Research, University of Oxford. Research
      presented to British Sociological Association, 7 April 2010.
      'Parents spend treble the amount of time on childcare now
      than in 1975, research shows', British Sociological Association
      press release, 7 April 2010. See also: Lewis, J., Campbell, M.
      and Huerta, C. (2008) 'Patterns of Paid and Unpaid Work in
      Western Europe: Gender, Commodification, Preferences and
      the Implications for Policy', *Journal of European Social Policy,*
      18 (21), 21–37, citing Warren, T. (2003) 'Class- and Gender-based
      Working time? Time Poverty and the Division of Domestic
      Labour', *Sociology* 37 (4), 733–52, which shows that childcare in
      the UK is shared by 40 per cent of working-class couples and
      28 per cent of those couples who are middle class.

22   'It's men who are increasingly left holding the baby', the
      Observer, 11 April 2010. http://www.guardian.co.uk/

lifeandstyle / 2010 / apr / 11 / home-father-childcare-leave. Accessed online on 26 April 2010. 'It was tough to stop work to look after my kids but lots of my mates wish they could too', the *Sun*, 20 April 2010. http:// www.thesun.co.uk/ sol / homepage / woman / parenting / 2939227 / We-talk-to-stay-at-home-dads.html. Accessed online on 26 April 2010. 'Stay-at-home dads "up ten-fold"', BBC news online, 6 April 2010. http:// news.bbc.co.uk / 1 / hi / education / 8605824.stm. Accessed online on 17 October 2010. 'Tenfold rise in stay at home dads', *Channel 4 News* website, 7 April 2010.http:// wwww.channel4.com / news / articles / business money / tenfold +rise+in+stayathome+dads / 3604507. Accessed online on 26 April 2010. 'Stay at home dads', *GMTV* website, 6 April 2010.http:// www.gm.tv / lifestyle / families-and-parenting / 47463-stay-at-home-dads.html. Accessed online on 26 April 2010.

23   'Fathers' clubs in London', *Time Out*, 9 January 2009. http:// www.timeout.com / london / kids / features / 6604 / Fathers-clubs in London.html. Accessed online on 6 September 2010. 'The rise of fathers' play groups', the *Independent*, 30 March 2010. http:// www.independent.co.uk / life-style / health-and-families / features / the-rise-of-fathers-playgroups-1930630.html. Accessed online on 26 April 2010. 'Full-time fathers find safety in numbers at local dads' club', *The Times*, 23 January 2010. http:// women.timesonline.co.uk / tol / life _and_style / women / families / article6999173.ece. Accessed online on 26 April 2010.

24   'It's men who are increasingly left holding the baby', the *Observer*, 11 April 2010, op. cit.

25   'Stay at home dads', *GMTV* website, 6 April 2010, op. cit.

26   'Stay-at-home dads "up ten-fold"', BBC news online, 6 April 2010, op. cit.

27   'Fathers' clubs in London', *Time Out*, 9 January 2009, op. cit. 'The rise of fathers' play groups', the *Independent*, 30 March 2010, op. cit. 'Full-time fathers find safety in numbers at local dads' club', *The Times*, 23 January 2010, op. cit.

28   Miller, T. (2010) *Making Sense of Fatherhood: Gender, Caring and Work*, op. cit.

29   36 per cent of women with children under the age of six requested flexible working between 2003 and 2005, 12 per cent of men with dependent children under six did the same. Working Families Policy Paper on Flexible Working, London, 2006.

30   Ibid.

31   17 per cent compared to 6 per cent of mothers. EHRC (2009) *Working Better: Fathers, Family and Work – Contemporary Perspectives*, op. cit.

32   Kelliher, C. (2008) *Flexible Working and Performance*. Bedford: Cranfield University School of Management for Working Families.

33   Government Equalities Office (2009) *Flexible Working: Benefits and Barriers – Perceptions of Working Parents*. London: Government Equalities Office, cited in Hunt, S. A. (ed.) (2009) *Family Trends: British Familes since the 1950s*, op. cit.

34   Dermott, E. M. (2006) *The Effect of Fatherhood on Men's Patterns of Employment: Full Research Report*. Swindon: Economic and Social Research Council.

35   Government Equalities Office (2009) *Flexible Working: Benefits and Barriers – Perceptions of Working Parents*, op. cit.

36   'I'd love to read *The Gruffalo* for the 777th time but, alas, duty calls', *The Times*, 13 May 2008. http://www.timesonline.co.uk/tol/comment/columnists/article3916988.ece . Accessed online on 27 November 2010.

37   Kilkey, M., Perrons, D. and Plomien A. (2010) *Fathering and Work Life Balance: Challenges for Policy – Draft Summary Report*. London School of Economics & University of Hull.

38   See 'Fatherhood Institute gives political parties Six Signposts to a better future for fatherhood', Fatherhood Institute press release, 20 April 2010.

39   Reynolds, T., Callender, C. and Edwards, R. (2003) *Caring and Counting: the Impact of Mothers' Employment on Family Relationships*. Bristol: Policy Press.

40   McConnell, H. and Wilson, B. (2007) 'Families'. In S. Smallwood and B. Wilson (eds.), *Focus on Families* (Basingstoke: Palgrave Macmillan), 2–17, cited in Hunt, S. A. (ed.) (2009) *Family Trends: British families since the 1950s*, op. cit.

41 Hunt, S. A. (ed.) (2009) *Family Trends*, op. cit.

42 Willets M. et al. (2005) *Children in Britain: Findings from the 2003 Families and Children Study (FACS)*, Department for Work and Pensions Research Report No. 249. Cited in *Recovering Child Support: Routes to Responsibility*, Sir David Henshaw's report to the Secretary of State for Work and Pensions, July 2006.

43 Ermisch, J. (2006) *Child Support and Non-resident Fathers' Contact with their Children*, ISER Working Paper 2006–14. Colchester: University of Essex.

44 'Why new dads don't always love their baby', the *Observer*, 7 June 2009. http://www.guardian.co.uk/lifeandstyle/2009/jun/07/accidental-guide-fatherhood-guilt. Accessed online on 23 June 2009.

45 For review see Lewis, C. and Warin, J. (2001) 'What Good are Dads?' *Father Facts*, 1 (1), Fathers Direct. Also Feldman, R., Gordon, I., Schneiderman, I., Weisman, O. and Zagoory-Sharon, O. (2010) 'Natural Variations in Maternal and Paternal Care Are Associated with Systematic Changes in Oxytocin following parent–infant contact.' *Psychoneuroendocrinology*, 35 (8): 1133–41.

6 The Enemy Within

1 'The Natural', *Vogue* magazine, September 2007. http://www.vogue.com/feature/2007_Sept_Michelle Obama/. Accessed online on 7 May 2010.

2 34 per cent of mothers agree that childcare is the primary responsibility of the mother, compared to 23 per cent of fathers. EHRC (2009) *Working Better: Fathers, Family and Work – Contemporary Perspectives*, op. cit.

3 Huang, C. C., and Warner, L. A. (2005). 'Relationship Characteristics & Depression among Fathers with Newborns', *Social Service Review*, 79 (9).

4 Allen, S. M. and Hawkins, A. J. (1999) 'Maternal Gatekeeping: Mothers' Beliefs and Behaviors That Inhibit Greater Father Involvement in Family Work', *Journal of Marriage and the Family*, 61, 199–212.

5   34 per cent. EHRC (2009) *Working Better: Fathers, Family and Work – Contemporary Perspectives,* op. cit.

6   For review see Henrekson, M. and Stenkula, M. (2009) *Why are there so few female top executives in egalitarian welfare states?* Stockholm: Research Institute of Industrial Economics.

7 Foreign Policy

1   Fairness in Families Index, Fatherhood Institute, Abergavenny, December 2010.

2   In Sweden men took only 7 per cent of the total number of parental leave days by 1987: Chronholm, A. (2009) 'Sweden: Individualisation or Free Choice in Parental Leave?' Kamerman, S. B. and Moss, P. (eds.) (2009) *The Politics of Parental Leave Policies. Children, Parenting, Gender and the Labour Market.* Bristol: Policy Press. Only 4 per cent of fathers took parental leave in Norway by 1992. Kvande, E. (2010) 'Norway's Policy Approach to Fathering'. Presentation at *Fathering and Work Life Balance: Challenges for Policy* seminar, Gender Institute of the London School of Economics, London, 5 March 2010.

3   Kvande, E. (2010) 'Norway's Policy Approach to Fathering', op. cit.

4   Duvander, A.-Z., Ferrarini, T. and Thalberg, S. (2005) *Swedish Parental Leave and Gender Equality: Achievements and Reform Challenges in a European Perspective.* Stockholm: Institute for Futures Studies.

5   Men in Sweden take 21.7 per cent of the total leave period. Figure for 2007. Haataja, A. (2009) *Fathers' Use of Paternity and Parental Leave in the Nordic Countries.* Helsinki: The Social Insurance Institution Research Department. Men take 11 per cent of the total available parental leave days in Norway. Figures for 2007 cited in Eydal, G. B., (2009) *Equal Legal Rights to Paid Parental Leave – the Case of Iceland.* The European Network for Social Policy Analysts (ESPANET).

6 In Norway parents also have the option of taking a shorter leave period of 44 weeks on 100 per cent of salary (with a cap). In Sweden most of the 480-day leave period is paid at 80 per cent of salary but ninety days are paid at a flat rate.

7 Duvander, A.-Z., Ferrarini, T. and Thalberg, S. (2005) *Swedish Parental Leave and Gender Equality: Achievements and Reform Challenges in a European Perspective*, op. cit. Also Brandth, B. and Kvande, E. (2003) *Fleksible fedre*. Oslo: Universitetsforlaget cited in Valdimarsdóttir, F. R., (2006) *Nordic Experiences with Parental Leave and its Impact on Equality between Women and Men*. Copenhagen: Nordic Council of Ministers.

8 In Sweden women do 1,050 hours of paid work, 1,180 hours of work in the home and 180 hours of childcare in a year. Men do 1,530 hours of paid work, 810 hours of work in the home, and 100 hours of childcare. Eurostat Standardised Time Use Survey data for 2000–1, cited in Henrekson, M. and Stenkula, M. (2009) *Why are There so Few Female Top Executives in Egalitarian Welfare States?* Stockholm: Research Institute of Industrial Ecomomics.

9 Chronholm, A. (2009) 'Sweden: Individualisation or Free Choice in Parental Leave?' In Kamerman, S. B. and Moss; P. (eds.) (2009) *The Politics of Parental Leave Policies – Children, Parenting, Gender and the Labour Market*, op. cit.

10 Duvander, A.-Z., Ferrarini, T. and Thalberg, S. (2005) *Swedish Parental Leave and Gender Equality: Achievements and Reform Challenges in a European Perspective*, op. cit.

11 'Female Power', *The Economist*, 2 January 2010.

12 For review see Duvander, A-Z., Ferrarini, T. and Thalberg, S. (2005) *Swedish Parental Leave and Gender Equality: Achievements and Reform Challenges in a European Perspective*, op. cit.

13 Johansson, E.-A. (2010) *The Effect of Own and Spousal Parental Leave on Earnings*. Uppsala: Institute of Labour Market Policy Evaluation.

14 Erler, D. (2009) 'Germany: Taking a Nordic Turn?' In Kamerman, S. B. and Moss, P. (eds.) (2009) *The Politics of Parental Leave Policies – Children, Parenting, Gender and the Labour Market*, op. cit.

15   Figure for 2004, BIB (Bundesinstitut fur Bevolkerungs-
      forschung) (2004) *Bevolkerung, Fakten – Trends – Ursachen –
      Erwartungen – Die wichtigsten Fragen*, Wiesbaden: Statistisches
      Bundesamt, cited in Erler, D. (2009) 'Germany: Taking a
      Nordic Turn?', op. cit.

16   Erler, D. (2009) 'Germany: Taking a Nordic Turn?', op.
      cit.

17   Quoted in 'Why Merkel is Not Enough', *Time Europe
      Magazine*, 22 January 2006. See http://www.time.com/
      time/europe/html/060130/story.html. Accessed online on 10
      September 2010.

18   Erler, D. (2009) 'Germany: Taking a Nordic Turn?, op. cit.

19   In Germany the 14 weeks' maternity leave is paid at 100 per
      cent of earnings with no ceiling on payments. It is obliga-
      tory to take eight weeks of this leave.

20   18 per cent of fathers took parental leave in 2009. Reich, N.
      (2010) *Who Cares? Determinants of Fathers' Use of Parental Leave
      in Germany*. Working Paper No. 1–31. Hamburg: Hamburg
      Institute of International Economics. Available at SSRN:
      http://ssrn.com/abstract=1619345.

21   Reich, N. (2010) *Who Cares? Determinants of Fathers' Use of
      Parental Leave in Germany*, op. cit.

22   Ibid.

23   *Closing the Gender Pay Gap: An Update Report for the TUC
      Women's Conference, 2008*. London: Trades Union Congress.
      Figures for 2006 calculated from *Equality Between Women and
      Men – 2008*, European Commission, 2008.

24   The crude birth rate per 1000 inhabitants in Germany has
      decreased by 16 per cent between 1999 and 2009; declining
      from 8.33 to 8.1 between 2007 and 2009, for example. Eurostat,
      May 2010.

25   *Consultation on Modern Workplaces*, HM Government, London,
      May 2011.

26   Gislason, I. V. (2007). *Parental Leave in Iceland: Bringing the
      Fathers In. Developments in the Wake of New Legislation in 2000*.
      Reykjavik: Ministry of Social Affairs.

27   Einarsdottir, T. and Petursdottir, G. M., (2009) 'Iceland: from
      Reluctance to Fast-track Engineering'. Kamerman, S. B. and

Moss, P. (eds.) (2009) *The Politics of Parental Leave Policies – Children, Parenting, Gender and the Labour Market*, op. cit.

28 Statistics for 2007. Eydal, G. B. (2009) *Equal Legal Rights to Paid Parental Leave – the Case of Iceland*, op. cit.

29 Gislason, I. V. (2007). *Parental Leave in Iceland: Bringing the Fathers In*, op. cit.

30 Hausmann, R., Tyson, L. D. and Zahidi, S. (2009). *The Global Gender Gap Report 2009*. Geneva: World Economic Forum. And Hausmann, R., Tyson, L. D. and Zahidi, S. (2010). *The Global Gender Gap Report 2010*. Geneva: World Economic Forum.

31 Organisation for Economic Co-operation and Development (OECD) (2007). *Babies and Bosses – Reconciling Work and Family Life: A Synthesis of Findings for OECD Countries*. Paris: OECD.

32 Statement by H.E. Mr Arni Pall Arnason, then Minister of Social Affairs and Social Security of Iceland, speaking at 54th Session of the Commission on the Status of Women, The Permanent Mission of Iceland to the United Nations, New York, 2010.

33 Gislason, I. V. (2007). *Parental Leave in Iceland: Bringing the Fathers In*, op. cit.

34 Eydal, G. B. (2004) 'Hvernig samhæfa íslenskar barnafjölskyldur atvinnupátttöku og umönnun ungra barna?' In Hauksson, U. (ed.): *Rannsóknir í félagsvísindum V*. Reykjavík, Félagsvísindastofnun Háskóla Íslands. Háskólaútgáfan, cited in Gislason, I. V. (2007) *Parental Leave in Iceland: Bringing the Fathers In*, op. cit.

35 Guðbjörg, A. J. (1995) *Launamyndun og kynbundinn launamunur*. Reykjavík. Skrifstofa jafnréttismála & Félagsvísindastofnun cited in Gislason, I. V. (2007). *Parental Leave in Iceland: Bringing the Fathers In*, op. cit.

36 Bryndis Jonsdottir, Capacent Gallup survey (forthcoming), cited in Gislason, I.V. (2007). *Parental Leave in Iceland: Bringing the Fathers In*, op. cit.

37 'Parental leave, care policies and gender equality in the Nordic countries'. Speech by Arni Pall Arnason, then Icelandic Minister of Social Affairs and Social Security, at Parental Leave, Care Policies and Gender Equalities in the Nordic Countries conference arranged by the Nordic Council of Ministers, 21–22 October 2009, Reykjavik, Iceland.

38 All figures from Ministry of Social Affairs in Iceland.

39 Ibid.

40 'Parental leave, care policies and gender equality in the Nordic countries'. Speech by Arni Pall Arnason, op. cit.

41 Ray, R., Gornick, J. C. and Schmitt, J. (2008) *Parental Leave Polices in 21 Countries: Assessing Generosity and Gender Equality*. Washington D.C.: Center for Economic and Policy Research.

42 *Maternity/Paternity Leave*. Momsrising.org. Available online at http://www.momsrising.org/maternity. Accessed online on 18 May 2010.

43 Nepomnyaschy, L. and Waldfogel, J. (2007). 'Paternity Leave and Fathers' Involvement with Their Young Children: Evidence from the ECLS-B', *Community, Work, and Family* 10 (4), 425–451.

44 The United States is ranked in the middle of the Gender Equality Index of twenty-one countries featured in Ray, R. Gornick, J. C. and Schmitt, J. (2008) *Parental Leave Polices in 21 Countries: Assessing Generosity and Gender Equality*, op. cit. The country is ranked fifteenth out of forty-six high-income countries in the Global Gender Gap index ratings 2010 compiled by the World Economic Forum. See Hausmann, R., Tyson, L. D. and Zahidi, S. (2010) *The Global Gender Gap Report 2010*. Geneva: Switzerland: World Economic Forum.

45 Organisation for Economic Co-operation and Development (OECD) (2007) *Babies and Bosses – Reconciling Work and Family Life: A Synthesis of Findings for OECD Countries*, op. cit.

46 Overall 67 per cent of UK mothers are in paid work as are 67 per cent of US mothers. 63 per cent of mothers with a youngest child aged three to five years of age work in the US. In the UK, 57 per cent of mothers with a child under five work. US stats from Organisation for Economic Co-operation and Development (OECD) (2007) *Babies and Bosses – Reconciling Work and Family Life: A Synthesis of Findings for OECD* Countries, op. cit. UK stats *Labour Market and Family Status of People, and Women with Dependent Children*. Statistics for 2009. Office for National Statistics, London. Released November 2010.

47 See for review: Henrekson, M. and Stenkula, M. (2009) *Why are There So Few Female Top Executives in Egalitarian Welfare States?*, op. cit.

48 Brennan, D. (2009) 'Australia: the Difficult Birth of Paid Maternity Leave'. In Kamerman, S. B. and Moss, P. (eds.) (2009) *The Politics of Parental Leave Policies*, op. cit.

49 'Parental Leave Pay may be transferred from the mother or the primary carer of an adopted child to another primary carer (such as the child's father).' *Questions & Answers about the Paid Parental Leave scheme*, Family Assistance Office, Australian Government. http://www.familyassist.gov.au/payments/family-assistance-payments/paid-parental-leave-scheme/faq/working-parents-faq-about-ppl.html#2. Accessed 10 September 2010.

50 Brennan, D. (2009) 'Australia: the Difficult Birth of Paid Maternity Leave'. In Kamerman, S. B. and Moss, P. (eds.) (2009) *The Politics of Parental Leave Policies*, op. cit.

51 Plantenga, J. and Remery, C. (2009) 'The Netherlands: Bridging Labour and Care'. In Kamerman, S. B. and Moss, P. (eds.) *The Politics of Parental Leave Policies*, op. cit.

52 Statistics from PricewaterhouseCoopers, 'Failure to Retain Competent Employees Costing UK Business £42 Billion a Year.' op. cit.

53 Statistics for 2007 for Sweden, cited in Eydal, G. B. (2009) *Equal Legal Rights to Paid Parental Leave – the Case of Iceland*, op. cit.

54 Organisation for Economic Co-operation and Development (OECD) (2007). *Babies and Bosses – Reconciling Work and Family Life: A Synthesis of Findings for OECD Countries*, op. cit.

55 Swedish National Agency for Education (2006) *Descriptive Data on Pre-school Activities, School-age Childcare, Schools and Adult Education in Sweden.* Stockholm: Skolverket.

56 Billari, F. C. (2008) 'Lowest-Low Fertility in Europe: Exploring the Causes and Finding Some Surprises', *The Japanese Journal of Population*, 6 (1).

57 Erler, D. (2009) 'Germany: Taking a Nordic Turn?' In Kamerman, S. B. and Moss, P. (eds.) (2009) *The Politics of Parental Leave Policies*, op. cit.

58 *Morgunbladid* newspaper, 10 February 2004, cited in Gislason,

I.V. (2007) *Parental Leave in Iceland: Bringing the Fathers In*, op. cit.

59   OECD average for female employment is 56.1 per cent. Iceland is 81.6 per cent, Norway 72 per cent, Sweden 72 per cent, Spain 54 per cent, Greece 47.5 per cent, Italy 46 per cent. Stats for 2006. Organisation for Economic Co-operation and Development (OECD) (2007). *Babies and Bosses – Reconciling Work and Family Life: A Synthesis of Findings for OECD Countries*, op. cit.

60   Organisation for Economic Co-operation and Development (OECD) (2007). *Babies and Bosses – Reconciling Work and Family Life: A Synthesis of Findings for OECD Countries*, op. cit.

61   Eydal, G. B. (2009) *Equal Legal Rights to Paid Parental Leave – the Case of Iceland*, op. cit.

62   Capacent Gallup (2006) *Launamyndun og kynbundinn launamunur*, cited in Gislason, I.V. (2007) *Parental Leave in Iceland: Bringing the Fathers In*, op. cit.

63   Although Dr Ingólfur V. Gislason, Associate Professor at the Department of Sociology, University of Iceland, fears that the pay gap between men and women in 'a society based on market economy' will always be around 10–12 per cent, as women's labour is devalued because of their ability to bear children. Gislason, I. V. (2009) 'Parental leave and gender pay gap – What, if any, are the effects of different systems of parental leave on gender pay gap?' In Sigurðardóttir, E. (ed.) (2010) *Parental Leave, Care Policies and Gender Equalities in the Nordic Countries*. Presentation to conference arranged by the Nordic Council of Ministers, 21–22 October 2009, Reykjavik, Iceland. Copenhagen: Nordic Council of Ministers.

64   Olah, L. S., (2001) 'Policy Changes and Family Stability: The Swedish Case'. *International Journal of Law, Policy & the Family*, 15 (1), 118–134.

65   See for review: Eydal, G. B. (2009). *Equal Legal Rights to Paid Parental Leave – the Case of Iceland*, op. cit.

66   Mothers were the primary carers for their three-year-old children in 77 per cent of cases where the father did not take parental leave but in only 43.8 per cent of cases where the father took three or more months of parental leave. The results for night-time care showed the same pattern. Eydal, G. B.

(2009) *Equal Legal Rights to Paid Parental Leave – the Case of Iceland*, op. cit.

67 Cooke, L. P. (2004) 'The Gendered Division of Labor and Family Outcomes in Germany', *Journal of Marriage and Family*, 66 (5), 1246–59. And Esping-Anderson, G., Guell, M. and Broadmann, S. (2005) *When Mothers Work and Fathers Care. Joint Household Fertility Decisions in Denmark and Spain*. Working Paper 5. Barcelona: Demosoc.

68 Eydal, G. B. (2009) *Equal Legal Rights to Paid Parental Leave – the Case of Iceland*, op. cit.

69 Organisation for Economic Co-operation and Development (OECD) (2007), *Babies and Bosses – Reconciling Work and Family Life: A Synthesis of Findings for OECD Countries*, op. cit.

70 Gislason, I. V. (2007) *Parental Leave in Iceland: Bringing the Fathers In*, op. cit.

71 2.05 children per woman average for 2005 – compared to between 1.77 and 1.84 in the other Nordic states. The OECD average is 1.63. Organisation for Economic Co-operation and Development (OECD) (2007). *Babies and Bosses – Reconciling Work and Family Life: A Synthesis of Findings for OECD Countries*, op. cit.

72 The other countries are Mexico, Turkey and the United States. Organisation for Economic Co-operation and Development (OECD) (2007). *Babies and Bosses – Reconciling Work and Family Life: A Synthesis of Findings for OECD Countries*, op. cit.

73 *Parental leave, care policies and gender equality in the Nordic countries*. Speech by Arni Pall Arnason, op. cit.

74 Ibid.

75 Olah, Livia Sz. (2003) 'Gendering Fertility: Second Births in Sweden and Hungary'. *Population Research and Policy Review*, 22: 171–200.

76 Knudsen, L. B. (1999). *Recent Fertility Trends in Denmark – A Discussion of the Impact of Family Policy in a Period with Increasing Fertility*. Research Report 11. Odense: Danish Centre for Demographic Research. Baizan, P. (2009). 'Regional Childcare Availability and Fertility Decisions in Spain'. *Demographic Research*, 21 (27), 803–842.

77 Mörk, E., Sjögren, A. and Svalelryd, H. (2009) *Cheaper*

Childcare. More Children. Discussion Paper 3942. Bonn: Institute for Study of Labour (IZA).

78   Esping-Anderson, G. (2009) *The Incomplete Revolution: Adapting to Women's New Roles.* Cambridge: Polity Press.

79   Organisation for Economic Co-operation and Development (OECD) (2007). *Babies and Bosses – Reconciling Work and Family Life: A Synthesis of Findings for OECD Countries,* op. cit.

80   See for review: O'Brien, M. (2009) 'Fathers, Parental Leave Policies, and Infant Quality of Life. International Perspectives and Policy Impact'. *The Annals of the American Academy of Political and Social Science* 624: 190–213.

81   Eydal, G. B. (2009) *Equal Legal Rights to Paid Parental Leave – the Case of Iceland,* op. cit.

82   O'Brien, M. (2009) *Fathers and work-family friendly policies: taking stock of the evidence.* Presentation at *Families in the balance: reconciling paid work and parenthood.* National Centre for Social Research, London, 14 October 2009. Cited in Fatherhood Institute Briefing on Paternity, Maternity and Parental Leave, 2010.

83   For review see Burgess, A. (2008) *The Costs and Benefits of Active Fatherhood. Evidence and Insights to Inform the Development of Policy and Practice.* Fathers Direct. Also Flacking, R., Dykes, F. and Ewald, U. (2010) 'The Influence of Father's Socioeconomic Status and Paternity Leave on Breastfeeding Duration: A Population-based Cohort Study'. *Scandinavian Journal of Public Health.*

84   Norway's child poverty rate is 2.9 per cent and Sweden's is 3.2 per cent, compared to the OECD average of 10.3 per cent, and 13.7 per cent for Spain and 14.3 per cent for Italy (stats for 2000). Organisation for Economic Co-operation and Development (OECD) (2007) *Babies and Bosses – Reconciling Work and Family Life: A Synthesis of Findings for OECD Countries,* op. cit.

85   The UK child poverty rate is 13.6 per cent (stats for 2000 as measured by the OECD), ibid. The OECD defines child poverty as those children in households with incomes less than 50 per cent of the median for the entire population. The UK's official measure is household income below 60 per

cent of the median: about one in five children in the UK falls into this category according to UK government figures.

86 Gislason, I. V. (2007). *Parental Leave in Iceland: Bringing the Fathers In*, op. cit.

87 World Economic Forum (2010) *Global Competitiveness Index 2010–2011*, Geneva: WEF.

8 The Birth of Equality

1 One of the reasons UK legislators are nervous about compulsorily splitting the existing leave evenly between parents is that European Union legislation prevents a reduction in member states' current maternity rights. In the UK, this legislation has the, presumably unintended, consequence of cementing deeply unequal leave provision for men and women. This itself directly undermines the EU's own equality and 'work–life' balance objectives. It also puts the UK at odds with much of the rest of Europe, which doesn't apportion leave so unevenly and proactively encourages fathers to take on more care. EU law should be challenged on this point.

2 Maternity Protection Convention, International Labour Organisation, Geneva, 2000. http://www.ilo.org/ilolex/cgi-lex/convde.pl?C183. Accessed online 28 September 2011.

3 *Fair Society, Healthy Lives. The Marmot Review*, Strategic Review of Health Inequalities in England post-2010. London, February 2010.

4 Equality and Human Rights Commission (2009) *Working Better: Meeting the Changing Needs of Families, Workers and Employers*. London: EHRC.

5 In the UK 50 per cent of a child's future earning potential is determined at birth, the highest percentage for any of the countries for which the Organisation for Economc Co-operation and Development (OECD) has data. *Social Mobility*, Trades Union Congress, London, 2010.

6 Ipsos MORI poll for the Chartered Institute for Personnel and Development, cited in Equality and Human Rights

Commision (2009) *Working Better: Meeting the Changing Needs of Families, Workers and Employers in the 21st Century*, op. cit.

7   Hrdy, S. B. (2009) *Mothers and Others: The Evolutionary Origins of Mutual Understanding*. Massachusetts:The Belknap Press of Harvard University Press.

8   See for review: Lamb, M. E. (ed.) (2010) *The Role of the Father in Child Development*. Fifth edition. Op. cit. And also *Briefing on Paternity, Maternity and Parental Leave: Supporting Families and Relationships through Parental Leave*, op. cit.

9   *Focus on Gender: Work and Family*. Office for National Statistics, London, September 2008.

10   *Making Britain the Place to Work*, Confederation of British Industry, London, 2010.

11   Equality and Human Rights Commission (2009) *Working Better: Meeting the Changing Needs of Families, Workers and Employers in the 21st Century*. op. cit, citing Hegewisch, A. (2009) *Flexile Working Policies: a Comparative Review*. London: EHRC.

12   These examples are drawn from a selection of those employers receiving awards and mentions from Working Families, Opportunity Now and the Equality and Human Rights Commission.

13   EHRC (2009) *Working Better: Meeting the Changing Needs of Families, Workers and Employers in the 21st Century*, op. cit.

14   Free childcare for disadvantaged two-year-olds to be guaranteed in law. London: Department for Education, 16 November 2010.

15   See Waldfogel, J. (2004) *Social Mobility, Life Chances, and the Early Years*. London: Centre for Analysis of Social Exclusion (CASE), London School of Economics. Also for review: Equality and Human Rights Commission (2009) *Working Better: Meeting the Changing Needs of Families, Workers and Employers in the 21st Century*, and *Fair Society, Healthy Lives The Marmot Review*, op. cit.

16   Personal well-being key stage 3 – programme of study, PHSE curriculum, National Curriculum online. http://curriculum. qcda.gov.uk/key-stages-3-and-4/subjects/key-stage-3/personal-social-health-and-economic-education/personal-

wellbeing/programme-of-study/index.aspx?tab=1. Accessed online on 29 June 2010.

17 98 per cent of the UK childcare staff are women. National Daycare Trust statistic, 2009.

18 *The Coalition: Our Programme for Government*, op. cit.

19 Children's Workforce Development Council research shows that 55 per cent of parents want a male childcare worker for their nursery-age child, this percentage increases to 66 per cent for lone-parent mothers. Statistics for England released on 1 January 2009.

20 Lambert, P. (2008) 'Comparative Political Economy of Parental Leave and Child Care: Evidence from 20 OECD Countries', *Social Politics*, 15 (4), 315-44. Quoted in Kamerman, S. and Moss, P. (eds.) (2009) *The Politics of Parental Leave Policies: Children, Parenting, Gender and the Labour Market*, op. cit.

21 Around forty countries have introduced national election quotas and in around fifty countries major political parties have introduced their own quotas for female representation. Figures for 2006. From the Quota Project: Global database of quotas for women. http://www.quotaproject.org/. Accessed online on 21 July 2000.

22 See for review: Flouri, E. (2005) *Fathering and Child Outcomes*, op. cit. Also Lewis, C. and Lamb, M. E. (2007) *Understanding Fatherhood: A Review of Recent Research*, op. cit. And Lamb. M. E. (ed.) (2010) *The Role of the Father in Child Development*, op. cit.

23 Solomon, S. E., Rothblum, E. D. and Balsam, K. F. (2004) 'Pioneers in Partnership: Lesbian and Gay Male Couples in Civil Unions Compared With Those Not in Civil Unions, and Married Heterosexual Siblings. *Journal of Family Psychology*, 18 (2), 275–286. Also Patterson, C. J., Sutfin, E. L. and Fulcher, M. (2004) 'Division of Labor Among Lesbian and Heterosexual Parenting Couples: Correlates of Specialized Versus Shared Patterns', *Journal of Adult Development*, 11 (3).

24 Dunne, G. A. (2005) *Balancing Acts: Lesbian Experience of Work and Family Life*. Swindon. Economic and Social Research Council (ESRC).

25   Dunne, G. A. (2005) *The Different Dimensions of Gay Fatherhood*. Swindon. ESRC.

26   *Invitation to Join the Government of Britain*, The Conservative Manifesto, 2010.

27   *The Coalition: Our Programme for Government*, op. cit.

28   Speech by the Deputy Prime Minister, Nick Clegg, launching the Children and Families Ministerial Taskforce, 17 June 2010.

29   Equality and Human Rights Commissin (2009) *Working Better: Meeting the Changing Needs of Families, Workers and Employers in the 21st Century*, op. cit.

30   Ibid.

31   Esping-Anderson, G. *Families and the Revolution in Women's Roles: How Women are Changing the World*. Unpublished paper available at www.esping-anderson.com. Accessed online on 6 December 2010.

32   Global Economics Paper No. 154 http://pslforum. worldbankgroup.org/docs/kevin_Daly_Global_Ageing_ Gender_Inequality.pdf. Accessed online on 15 September 2010.

33   Portanti, M. and Whitworth, S. (2009) 'A comparison of the characteristics of childless women and mothers in the ONS longitudinal study', *Population Trends*, 136, 10-20. This analysis of the Office for National Statistics Longitudinal Study shows that, of women born between 1956 and 1960, 17 per cent hadn't given birth to a child by December 2005. Although more often single than mothers in the same age group, these women shared other telling characteristics: women without children are much more likely to be educated to degree level or above (26.8 per cent compared to 19.2 per cent) and more likely to be employed in professional and managerial/technical occupations (42 per cent compared to 30 per cent in the 40–45 years age group) than mothers. They are also more likely than mothers to be more highly educated than their partners (13 per cent compared to 8 per cent). Therefore, I'd suggest it's reasonable to conclude that these are women for whom their professional life is central to their sense of identity and vital to the household finances and so, even if some of them never wanted children, others have decided that motherhood is incompatible with their work.